Impressions
Of America
Vol.1

by

Tyrone Power

IMPRESSIONS OF AMERICA
Vol.1
by TYRONE POWER

ISBN: 978-93-59327-72-3

Published by

DOUBLE 9 BOOKS
2/13-B, Ansari Road, Daryaganj
New Delhi – 110002
info@double9books.com
www.double9books.com
Tel. 011-40042856

This book is under public domain

ABOUT THE AUTHOR

Tyrone Edmund Power III was an American actor that lived between May 5, 1914 to November 15, 1958. Power featured in scores of films from the 1930s to the 1950s, frequently as a swashbuckler or a love protagonist. Jesse James, The Mark of Zorro, Marie Antoinette, Blood and Sand, The Black Swan, Prince of Foxes, Witness for the Prosecution, The Black Rose, and Captain from Castile are among his more well-known films. Nightmare Alley was Power's personal favorite among the films in which he appeared. Though he was primarily a matinée idol in the 1930s and early 1940s, and was noted for his striking good looks, Power acted in films ranging from drama to light humor. He began limiting the quantity of films he would produce in the 1950s in order to dedicate more time to theater performances. As a theatrical actor, he was most known for his performances in John Brown's Body and Mister Roberts. At the age of 44, Power died of a heart attack. In 1970, his eldest daughter Romina Power married Italian music superstar Al Bano, with whom she developed a musical duet that became enormously popular around the world.

CONTENTS

PREFACE

Although I have hitherto forborne all preface or dedication on exhibiting my small ware to the public, concluding that the less I said about the matter the better, and from having some scruples about tacking any lady's or gentleman's name to bantlings from which I had withheld my own; yet, in the present case, do I consider myself bound, in a like spirit of honesty, to provide this book with a few words descriptive of its quality, lest my Readers, being disappointed, may charge me with having deluded them under false "Impressions."

I seek, then, to describe America as I saw it, — a mighty country, in the enjoyment of youth and health, and possessing ample room and time for the growth, which a few escapades incident to inexperience and high blood may retard, but cannot prevent. Heaven has written its destinies in the gigantic dimensions allotted to it, and it is not in the power of earth to change the record.

I seek to describe its people as I saw them, — clear-headed, energetic, frank, and hospitable; a community suited to, and labouring for, their country's advancement, rather than for their own present comfort. This is and will be their lot for probably another generation.

To those, then, who seek scandalous innuendos against, or imaginary conversations with, the fair, the brave, and the wise amongst the daughters and sons of America, I say, Read not at all; since herein, though something of mankind, there is little of any man, woman, or child, of the thousands with whom I have reciprocated hospitality and held kind communion.

On the other hand, it can be objected that I set out by giving evidences of a partiality which may cause my judgment to be questioned.

Frankly do I avow this fault, and in my justification have but to add, that the person who, for two years, could be in constant intercourse with a people, to the increase of his fortune, the improvement of his health, and the enlargement of all that is good in his mind, yet feel no partiality in their favour, I pity for coldness more than envy for philosophy.

But whilst I am by nature incapable of repaying kindness by aspersion, I feel that I am no less above the meanness of attempting a return in that base coin—flattery; that which I saw I say, and as *I* saw it. I blame none of my predecessors for their general views, but claim the right of differing from them wherever I think fit; and if my account of things most on the surface even, should sometimes appear opposite to theirs, I would not, by this, desire to impeach their veracity, since the changes working in society are as rapid, though not quite so apparent, as those operating on the face of these vast countries, whose probable destinies do in truth render almost ridiculous the opinions and speculations of even the sagest of the pigmies that have bustled over their varied surface.

EUROPE

THE EVE OF SAILING

In youth's wild days, it cannot but be pleasant
This idle roaming round and round the world,
With wildfire spirits and heart disengaged.
Anster's Faustus.

When one first contemplates a voyage of many thousand miles, attended with long absence, loss of old associates, together with all the charms of home, country, and friends, often too lightly estimated whilst possessed, but always sorely missed when no longer within call; one is yet, and this through no lack of sensibility, apt to regard the sacrifice about to be made to duty as sufficiently light, and, with the aid of manhood and a little philosophy, easy of endurance. The very task, which a resolution of this grave nature necessarily imposes, of making as little of the matter as possible to those dear ones who yield up their fears, and subdue their strong affections, in obedience to your judgment, serves for a time the double purpose of hoodwinking oneself as well as blinding those on whom we seek to practise this kind imposition. Next comes the bustle of getting ready, assisted and cheered by the redoubled attentions of all who love, or feel an interest in one's fortunes. Amidst the excitement, then, of these various feelings, the deep-seated throb of natural apprehension, or home regret, if even felt, struggling for expression, is checked or smothered in the loud note of preparation. The day of departure is fixed at length, it is true; but then it is not yet come: even when contemplating its near approach, one feels wondrous firm and most stoically resolved: at last, however, come it does; and now our chief friend Philosophy, like many other friends, is found most weak when most needed. In vain do we invoke his approved maxims, hitherto so glibly dealt out to silence all gainsayers; yet now, they are either found inapt or are forgotten wholly, until, after a paltry show of defence, braggart Philosophy fairly takes to his heels, and leaves us abandoned to the will of old mother Nature. Now, indeed, arrives the tug; and I, for my part, pity the man who, however savagely resolute, does not feel and own her power. The adieus of those one loves are, at best,—that is, for the shortest absence,—sufficiently unpleasant; but when there lie years, and, to the eye of affection, dangers, in the way of the next meeting, as the old Scotch ballad has it, "O but it is sair to part!" I should, I confess, were I free to choose, prefer the ignominy of cowardly flight, to the greatest triumph firmness ever yet achieved, and be constrained to hear and respond to that last long "good-b'ye!"

As I honestly own that, for various good reasons, I set out with the intention of keeping such a close record of my feelings and doings as my errant habits might permit, with the premeditated design also of giving them to that public which from the beginning had decided that I should do so, I concluded there was nothing like an early start; and finding these thoughts preface, or rather commence, my journal, so do I give them like precedence here.

SAILING DAY

Liverpool, Tuesday, July 16th, 1833.

I am not usually very particular about dates; but, as there is an odd coincidence connected with the 16th, I desire to note it. On this day, then, about 3 P.M. I was rumbled from Bold-street down to St. George's Dock, accompanied by a few friends, who were resolute to extend their kindness to the latest limit time and tide, those unyielding agents, might allow.

Arrived at the ship's side, I found a number of my own poor countrymen, *agricultural speculators*, filling up a leisure moment before seeking harvest, in seeing "Who in the world was going to America, all that way," with which country there are now few of the humbler class of Irish but have some intimate associations. Disposing amongst *the boys* the few shillings I had left in my pocket, I jumped on board the packet-ship Europe, without cross or coin, saving only a couple of luck-pennies, the one an American gold eagle, the present of an amiable gentlewoman; the other a crooked sixpence, suspended by a crimson ribbon, the offering of a fair "maid of the inn," given to me on the very eve of sailing-day with many kind wishes, all of which have been realized.

The wind had been all the morning, and was still, away from the south-west; that is, right into the harbour; and I had heard many doubts expressed whether or not we should sail at all before night tide; doubts which, I am almost ashamed to confess, did not offend my ears so very much, considering my avowed impatience to be gone; nay, I do further admit having observed carelessly that I would as soon we did not sail until night tide, though wherefore I should thus have sought to keep chords on the stretch already too painfully braced, I leave to the wise to resolve.

Once on board, however, doubt was at an end; since the task of warping out from the tier was already commenced, and the noisy steamer might be heard bellowing and fuming, impatient of delay, from where she awaited us without the pier. We were moored inside several other ships; and the dock being quite full of craft, to the unpractised eye there appeared no possibility of winning a passage without doing or sustaining damage. However, what with warps and checks, careful and well-timed hauling, and ready backing, the gallant-looking Europe was quickly and safely handed over to the turbid waters of the Mersey without suffering a rub on her bright sides.

The steamer now took us in tow, and in a few minutes the busy docks and crowded pier-heads had passed away. Our companion vessels at parting were three only — a large private Indiaman, (the Albion,) a smaller ship for the coast of Africa, and a little gaily-painted Irish schooner called the Shamrock. These, it appeared, were dependent upon their own resources, and were soon left behind contending hardily with a strong beating wind; whilst the Europe, with yards pointed and sails closely furled, steadily and swiftly followed in the wake of the George the Fourth, looking like a noble giant led captive by some sooty dwarf. The Black Rock was soon gained, Crosby and its pretty cottages showed dimly distant; the mountains of Wales opened grandly forth before us; and, after one last long look, I dived to my state-room, partly to busy myself with seeing all my traps arranged and set in trim for sea, and partly to be alone.

THE EUROPE PACKET

"This goodly ship our palace is,

Our heritage the sea."

It will doubtless appear to many who shall win their way thus far into this book, a work of impertinent supererogation to describe at large an American packet-ship, together with the mode of living on board a regular *Liner*, considering that there are some three or four of these departing every week from Liverpool, London, and Havre, and at this same point I can fancy some hot fellow, who has performed his twentieth trip, here toss by my unoffending volume, with "Devil take the chap! does he think he knows about all this better than *us*?"

But, hold hard, my fiery friend, whilst I remind your worship that there are some thousands of the lieges out of the countless numbers who will be our readers, who, insular though they be, and well used to ships, have yet no conception of these wonders of the water; that is, provided the "Europe" is to be taken as a true sample of the service she belongs to: not to mention that what was new and notable to me, who have voyaged much, can hardly fail to interest some gentlemen "who live at home at ease."

Let, then, the reader who knows what a "between-decks" is, step below with me, and there picture to himself a room forty feet long, not taking in the deep transom, by sixteen in breadth, having on either hand a range of inclosed state-rooms about eight feet square, each with its own door and window, of bird's-eye maple curiously inlaid with variously grained wood, polished as glass. The upper part of the door and the whole of the side window are latticed; so that on both being closed, the occupant is hidden, yet the air admitted freely.

Each of these state-rooms is furnished with a washhand stand, containing a double service, a chest of drawers, with handles of cut glass, a shelf or two for books, &c. and a brace of berths or bed-places of ample dimensions, well appointed with mattress and linen, white as ever lassie lifted off the sunny side of a brae, at whose foot brawled the burn to which her labour owed its freshness.

Now, although each room is fitted up for two insides, you may nevertheless conserve your individuality,—the which I recommend,—at the cost of an additional half-fare, or, in all, about fifty-five pounds sterling.

Being here installed, then, *solus*, you will be roused from your sound night's sleep in the morning at eight bells, or eight o'clock A.M., by the tinkling of a shrewish-sounding hand-bell, which says, as plainly as ever the chimes of Bow hailed Whittington lord mayor of London, "Arise, and shave, and make your toilet, and prepare to come forth; for the cow is milking, and the kettle is screeching, and the hot rolls beginning to get over-brown."

Upon this welcome summons, if you are not sea-sick, which Heaven forbid! or insensible to the goods here by the gods provided for you, you will bounce or creep out of your crib, according as the waves and your agility may determine; and popping your head out of window, loudly bawl "Thomas!" or plain "Tom!" or "Steward!" according to the terms of friendship and familiarity on which you may stand with this dignitary, who, by the way, has a vote on board worth canvassing for;—I say bawl out, because, firstly, your mincing and Clarendon-like lisp of "Waiter!" would not be heard by one used to listen to the rush of the tempest and the shriek of the scourged Atlantic; also, for that your stirring call may remind some wretched skulker of a circumstance which he is miserably dozing out of remembrance, viz. that breakfast is under weigh. "Yes, sir!" is the prompt response from the larboard corner of the cabin, where the steward and his gang are installed with all their appointment of glass and crockery ranged neatly within reach. Your next call will be, "Bring me a bottle of Saratoga water"—a chalybeate, cool and brisk on the palate as soda water, a commendable morning draught, and such a trumpet to appetite!—well, having swallowed of this, your pint or so, dress, mount the deck, and inquire "how she heads," and what she has done during the long hours of night whilst you lay sleeping like a sea-bird in your wave-borne nest.

You next take a look over the weather quarter, sweep the horizon knowingly with your best eye, and after, walk forward towards the galley or kitchen, pricking your ears at certain sputtering and hissing sounds, the which, backed up by sundry savoury sniffs caught under the tack of the main-sail, give you foretaste of broiled ham, spitch-cock, eggs, frizzled bacon, and mutton cutlets.

One by one your messmates tumble up the companion, or cabin-stair; some hungry and blooming as sound stomachs and clear consciences can make them, others showing a *leetle* blue and bilious-like; but each and all resolute to essay the onslaught, which the train of polished covers, making rapid transit from the caboose down the steward's hatchway, proclaim about to begin.

Tinkle, tinkle, ting! again sounds the steward's bell; and, without any pauses of ceremony, down dive the *convives*, turning *en qûe* the foot of the stair, some to windward, others to leeward, but all facing right aft — a double game of "follow my leader."

"Oh! 'tis a goodly sight to see," the show which here presents itself; — covers of all sizes glisten under the flickering rays of the morning sun, stealing in through the open deck-light, and dancing about to the heave of the ship over a well-laid cloth flanked by ready plates and the weapons of attack.

The signal is made, the covers drawn; and, appetite or no appetite, here is temptation for all. If the incipient voyager will benefit by my experience, as he might well have done by my example had we been happy enough to have possessed his amiable society on board the Europe, he will develope his main battle against the mutton chops *au naturel*; then gossip over a slice of broiled *Virginy* ham, with an egg or twain, whilst his souchong is getting pleasantly cool; then, having emptied his cup, flirt with a couple of delicate morsels raised from the thin part of a salted shad-fish, the which shad, for richness and flavour is surpassing.

To his second cup he will dedicate the upper crust of a well-baked roll with cold butter; and, after having duly paused a while, choose between Cognac and Schiedam for a *chasse*. If he will yet walk with me, I say unhesitatingly, try Schiedam, in the absence, reverently be it spoken, of Isla or Innishowen.

Now, my pupil, if this breakfast would, which it could not fail to do, raise the bastard appetite of your close-curtained, feather-bedded coal-smoked, snivelling in-dweller of the city, judge of the influence it must exercise over a child of ocean, who inhales the breath of heaven freshly as generated beneath the blue sky that vaults his watery world, pure, uncorrupted, untainted by touch of anything more earthly.

Why, man, it is worth a life of ordinary vegetation to be stirred but for once by the sensations, such a morning as I draw from, in such a place, create; and to those who sagely shake the head and doubt, if any such cavillers there be, I say, "Pay your just debts; make your tenants easy, that their prayers may be in your sails; forgive your enemies, kiss your wife, draw up and add in her favour a codicil to your testament; and your duties being thus fulfilled, with a clean heart, backed by forty-eight clean shirts, go and try; and if you 'fall not' of my advice before you again embrace your mother country, curse Fortune for a perverse wench, and set your humble servant down for false counsel."

Leaving you now, my pupil, to write, to read, to practise shooting with ball at a bottle swinging from some outstanding spar, or to follow whatever pursuit most engages your fancy, for the space of some four hours, we will just name an intermediate and somewhat tempting meal, ycleped luncheon, chiefly indeed for the purpose of advising you to eschew it as you value unimpaired digestion, and would appreciate a four o'clock dinner. If, however, you are obstinately self-willed, and choose to obey a villanous unappeasable appetite, in place of following my wholesome advice, I pray you, at least, not to sit down knife in hand, as I have noted "some shameless creatures do;" but lift a piece of pilot biscuit, request some kind soul to shave the under side of the corned round for you, then desiring the steward to follow with a tumbler of Guiness's porter, fly the place and seek the deck.

Shuffle-board, chess, and backgammon, with exercise and pleasant converse, will while away the intervening hours so quickly, that, if you do not keep a bright look-out, you will be surprised by the dinner-bell before you think of your toilet, which, if a luxury to you on shore, will be thrice welcome at sea, besides being a pleasant way of disposing of twenty minutes; not to mention the ladies, who, at all times sensibly alive to any neglect in us, become doubly so here, where there is so much to remind them that they are not ruling in their own pretty drawing-rooms, though, as the old song has it,

"Queens they be

On the boundless sea,"

as indeed they are, and ought to be, everywhere.

Mem.—Do not trust your appetite to forewarn you of approaching dinner, since I have been more than once deceived by over-confidence in that quarter: truth is, you have the cry of "wolf" from that insatiable look-out so early and so often, that you learn after a time to treat the call as impertinent and troublesome, and so strive to cut it until the cutting moment really and unexpectedly comes upon you.

I have been so elaborate upon the head of breakfast, which meal, I freely confess to be my foible, that I feel as though any description of dinner would now come comparatively weak; besides, to speak verily, one might, with time and prudent choice, get as good a dinner, perhaps, a-shore in favoured countries: but for a breakfast, pho! the thing is beyond reach, away from the stores of a well-regulated Yankee packet. I challenge Europe, including Scotland, with all her *Finnanhaddies, herrin's,* cakes, and preserves, to back her.

Suffice it then to say, that here is a dinner of three courses, with pastry and various *confitures* which would not shame Gunter; and, for *boisson,* sherry, madeira, hock, and claret, with port for those who indulge in strong potations, and three or four times a week well-iced champagne.

A variety of dried fruits compose the dessert, since, although they sometimes raise small salad, I feel bound to admit that they have not yet attained to the comfort of a pinery on board: nor, let me add, did I see finger-glasses in use; and how persons get on who have never dined without them, I cannot guess, this not being my case, since luckily, even in England, I had sometimes roughed it in very good society without these necessaries. Once seated to dinner, there you remain, and imbibe until discretion bids you hold your hand, for other check have you none, cellar and servants remaining at your disposal.

After a walk on deck, and a cup of tea or coffee, you form your party for whist or some round game, or join the ladies in their *boudoir,* which I ought to have mentioned before as leading out of the great room forward, being a pretty square apartment, fitted up with sofas, mirrors, loo-table, and other little elegancies which ladies love to look upon and be surrounded by. *Entre nous,* between the lights this snuggery affords tolerable convenience for a little flirtation, if you are lucky enough to get one up; — this broken off, you play your play, and at the conclusion of your rubber of whist, or *parti d'ecarté,* you prepare for bed, — early hours forming here one of those sanitary laws which the wise feel little inclined to impinge.

Now I am quite well aware that on the head of night-caps every biped has his own fancy, and most of the genus I also know to be infernally pig-pated on this seemingly simple point; such incurables I abandon, to supper, porter, night-mare, and all the other nameless horrors that rouse them to avenge an ill-used stomach; but to the willing ear and ductile mind I whisper again, "try mine." *Imprimis* — one cigar, one tumbler of weak Hollands' grog, better named swizzle, all to be disposed of in pleasant company during some half-hour's walk on deck; when, if you should sometimes, as I hope you often may, fall in with a soft downy south-west breeze, a clear deep-blue sky over head, gemmed full with little stars, and fringed about, down into the watery round, by a broad border of jet-black cloud, against which each curling wave appears to break, and the goodly ship seems as though delving through a lake of quick-silver—when the track of the swift porpoises show like long furrows of dazzling flame, and over the whirling eddies of the keel's deep wake is seen to hover a strange unearthly light,—a thin bluish, devilish, vaporous haze, which, in the silent watch of night, maketh the lonely gazer's flesh to creep, and conjures through the brain every wild legend whispered of the "vasty deep," fascinating the eyes, and holding them with spell-like power, until—until what?—why, until a sharp twitch on the lip from the fire of the close-burned cigar we recommended awakens you to a due sense of such a "lame and most impotent conclusion."

Jump off the spare spar on which you have been perched whilst gazing so dreamily over the ship's quarter, give the last half of your grog to the old lad at the wheel, peep in on the compass, find she heads about west-north-west, and, well satisfied, descend the stair. The steward lights the waxen taper which fixes on a branch before your glass; when, having performed such ceremonies as you delight in, thank God and sleep: and thus ends the chapter of a day.

And, gentle pupil, if you would learn yet more especially to enjoy all this, which I have for your benefit somewhat *lengthily* detailed, give directions to the steward to rouse you at deck-washing; that is, about six A.M.; put on drawers and jacket of fine cotton, and, sunshine or cloud, calm or squall, run on deck, leave your *robe de chambre* in the round-house, and slide down into the lee gangway, where, according to previous contract, you see a grim-looking seven-foot seaman—pick out the tallest—waiting for you with a couple of buckets of sea-water, one held ready in his claw, with a half-grin upon his puckered phiz as he inwardly blesses the simplicity of the landsman who turns out of his hammock in the morning-watch to be soused like the captain's turtle in cold salt water; and i' faith! startlingly cold it gets when on the Banks, even in July, especially if within the influence of an ice-berg or twain: think not, however, of this, the infliction is light in comparison with the after enjoyment.

Being seated in the lee-scuppers, give the word; up goes the bucket, and wush! down pours the deluge on your oil-capped crown. "Hah!" you cry involuntarily, for the flesh will quiver, &c. You then compress your lips a little closer, whilst Jack's giggle expands into a broad grin, and in a steadier stream descends the second shower; which, having abided to the last drop, away you scurry along the wet deck, that is, always provided you avoid a fall or two by the way, into the round-house, on gown, and down to your little den; where a coarse towel, and a couple of flesh-brushes smartly applied for five minutes, will produce such a circulation throughout your inward man, that, like bold Waterton, you feel as though you could back an alligator, take the sea-serpent by the beard, or kick a noisy steamboat fairly out of water.

I have, since I am at confession, sometimes in very bad weather been tempted into bed after this ablution, when such an hour's nap awaits one! But this is a luxury Xerxes would have given a Satrapie to have tasted, and not to be indulged in over-often, lest it lead to effeminacy, which is as far removed from comfort as is sensuality from pleasure.

I have often heard objected to these fine ships the discomfort and difficulty attending toilet; but, for my own part, I did not discover these. Having a state-room, and possessed of the same appliances, with perhaps a little more trouble, a man may be as scrupulously nice as in any other dressing-room; provided always he be not prostrated by that unsparing nausea, sea-sickness; from the which I wish you, gentle reader, the full exemption I enjoy, and so commend you to repose.

THE EUROPE CONTINUED.— CHANGE OF AFFAIRS

"Life's like a ship in constant motion:
Sometimes smooth, and sometimes rough." — *Song*.

"Oh! the pleasures of a summer trip across the Atlantic!" Thus sung and chorused my good friends one and all; some from experience, most from hearsay, but ever in unison.

"You'll have quite a party of pleasure," says one. "The only thing to be dreaded will be the *ennui* arising out of long calms, gentle breezes, eternal sunshine by day and moonlight by night," says another.

One would have fancied, according to their account, that sun and moon alternated like buckets in a well, one up, the other down, with the exception that both were to be always at full.

So constant, however, were these remarks about heat, and sun, and summer air, that I packed up every article of clothing heavier than duck or cachmere; nay, had not some worthy matter-of-fact soul let slip a stray hint about ice and sleighing parties in December, I verily believe, hating as I do all superfluous baggage, I should have left my greatcoats to the moth and fog of Old England.

But whew! from such *airs* the Lord preserve me!—whilst at the tail of our honest, grimy, grumbling steamer, cutting through the Mersey or along the coast of Wales, we were, I admit, tolerably sunned and warm enough, though not even here bedazzled or over-heated; but on the second morning out, what a change!

I came on deck just before six A.M. to take my shower-bath; the wind was about west by south, blowing a brisk gale, the ship under double-reefed topsails, with top-gallant sails set over them, making all smoke again—on one hand lay the Isle of Rathlin, with the north coast of Ireland, bleak and bare; on the other, the Mull of Kyntyre, with a tide of its own rushing by like a mill-race, and over it the cloudy crest of Isla, looming through the flitting vapours, cold, dark, and hard-visaged, as though no drop of whisky had ever been brewed therein. One could not recognise the misty monster, thus grimly shadowed forth, to be the parent of that glorious sunny spirit.

We had full time afforded to become well acquainted with the changing aspects of these and the other localities hereabouts, for we had to battle it with their ally the wind, and with their waters, for full sixty hours; and although we at length fought our course seaward, it was to feel that such another victory would be anything but serviceable to the gallant ship.

Oh that infernal Rathlin! I shall not soon forget it; it is a spot I always held in ill odour ever since Miss Porter's "Scottish Chiefs" taught my unsophisticated youth to weep over the wrongs of Wallace wight. Now, although I abominate the place more, I have learned to compassionate her ill-starred hero less, since to have been carried southward through "merrie England" from such a place of exile, albeit the journey ended in hanging, was yet a deliverance especially to be rejoiced in.

We had a near view of the natives too, one day, trying to catch us in a whale-boat, whilst we were hugging the land sculking from the strength of the tide of flood: but, thank Heaven! they missed taking us as we went about on the opposite tack, the which I shall ever consider a providential escape, although at the time, a heedless confidence in our numbers led Captain Maxwell to throw them the end of a rope. They failed to lay hold on it, however, and away we dashed by them like a whirlwind; whilst the disappointed men gesticulating fiercely, with their red "fell o' hair" blowing to the four corners of the earth, and their wild eyes and ogre mouths agape, yelled forth a volley of strange sounds, soon drowned by the louder roar of these summer waves. This was happily the only danger we incurred from the natives; we saw no more of them,[2] and right glad were all-hands when the last glimpse of the Hebrides, or Western Isles, as they are called in their charts, faded away in their mist.

After this date one heavy blow succeeded another until the first of August, with seldom sun enough to afford an observation: yet it mattered not; like sea-birds we "rode and slept," for the excellence of the boat, and the way in which she was handled, was evident enough to inspire even the nervousness of inexperience with confidence; and the efficiency of our domestic arrangements bade defiance to the anger of the elements; — uninfluenced by their frowns as by their smiles, on went the work, and meal succeeded meal with faultless regularity.

On the second of August we passed within the immediate atmosphere of a huge iceberg. We had for some time previous been enveloped in fog, which suddenly lifting, showed us this isle of ice, and two other smaller ones.

The main island, by which we were most attracted, lay about a quarter of a mile to leeward, of dazzling whiteness, and picturesque of form, having at one end a lofty cone-shaped mountain, and at the other an angular bold mound, crowned by what we decided to be an extensive Gothic fortalice or castle, not unworthy the Ice-king himself if bent on a summer trip round the gulf stream: between these promontories lay a deep valley thickly tenanted by tribes of the white gull.

Three sides of Castle-hill were regularly scarped, the fourth communicated by a neatly kept slope with the valley, and along this radiated a number of well-trodden paths, all uniting at the castle gate, at once giving evidence of considerable population, and great hospitality on the part of the worthy castellan.

The position of these islands was unusual, and their appearance occasioned a little surprise, although the fall of the thermometer, and the change in the temperature of the water, had led Captain Maxwell, some hours before we met them, to decide upon their vicinity.

On the banks of Newfoundland they are common at this season of the year, and form, indeed, the danger most to be dreaded of the voyage; since, if the weather should prove thick, and the ice swim deep, scarce showing above the surface, as is commonly the case, a ship going quickly through the water may strike before any measures can be taken to avoid the encounter.

A fine packet, the Liverpool, but nine days out, on her first trip was totally lost on one of these in the summer of 1822; and this very year our captain coasted to the southward for seventy miles along the edge of a field of ice, in which he had previously been locked-up for fifty hours, till released by a lucky shift of wind. On this occasion he had one on board whose experience among ice had been well tested, and was about to be yet again tried; for Lieutenant Back was here on his perilous adventure in quest of the long lost Captain Ross and his crew.

For the succeeding sixteen or seventeen days of our voyage the weather was generally fine. Upon the western edge of the Banks we had a few days' calm, which taking advantage of, I turned my morning shower-bath into a plunge from the bowsprit, and had a delicious swim round the ship. The passengers, however, got wind of my fun, and in obedience to the kindly meant remonstrances of one or two of them, I forbore a pleasure which never occurred to me to be perilous, for I have practised it in many parts of the ocean, always taking care that there was no way upon the ship.

We had no casualties except amongst the pigs, sheep, and poultry; and as yet no great loss of spars, indeed in all our blows, we only sprung a main-topsail yard, carried away a fore-topmast, and made a few stu'n-sail booms, — for the latter, we had very little use, not having the wind abaft the beam over five days, all counted, out of a passage of thirty-five; and how it was accomplished in the time under the circumstances, is yet to me a matter of some wonderment.

FOOTNOTE:

[2] To homeward-bound ships these visits of the *Rathlineans*, often prove sufficiently welcome, as they generally provide themselves with a cargo of ancient, fish-like milk, and fine potatoes. The Europe having an excellent dairy and a poultry-yard of her own, stood in no need of their supplies.

JOURNAL AT SEA

This is usually a very monotonous task to the journalist, and can hardly fail of soon becoming tiresome to the reader, since a voyage away from the land affords but little to record; still, as it is my intention occasionally to refer to this current report of my *Impressions* and every-day-doings, I may as well transcribe literally a page or two illustrative of every-day life in this, our "Europe."

July 31st. — Sixteen days out this afternoon; during which time, with but forty-four hours that we could fairly lay our course, the good ship has knocked off forty degrees of westing, a prodigious slant under the circumstances. The last two days up to meridian, we have run ten degrees of longitude and two of latitude.

Thursday, August 1st. — Going about seven knots, heading west by north; all well and mighty agreeable. Rifle-shooting and backgammon the great antagonists of time before dinner — whist after. Various wagers are daily made against time, as to the length of our passage, as well as for or against certain ships that preceded or were to follow us. Most persons have named some date for our arrival at New York, and backed it for more or less; finding that these days were selected more in accordance with the desires of the betters than their judgment, I selected an outsider, and took the longest date named for my day, August 20th. The odds fluctuate daily in the market, according to the view the knowing ones take of the weather: these bets form a subject of interest and banter which daily rises in importance.

Wednesday, 7th. — About meridian carried away our main-topsail yard, whilst two hands were employed rigging in the studding-sail boom; one fell into the top, and the other caught hold of the rigging, receiving much fright but small damage. Had they fallen on the deck or over-board, why their chance would have been exceeding small. There surely is "a sweet little cherub that sits up aloft," &c. or these careless rogues could not escape so often scot-free.

To-day we have a rattling north-easter with sunshine: and the sea, which yesterday was wild, dreary, and dark, is now beaming and light as a beauty at a birth-day ball; and as radiant, for it sparkles in diamonds of its own.

All hands in high spirits, the ship the favourite for odds; Time gone back sadly; the 13th inst. named for very long odds; I offered eight to one against it, and was taken up at a word. Made two or three entries in my book after dinner; against the 20th, my day; take all that offers, but have made a *leetle* hedge on the 18th by way of a break-water.

Saturday, 9th.—A very heavy gale from north-west, a rare occurrence at this season; it stuck to us for fifty hours, hauling gradually round to the south'ard. No business done to-day; 'change deserted; not a time-bargain to be had for love or money; most of the bulls in bed.

Tuesday, 13th.—One of the most lovely days possible: all the morning we have been observing a large ship right a-head, on which we draw rapidly, though a stern chase is proverbially a long chase. The alley all alive, books and pencils in great demand: odds offered freely that this ship is the Tallahassie, Captain Glover, which sailed from Liverpool on the morning of the day we left; but owing to our taking the north channel, whilst she pursued the south, had thus gotten a decided pull upon us, besides being a very fine ship. Consultations frequent, as we neared, between the mate and the backers of the Tallahassie, adjournments to the top-gallant forecastle constant; every spy-glass in requisition.

We drew near; the odds rose in favour of this being the ship in question—she was a large ship, square-built and long, so was Tallahassie— she was flush deck, so was Tallahassie—had stump-royal masts, and a storm-house abaft, so had Tallahassie, hurrah! Nearer we came, less ardour amongst the backers of Tal.—nearer still, they are all silent; the alley is deserted for the forecastle—a straggler now comes aft, with a sneaking offer of a hedge: no takers.

One of the opposite side's scouts next comes aft. "This can't be the Tallahassie—this ship has no copper, Tallahassie had; she has a white line over her bright side, Tallahassie had not—her top-rail is white, and the yards tipped with the same colour, the Tallahassie's were black.—In short, it could not be the Tallahassie, as any one with half an eye might have seen from the first, and might see now."

The latter part of the proposition was already demonstrated, for we were by this time right a-beam; the former might have been disputed, although it certainly was not the Tallahassie.

Trifles like this were all-sufficient occupation for the day, and served as subjects of conversation after. On this occasion we had for nearly the first time a complete muster of our crew, the exceeding fineness of the day brought out even our sick, and there they lounged about in the sun, like weary birds plumeing their ruffled feathers.

Sunday, 18th.—Wind north-west; weather fine. We are now within one hundred and sixty miles of our port. Betting-market a little anxious, but a good deal of business doing in a quiet way; my odds looking well, but to-morrow, the 19th, by far the favourite, Captain Maxwell himself indeed, considering it a hollow thing. Got a notion in my head, however, in favour of my day, and accordingly took the odds; resolute to abide by the 20th, and either "mak' a spune or spoil a horn."

All hands well and in motion; the crew busily employed getting the sea-service off the rigging, and setting it all up in holiday order. The mate is peering about jealously on all sides, eyeing his ship as a mother would a beauty dressing for her first drawing-room, and to the full as anxious about her appearance.

Monday, 19th.—In the middle watch had a heavy squall, and carried away our foretop-gallant mast. At nine o'clock, A.M. made the American shore off Jersey, to the southward of Barney Gat. Wind light, no betting, but anxious speculations on the probability of our getting within Sandy Hook this day. Tuesday a hollow thing, feel "cock sure:"—about noon, wind died away; and, right enough, it was not until

Tuesday, August 20th, that at three o'clock, A.M. I was called on deck to look upon the Hook lights, and count my wagers won. I received the omen as a good one, and so it proved.

LAND, HO!

I had often, and with much pleasure, heard intelligent Americans describe the restless anxiety with which they approached the shores of Britain; the almost painful degree of excitement created by the various associations crowding on the imagination, and jostling each other for supremacy, as they looked for the first time on their father-land.

The veneration with which they pictured her ivy-clad towers, and the throb with which they caught the names of places long familiar to memory and hallowed by historical events, to all of which they felt their claim inherited from their ancestors, whether from Thames, or Tweed, or Shannon.

To all of this I have, I say, listened with great pleasure, and with a full sympathy in feelings at once natural and generous, yet can I hardly admit them to possess more force, or their nature to be more exciting, or richer in the material whence Fancy frames her chequered web, than the recollections awakened in a well-stored imagination by a near approach to the shores of America. Although differing widely, these are to every philosophic mind, especially to a subject of Britain, at least equally stirring.

When it is first remembered, that on all the long line of coast extending from the St. Lawrence to the Gulf of Mexico there was not, in the beginning of the sixteenth century, one European family settled, or a Christian voice that woke the forest with the name of God, — not a civilized man from Canada to Florida, who placed his foot upon the soil to call it home. Yet now, within this immense range may be reckoned the mightiest States of the Union; and over its wide circumference are scattered great cities, towns aspiring to be cities, and villages fast growing into busy towns — possessing a population which for wealth hardly need yield to the oldest countries of Europe, and in the general diffusion of intelligence and education offering indeed to most of these an example worthy of their imitation.

When it is called to mind that the waters of her vast line of coast, now daily ploughed by thousands of busy prows, were at this same not very distant day as desert as her swamps and as unfurrowed, except where the canoe of the scared Indian left its light track behind, when driven from the shelter of some near river: — silent and shadowless, except when the sail of the adventurous explorer flitted slowly over the waves, as he steered his doubtful course filled with the many wonders seen and fancied by his watchful, credulous crew, — some band of daring spirits tempted hither in search of gold, or wild adventure, perhaps to perish suddenly by the arrow of the savage, or slowly to wither beneath the influence of the climate — God! what wonderful changes have been wrought here, and what a living marvel is this land! Changes, which it has required the labour of ages to accomplish elsewhere, have here been effected by the energy of a few busy generations, whose toil was begun and carried on amid want, and sickness, and a struggle against ignorance and neglect without, as well as a war of extermination within; a war which may be said to exist even to this day, for yet is the ever-growing frontier from time to time awakened by the night whoop of the savage and the answering shot of the hardy pioneer.

Then come the recollections connected with the war of the Revolution, — the noble declaration of independence, for truly noble it was: no dark compact of a crew of ruffian conspirators, but a generous bond that their aggrieved country should be freed, given by a band of citizen gentlemen, husbands, fathers, and brothers, to the fulfilment of the which they pledged unto each other their lives, their fortunes, and their sacred honour; and having placed their hands to this bold deed, they gave it to their people and the world.

Their bond is cancelled, and they are dismissed beyond the hearing of praise or censure; yet shall these, the names of their country's fathers, be read and blessed by ages yet to come, and shall stand for ever, each a synonyme for patriot honour.

Washington, and the long wars he conducted through defeat and disaster to such a glorious end for his country, together with that large list of famous names connected with those and later events formed no mean subject for reverie, and these were the fancies conjured through my brain by a near approach to the shores of America. I confess I contemplated her triumphs with a participation in her glory where England was not a party, with no other feeling than regret when she was, — with regret that the hands of brothers should ever have been opposed in deadly enmity.

I give back in love of country to no man, and to no foe under heaven would I yield up one jot due to Britain's well-won supremacy, but to the United States we may surely spare without envy the leaf she so hardily plucked from our thick laurels. The glory of having given her birth, language, and laws, she cannot rob us of; this will endure until her mountains crumble: and all else she has acquired at the expense of Britain, Britain can well spare, and still stand foremost on the roll of Fame.

PORT

On the morning of Tuesday, August 20th, I was roused, according to a request I had left to that effect with Captain Maxwell, to look on the Hook Lights, the entrance to the outer bay and harbour of New York. It was three o'clock in the morning, a fresh yet bland breeze was just giving motion to the smooth sea, and above, the firmament showed thickly studded with heaven's lights; but the dazzling pharos of the Hook, to my mind, were brighter at this hour than the best twinklers on the floor of heaven, — so welcome were they.

While waiting on deck, a couple of sky-rockets were discharged from the storm-house by way of signal for a pilot. The effect of the sudden blaze was fine; and the rush of each fiery messenger on its upward mission, as it burst away from the Europe's deck, seemed a glad sound of welcome, for it spoke of safe arrival, and consequent freedom from our present thrall; for, however pleasant a ship may be, and however poetical our notions about the "deep sea," after having been in the one and on the other for five or six weeks, there are few bipeds who do not hail the shore as a type of recovered liberty, and, however barren it may be, right joyfully embrace it.

About 7 A.M. — for here it appears pilots do not hurry themselves — we made out a couple of schooner-rigged boats standing right for us, which were at first taken for pilots, but proved to be news-boats. Several such are, as it appears, kept in commission by the New York journals, and the struggle for early intelligence between the rivals occasions a display of considerable adventure not unattended with risk, since these news-boats are out in all weathers, and from a great distance often bring to the city a ship's letters, &c. many days before she makes her own appearance.

The news-collectors were welcomed civilly by our captain, bagged their papers, made out a list of the passengers, and in a few moments were again on the wing for shore, looking right into the wind, and with smooth water and a light breeze, they drew rapidly away from the heavier ship. I must observe that our Mercury's correctness was by no means commensurate with his activity; for such ingenious changes did this worthy contrive in the names of the passengers, that the mothers of some would have failed to have discovered the arrival of their sons, except upon instinct.

At length, after long watching, a couple of pilot-schooners were discovered standing out from under the high land, and in due time their boats boarded us nearly together; and hence arose a dispute as to whose particular prey the good Europe was to be considered.

Each Pilot was voluble, and accused the other of violating the laws made and provided in such cases for their better government: who was wrong in this case it was difficult to say, but I very clearly made out that both parties had cheated on former occasions, were willing to cheat in this, and resolute to continue a like commendable practice in all others that might offer, as far as in them lay. What arrant rogues are we in all climes and under whatever rule, quoth I, internally, as I listened to these wordy disputants; for, to do messieurs the pilots justice, the matter was conducted in a manner more worthy the courts, better argued, and in language less offensively figurative, than similar disputes at which it has been my chance to assist between angry members of our own *bars*.

At length the elder pilot left the deck, and returned to his attendant yawl, in evident dudgeon and disgust; when the junior, being hailed by his comrades in the schooner on the opposite quarter, was advised to give up the Europe, since they had made out a second ship quite as large in the offing.

Whether this information, or a latent sense of justice prevailed, it is hard to say; but on the tidings our man hailed his irate senior—who was borne away amidst deeply-muttered vows of vengeance—desired him to return, and told him he would give up the ship. Thereon, back rowed our ancient mariner; and after a few explanatory sentences, mutually offered as salvos to their hurt honour, the rivals parted, to all outward seeming as good friends as ever.

Which had right I know not, but one of them had fish, and we of the Europe had no cause to mourn the departure of that one, since, having gained his deck, he sent us back a basket of newly-taken porgies, and various other fishes with unpoetical names but of marvellous sweetness, and sumptuous was our *déjeuner* in consequence of this unlooked-for addition.

Henceforward, all between-decks presented a scene of bustle and preparation; the most sluggish natures amongst us appeared now inspired, whilst on all sides were heard good-humoured congratulations and glad anticipations. I confess, although a very experienced voyager, I felt a little touch of softness striving to sneak into and coil about my heart, as the words, — home — friends, with other household sounds, fell thick upon my hearing; for, all our passengers being American, I stood alone here on this day of happy greeting, a stranger amongst strangers.

Let me add, that this was the last day on which I felt so during my long sojourn in the hospitable land; and even on this I possessed buoyancy enough of spirit to keep down these selfish reflections, and, I thank Heaven, sympathy enough to rejoice in the gladness of my comrades.

I did not lack amusement, either after the first hurry was past; an intelligent friend or two busied themselves pointing out to me the various localities in detail, with whose general character Carey's excellent atlas had already made me tolerably conversant.

The day was clear and cloudless; and when to this advantage is added a light head wind, which compelled us to work our way inward, no harbour could be approached under auspices more favourable, or better calculated to afford a complete and varying view of its beauties.

Just as we had opened the Narrows, the entrance to the inner bay so called, the wind grew so unpromising that a party of us decided to engage the pilot vessel to take us as far as Staten Island, which they "calculated" they could reach before the departure of the steamer for New York.

Bidding adieu to the Europe, away we dashed in the little witch of a pilot, a craft of some eighty tons' burthen, but, viewed from a short distance, not looking more than half that size, so snug was her build, as well as from the absence of every kind of hamper; her shrouds were without ratlins, and her deck without even the protection of a rough-tree — a nakedness I should by no means like in bad weather. The afterpart, however, or stern-sheets, is sunk about four feet; and as the bowsprit is a mere stump, and the sheets of both foresail and jib lead aft, all the work may be done here when under snug sail.

The necessity, during our trip in the schooner, of working up between the shores of Long and Staten Islands, was a chance that added to the charm of our approach.

Standing into the Narrows, under the guns of a formidable fort, the pretty-looking village of Staten, where quarantine is performed, first presented itself: the smoke of the steamer assured us she had not yet departed, and two or three tacks brought us within signaling distance, just as she broke away from the shore: our desire was readily understood, and, slightly changing her course, she soon after received us in addition to her already crowded freight.

I found the upper deck of the Bolivar, the name of our steamer, uncommonly hot, but it afforded a good place from which to view the harbour and city as they were now rapidly unfolded: here, therefore, I planted myself, all eyes; and certainly have rarely been better repaid for a broiling.

As we neared the Battery, we were afforded a passing glance up the East and North Rivers, — the great waters which give wealth to Manhattan, and jealously clip her beauty about, in equal participation. The *coup d'œil* thus taken is very imposing, and at once awakens the stranger to a sense of the commercial importance of the *entrepôt* whose walls he perceives shaded by such a forest of lofty masts.

NEW YORK

FIRST IMPRESSIONS OF THE CITY

On landing at the Battery, our first visit was to an office of the customs here; and, instead of the dogged, sulky, bribe-demanding scowl, too commonly encountered from our own low-class officials, who seem to consider the custom-house as a means rather of annoyance to the lieges than a protection to trade, we were met by civility, respect, and prompt despatch. The luggage we had brought with us on shore was not subjected to the least examination, and we went on our way highly pleased. First impressions give their colour to succeeding matters; and surely those derived from my encounter with the officials of a service at best annoying, were much in favour of the land.

On entering the quiet Bowling Green, where many of the houses have coloured fronts, and all gaily painted jalousies, with trees shadowing the *stoups*, I was reminded of Cape Town: but the impression was momentary; a few yards on, and the long line of Broadway, with its crowded side walks, showy shops, and numerous hotels, at once transports you back to Europe; and, were it not for the sprinkling of black faces with which the mass is chequered, one might swear oneself in Paris on some portion of the Boulevards not altogether familiar to the eye, but offering most of the points needful to prove identity, from the monkey and hurdy-gurdy of the Savoyard, the *blouse* of the carman and *Conducteur*, to the swagger of the citizen-soldier, and the mincing step and *"tournure charmante"* of the *belles*. The fronts of the *cafés* and hotels, too, as you pass along, you perceive to be covered by chairs occupied by similar loungers to those on the Boulevards.

Such were my impressions whilst moving on a hot day from the Battery to the City Hotel, and so give I them place here; since I have often, after a long residence in a place, found myself referring back to these first glimpses, when desirous to present it at once fresh and comprehensive to the eye of the stranger, and for such these sketches are chiefly designed.

A BIVOUAC

The day after my arrival, I was both interested and amused by accidentally falling on the bivouac of a Swiss family of emigrants.

I had risen early for the purpose of bathing, and was making my way to the fort through the grounds of the Battery as the rising sun was just adding new light and life to the most beautiful of harbours, when I came suddenly upon the barriers of a little encampment perfectly Teutonic in its arrangement; it was, however, no surprisal to the hive within, for their morning operations had already begun.

Within a circular rampart, formed out of various articles of household gear, — three or four antique-looking spinning-wheels, a pair of churns, a few clumsy chairs, a large chest, together with a couple of small heavy waggons not yet placed upon the wheels, — were a few as lively recruits as any land desirous of population could wish to welcome.

The party consisted, first, of a right venerable-looking old man, the patriarch of the tribe, as he told me, seventy-four years old; six men, his sons and grandsons; seven lively boys, his great-grandchildren, and about an equal number of girls, the patriarch's wife, nearly as aged as himself, but with a shrill piercing voice and the activity of a girl of nineteen, with four other women, the wives of the ancient's sons.

At the moment I came upon them the whole camp was rousing into full activity. The grandmother, assisted by a couple of her young women, found ample occupation in first catching and next washing the junior branches of the colonists: these appeared already aware of their being in a country where every individual thinks for himself, or at least thinks he does, which comes to the same thing, for they stoutly resisted, to the last extremity, the soapless saline ablutions profusely administered by their great grandam.

Meantime a couple of the more staid of the youngsters, who had been passed outside the lines, were busied beneath the trees collecting fallen sticks, leaves, &c. for keeping up the fire already lighted and presided over by one of the females, whose task it evidently was to prepare breakfast.

A couple of the men yet slept soundly; another pair were composedly leaning against a waggon smoking their pipes; whilst a third, the youngest of the grown men, and evidently the *beau-garçon* of the party, was busied about the completion of a careful toilet before six square inches of looking-glass, held up to him by a young lass, rather good-looking, who, kneeling before this Adonis in evident admiration, most patiently abided the completion of his equipment previous to commencing her own.

My course was at once arrested by a scene so new and unexpected; and I stood for a long time contemplating the repose of this little group, camping here in the midst of a busy population on the banks of the Hudson, in the same manner and after the same fashion their ancestors are described to have followed by the Rhone and the Danube in the time of Cæsar.

There was an air of confident security about the whole arrangement, that spoke equally in favour of the hardy simplicity of these strangers and the courtesy and honesty of their adopted country; for I know no European capital wherein such a group could have sat them down and passed a summer night, unhoused and unwatched, without receiving annoyance, if not suffering loss.

I learned that the family had been landed late on the preceding afternoon from a French ship; so that, not being able, as is the wont of this people, to depart for their destination immediately, they had in the most prompt and orderly manner pitched their tents here for the night, and were now preparing for their march into the wilderness.

This sight, striking in itself, was no less illustrative of the country and the time: these arrivals are of daily occurrence here during the season; every one of the northern nations of Europe is contributing her quota out of the most enterprising of her children to swell the numbers, and give additional pith and vigour to the population, of this land of wonder.

About three hours after this first rencounter, whilst seated in our parlour at breakfast, I pointed out to my friend P— — the whole family passing the city hotel *en route*.

They had now gotten one of their clumsy waggons mounted, and rudely harnessed to a stout-looking horse, and on this vehicle was piled all their worldly store. The males, pipe in hand and marching four abreast, strode boldly on before; next came the waggon, surrounded and followed by the women and children: the heads of one or two of the youngest of these, by the bye, might just be seen poking out from the lumber amongst which they were ensconced upon the car.

I observed that the old dame now carried in her hand a wicker-cage, containing a little captive of the goldfinch tribe, some home-bred favourite, whose simple notes will often call up the memory of father-land, when this family of humble adventurers shall be located, happily I trust, on some wild stream of the far west, for thither were they bound, and, with the appliances I have sketched, were cheerfully setting forth to perform a journey of some two thousand miles. These, however, are the sort of persons who may look most to benefit by such a change; after a few to them trifling privations, and an industrious struggle, they have the certain satisfaction of beholding their offspring surrounded by comfort, and their means yearly increasing. They presently exchange want for plenty, and cease to look upon the coming time with fear or doubt for even their children's children; since generations must rise and pass away before enterprise and honest industry will feel any lack of elbow-room here.

The weather was awfully hot during the last week of this month; and great was my delight, on entering the parlour of a morning, to look upon the butter luxuriating beneath a large wedge of clear ice: only for the cutting up, I should have gloried in being a *Pat* of butter myself. This article of ice is presented here in a purity of form, and is withal so plentiful, that it almost makes amends for the dog-days.

Our breakfasts were excellent—fish, fruit in abundance, chickens, omelette, &c. with good coffee, and the best black tea I ever drank. The parlour was a very large well-furnished room, level with and fronting on the busiest part of Broadway; and a more amusing stand than one of the windows, for a stranger, it would be difficult to select. The whole busy population, I should imagine, passed in review here once, at least, in six hours; together with samples of all the nondescript vehicles city or country rejoices in.

To one worthy I owe many a hearty laugh,—who knows but I may have repaid the good soul in kind?—I hope I have, for my gratitude is his. Let the reader imagine a long street, very crowded, and about noon shadeless, with the thermometer at 98° in the sun. In the very middle of this broiling thoroughfare, fancy a low carriage on four wheels, ycleped a Jersey waggon, having a seat with a high back hung by straps athwart-ships; over this seat a buffalo robe of vast dimensions, the thick fur outside and a red lining within, falling in heavy folds to the waggon floor; upon this buffalo skin, seated right in the centre, with knees and elbows spread as far apart as possible, a huge mass of humanity clothed in a dark jacket of home-spun cloth, with vest and trousers of blue cotton; his pumpkin-like head covered by a broad-leafed straw hat, a Dutch pipe on his lip, and before him a hard-mouthed awkward little horse pulled about by both hands, now right, now left, but rarely going out of a walk. Above a high shirt-collar his full-blown cheeks might be seen, as he sucked in the hot air and rejected it again like a blowing porpoise: cravat he had none, because he had no neck to tie it about; but in lieu of this article he carried, knotted over his broad shoulders, a little red handkerchief. Daily did I ask myself for a whole week "Will it walk again?" and, so surely as the shadeless hour of noon arrived, did my Dutch fire-king arrive with it, steering his waggon through the sweltering mass with a composure—coolness I could not call it—most enviable.

I would have given anything to have known him and his history; but though I had opportunities of pointing him out to my friends occasionally, no one knew him. Son of a thousand burgomasters, may your shadow never grow less! for I owe to you the beguilement of many a hot hour: but I fear me my friend must be "larding six feet of lean earth," somewhere in the vicinity of Manhattan, since for the last year I have, on every day that the sun shone intensely with the glass over 90°, watched in vain for his coming.

In the cool of the afternoon, if there chance to be any cool, it is a common custom for the young men of all classes to drive or ride some five or six miles along the north avenue,—an excellent road leading to the pretty village of Harlaem; and on this line, about sunset, the amateur of horse-flesh may see done, the fastest pace in the trotting world; double-horse waggons of the neatest and lightest construction, gig, sulky, and saddle, all are alike borne along by trotters or pacers at a speed varying from the pair that are doing their mile in three minutes, to the sulky or saddle nag flying at the rate of a mile in two minutes, thirty seconds.

The first time I was whirled along this road at the heels of one of the crack goers of the city, amidst clouds of dust through which the rushing of other vehicles might be dimly made out, and startled by the wild cries used by the rival drivers, at once to encourage their horses and prove the impossibility of scaring them into breaking up, I thought it one of the most exciting things I had ever met; and on getting down at Cato's, involuntarily found myself drawing a long breath.

CATO'S!

And what is Cato's? and who is Cato? Shade of Rome's patriot and sage, anger not! for Cato is a great man, foremost amongst cullers of mint, whether for *julep* or *hail-storm*; second to no man as a compounder of *cocktail*, and such a hand at a *gin-sling*!

Cato is a gentleman of colour who presides at a little tavern, named after its proprietor, lying just off the dust of the road between two sharp hills, and situated some four miles from New York—a good breathing distance for a fast burst—and here consequently most men halt to give their horses breath, and wash the dust out of their own throats with some one of Cato's many excellent compounds. The convenience of the place is enhanced by the manner of its master, who for courtesy and *bienséance* might serve as a model to most of his young friends. His society indeed is of the very best, including all the first sporting youths of the city; and his liquors are equal to his breeding.

Cato will give a few select friends breakfast too on a hot morning, if it be especially ordered; and, certes, a woodcock and toast as served up by him on these occasions is a thing not to be forgotten. It was my fortune, under the auspices of my friend, Mr. M'L—d, an especial favourite of "mine host," to pay several visits to Cato's, and to come away at each with added respect for the great man, and increased regard for his excellent entertainment.

THEATRE

Great heat – doubts, dubitations, and début.

I do not intend to bore my readers with a series of play-bills, or a journal of my theatrical career; but I feel that on this head there may be some little curiosity, and that it would on my part be an affectation to eschew the subject, as well as an injustice to my American comrades of the buskin, to whom I owe some kind mention, since it was my lot to add considerably to their labours. I will therefore just notice my appearance in each city as it occurred, and that as briefly as may be consistent; when any fun turns up, I promise the reader the benefit of it. I shall also give my impressions of the various audiences I encountered; because I think there is no place where the characteristics of a people are more clearly shown than at a theatre, where all mix upon a footing more purely democratic than in any other whatever, and each man having a right to evince his taste after his own fashion, opinion becomes the only conservation of propriety.

To my first night at New York, then, I looked with much anxiety, and not without reason. I had, contrary to the advice of many friends, given up a large income, the continuance of which the increasing favour of the public gave me reasonable promise of. I had vacated my seat and quitted my country on no other engagement than one for twelve nights at New York, the profits of which were wholly dependent upon my success, as were my engagements in other cities dependent upon my reception in this.

One kind soul assured me that every drama I possessed had been already anticipated; another, that they had no taste for Irish character, or that accustomed, as they had long been, to associate with the representative of my poor countrymen a ruffian with a black eye, and straw in his shoes, the public taste was too vitiated to relish a quiet portrait of nature undebased.

This was flattering, but not pleasant: the only man whose views appeared sanguine was Mr. P— —, who had been my companion on the voyage, and whose cheering reply to all doubters was, "I tell you, sir, it must do."

The theatre was announced to be re-opened on the 28th of August, with the "Irish Ambassador" and "Teddy the Tiler." The day was one of the hottest we had known, and towards night it became oppressively close.

No strange actor of the least note could open in New York, to anything short of a full house; it seems to be a hospitable principle to give the aspirant for fame a cordial welcome and a fair hearing; let it not be considered egotistical, therefore, when I say that the house was crowded; from pit to roof rose tier on tier one dark unbroken mass; I do not think there were twenty females in the dress circle; all men, and enduring, I should imagine, the heat of the black hole at Calcutta. I at the time regretted the absence of the ladies, when, had I been less selfish, I should have rejoiced at it.

The moment came when "Sir Patrick" was announced; and amidst greetings as hearty as ever I received in my life, I made my first bow to the Park audience. I saw no coats off, no heels up, no legs over boxes—these times have passed away; a more cheerful, or apparently a more English audience, I would not desire to act before.

I was called for at the end of the play, and thanked the house for its welcome. If the performance had not gone off with that electric and constant laughter and applause to which I had grown accustomed at home, I had received positive assurance that my new clients were intelligent and very attentive, and I therefore no longer entertained fears for the result.

Not so, however, one or two of my friends, whose anxiety and kind wishes it would have been hard indeed for any measure of applause to have satisfied: amidst the congratulations they brought me were therefore mixed up little cautionary drawbacks.

"It was capital," said one; "but you must not be so quiet: give them more bustle."

"In some other piece," replied I; "here it is not in the bond."

"You must paint a little broader, my dear fellow," says another:—"you're too natural for them; they don't feel it."

"If it's natural they must feel it," said I, adding, "each of my characters are, according to my ability, painted from nature; they are individual abstractions with which I have nothing to do; the colouring is a part of each, and I can't change it as I change my audience:—'tis only for me to present the picture as it is; for them to like or dislike it."

For the six following evenings the houses, though not great, were equal and good; each night I found my audience understanding me better, and felt that I was grappling them closer to me. The arrival of Mrs. and Mr. Wood earlier than the manager counted upon, created a difficulty; to obviate which I waived my claim to six of my nights, as my acting must have kept them idle.

A day or two before my departure for Philadelphia, I witnessed the first appearance of this lady and her husband. Her reception was enthusiastic, but Malibran had left impressions it was difficult to compete with; and, although her brilliant talent was on all hands admitted, I am not sure whether her husband's manly style of singing a ballad was not to the full as much considered as her execution of the most brilliant scéna.

The Park Theatre is, as well as I could judge, about the size of the old Lyceum, of the horse-shoe form; has three tiers of boxes; is handsome, and in all respects as well appointed as any theatre out of London.

The orchestra is at present excellent, and under the direction of a very clever man — Penson, formerly leader at Dublin. The company I found for my purpose a very fair one, my pieces requiring little save correctness from most of those concerned, except where old men, like "Aspen," "Frederick II." &c. occur, and all such parts found an excellent representative in an American actor, called Placide. Descended of a long line of talented players, he possesses a natural talent I have rarely seen surpassed, together with a chastity and simplicity of style that would do credit to the best school of comedy; yet he has never been away from his own country. I trust the model may not be lost on those who have to follow him.

There is a representative of old women here, too, a native, Mrs. Wheatley, an inartificial charming actress, with a perfect conception of all she does, and a humorous *espièglerie* of manner that is admirable. This lady has a daughter, a girl of fourteen, one of the cleverest mimics I ever saw: she would imitate Miss Fanny Kemble throughout a whole character, or think, talk, and walk, like her in private, — all with a slight dash of caricature, but in a spirit of truth and acute observation worthy of the inimitable Matthews himself.

With these exceptions, the company is, I think, made up of English actors, many of whom have held respectable situations in the London houses.

I had heard a good deal of the disorder of the American stage, and the intractability of American actors; with this specimen I had therefore every reason to be pleased. I am rather a hard drill, too; but I also know how painful is the task of studying and practising long parts for the star of the day, to be thrust out by some fresh stuff got up for his successor: I am aware of this, and therefore strive to make the pill less bitter by doing my "spiriting gently," where I see a desire to be attentive on the part of my friends.

As I may not have occasion to revert to New York theatrically again, let me here say that, after repeated renewal of my engagements during two years, my last were amongst the greatest I made in this city: how, after this, the American public can be called cold or fickle, I at least have no means of judging.

After a stay of three weeks in New York, rendered as agreeable as fine weather, kind friends, warm welcome, and success could make it, I took my departure for Philadelphia by the Camden and Amboy line of steam-boat and rail-road. Punctual to the minute advertised, we left the wharf; and, although the day was cold for the season, I was charmed with our trip across the harbour towards Raritan Creek.

From about half-way over this channel, which separates Staten Island from the city, I should say, after some experience, the best general view of New York and its most prominent environs may be obtained.

Behind you rise the heights of Brooklyn, undulating along your left to the passage of the Narrows, through which you catch a glimmer of the sea beyond; close on your right lies the picturesque-looking old city of Jersey; and immediately beyond, the village of Hoboken, famous for turtle and pistol-matches: its neighbourhood to the Elysian fields renders it a singularly lucky site for the fire-eaters, since, if shot, they have no Charon to pay; the turtle-eaters here find, no doubt, equal facilities. Far to the north, the dark promontory of the Palisadoes beetles broadly forth, marking the course of the Hudson.

In the middle distance lies the city, looking as though it floated deep upon the bosom of the ready waters that encompass it about. It is happier in its place of rest than most Dutch towns, and well merited the name of New Amsterdam, given it by its founders. The ground it covers was at one time divided into hill and dale; but with eyes wide open to business, and close sealed against taste, the conscript fathers of our infant Rome shaved smooth every ant-hill that rose in their path, and to their inheritors have bequeathed a love of their trim lines of beauty, for they are proceeding on the levelling system with a worthy pains-taking that will in due time render the whole island as flat as a tulip-bed.

The passage up the Raritan or Amboy Creek, between Staten Island and the main, is uninteresting enough; the channel reminding one very much of the left bank of the Thames about Erith,—swampy levels, with flat barges, and river-side public houses. The village of Perth Amboy is the first attractive object; it is built upon the face of a hill rising gently from the water, and is well shaded, looking healthy, fresh, and neat. Here the steamer stops for a minute to land or receive passengers, and then makes for Amboy landing, about a couple of miles distant. Here we left our boat, and were immediately transferred to the cars of the new railroad connecting the Raritan with the Delaware, and pursued our way to Bordentown, through a dreary, barren-looking country, whose only attractions were occasional orchards of a most fruitful kind, if one might judge by the plenteous gathering already in progress. In many places were piled up little mountains of apples, destined chiefly for the cider press.

The loco-motives not being in condition to do duty, the horses occupied as yet their legitimate station, going at the rate of about eight miles per hour.

Near the entrance to Bordentown, the present mansion of the ex-king of Spain was pointed out: it does not appear to be very happily located, but commands, I understand, an extensive view of the broad Delaware, and affords room enough to bustle in, even for one whose domain was once royal.

Here we once more embarked; and hence to Philadelphia the Delaware is a broad placid stream, with low banks of alternate wood and meadow, having sprinkled along them numbers of well-built houses of all sizes, from the shingle cottage to the imposing-looking mansion with its lofty portico of painted pine.

The boat touches on its way at two very charming-looking villages, Bristol and Burlington, situated at opposite angles of a fine bend of the river. On the quay of the latter I noticed, as we halted, a group of fairy-looking lassies watching for the landing of some friend; and their animated expression, delicate proportions, and graceful *tournure*, did much to bespeak favour for the girls of Pennsylvania.

It was night before we gained the Quaker city, and exceeding dark withal; so that the long dotted lines of lights, regularly intersecting each other until lost in distance, had the effect of a general illumination, whilst it gave evidence of a widely-spread and populous city.

We drove to Mr. Head's hotel, the Mansion House, where we were welcomed by the worthy host in person; although he had not bed-rooms for us that night, for we were three in company. We were, however, soon furnished with a most excellent supper; and after, two of us got, not "three chairs and a bolster," but a couple of camp bedsteads with good mattresses, and sheets white as snow. Our senior companion, Mr. P— —, was provided with a bed-chamber; and what could the heart of weary traveller wish for more?

On the morrow I also was installed in a capital chamber; and if those incarnate demons the musquitoes would have made peace with me, I should have scorned comparisons with the Nabob of the Carnatic. But, oh! immortal gods, how they did hum and bom, and bite and buzz! and how I did fume, and slap, and snatch, and swear, partly in fear, and partly through sheer vexation of spirit, at having no means of vengeance against a foe whose audacity was open and outrageous, whose trumpets were for ever sounding a charge, yet who were withal, as impassable as Etna.

I would rather hear the roar of lions about my resting-place than the vicious hum of these infernal wee beasts; and I may be allowed to decide, having listened to both: the latter never failed to keep me wakeful through fair fright; but when well worn with fatigue, after a shiver and a start or two, I have slept sound, in safe company, although the crunch and roar of the nobler *varmint* sounded near enough to make our terrified horses press to the watch-fire with breathings thick and loud, — a neighbourhood anything but agreeable, but, I swear, infinitely preferable to an incursion of hungry musquitoes.

The next morning, Sept. 12th, rose early, took a hot bath, and dressed for a hot day; but the day was resolute not to be hot: a north-east wind had set in after breakfast, and down went the thermometer from seventy-nine to forty-five. "Zooks, what a tumble!" as Mister Poll says: all the time too the sky was cloudless, and the sun shining most treacherously. I wasn't to be done, however; so, after an hour, jumped again into my broad-cloth for comfort.

During my first week here I occupied private apartments, — which may be had at every hotel, by the way, — and being in company with a friend, we had our meals at our own hours, all of which were excellent and well served, with wines most unexceptionable. My friend leaving me, however, I took the advice of my good host, Mr. Head, and, quitting my sulky solitude, joined the public table, — a change I had every reason to be satisfied with, since, however, unpleasant the bustle occasioned by a hundred or a hundred and fifty persons dining *ensemble,* no such objection can apply here, where the guests rarely exceed twenty-five or thirty, including from time to time men of the first rank and intelligence in the States. This dinner-table indeed is as well appointed in every way as any gentleman could desire; the attendants numerous and well ordered; the service, including every luxury the season can furnish, is of three courses; and the cloth is never drawn under an hour. I am thus particular, because, as much has been said of the badness of hotels in America, it is but fair to give place to a notice of those which are good; and so essentially good a *table d'hote* as that of the Mansion House at Philadelphia, whether for variety, cooking, wine, or all these things combined, I never yet met in any country of Europe.

PHILADELPHIA

I pity the man who, on a fine morning, can walk through the shady and clean streets of Phildelphia and cry, "all is barren!" In my eyes, it appeared, even at first sight, — and no place improves more upon acquaintance, — one of the most attractive-looking towns I had ever beheld.

Coming immediately out of the noise, bustle, and variety of Broadway, its general aspect appears quiet, almost *triste*; but the cleanliness, the neatness, the air of comfort, propriety, and health, that reigns on all sides, bespeaks immediate favour.

The progress of improvement, and enlargement too, are sufficiently evident, for at either extremity of the city, the fall of hammer and chisel give unceasing note of preparation. The circle designed and marked out as the limit of its future greatness by the sanguine mind of its sagacious founder has long since been overleaped; the wide Delaware on one side, and on the other the Schuylkill, seem incapable of bounding the ambitious city. Already does Market-street rest upon these two points, which cannot be less than three miles apart.

Touching Market-street I ought to know something, since, on two occasions, I got out of my bed to visit it at four A.M. I am curious in looking upon these interesting *entrepôts* whence we cull the dainties of a well-furnished larder, and a view over this was truly worth the pains; for in no place have I ever seen more lavish display of the good things most esteemed by this eating generation, nor could any market offer them to the amateur in form more tempting. Neatness and care were evident in the perfect arrangement of the poultry, vegetables, fruit, butter, &c.; and the display of well-fed beef, with the artist-like way in which it was dressed, might have excited our Giblets' spleen even in the Christmas week.

Poultry of all kinds here is equal to that of any country, and the butter almost as good as the best Irish, which I think the sweetest in the world. The market, at the early time I mentioned, offered a busy and amusing scene, and I passed away a couple of hours here very much to my satisfaction, besides cheating those souls of d — — d critics, the musquitoes, out of a breakfast; for each day, about the first light, I used to be awakened by their assembling for a little *déjeuner dânsant*, whereat I was victim.

One of the pleasantest visits a man can pay in Philadelphia on a hot day, is to the water-works at Fair-mount, on the Schuylkill: the very name is refreshing with the mercury at 96° in the shade; and, if there be a breeze in Pennsylvania, you will find it here. No city can be better supplied with water than this; and I never looked upon the pure liquid, welling through the pipes and deluging the thirsty streets, without a feeling of gratitude to these water-works, and of respect for the pride with which the Philadelphians regard their spirited public labour. They have evinced much taste, too, in the quiet, simple disposition of the ground and reservoirs connected with the machinery; the trees and plants are well selected for the situation, and will soon add to the natural beauty of this very fine reach of the river.

Mounting the east bank of the stream, from this to the village of Manayunk, you have a very pretty ride; and crossing the bridge at the "Falls of the Schuylkill," — falls no longer, thanks to the dam at Fair-mount, — the way back winds along by, or hangs above, the canal and river, here marching side by side; offering, in about four miles, as charming a succession of river views as painter or poet could desire. It is a lovely ramble by all lights, and I have viewed it by all, — in the blaze of noon, and by the sober grey of summer twilight; I have ridden beneath its wooded heights, and through its overhanging masses of rare foliage, in the alternate bright cold light and deep shade of a cloudless moon; and again, when tree, and field, and flower were yet fresh and humid with the heavy dew, and sparkling in the glow of early morning.

At the period of my first visit, the huge piers of a new bridge, projected by the Columbian Railroad Company, were just appearing in different degrees above the gentle river's surface. The smoke of the workmen's fires rising from the wood above, and the numerous attendant barges moored beneath the tall cliff from which the road was to be thrown, added no little to the effect. I have since seen this viaduct completed, and have been whirled over it in the train of a locomotive; and, although it is a fine work, I cannot but think every lover of the picturesque will mourn the violation of the solitude so lately to be found here.

I could not refrain from picturing to myself the light canoes of the Delaware Indians as at no very remote period they lay rocking beneath the shelter of that very bluff where now were moored a fleet of deep-laden barges: indeed these ideas were constantly forcing themselves, as it were, into my mind as I wandered over the changeful face of this singular land, where the fresh print of the moccasin is followed by the tread of the engineer and his attendants, and the light trail of the red man is effaced by the road of iron: hardly have the echoes ceased to repeat through the woods the Indian's hunter-cry before this is followed by the angry rush of the ponderous steam-engine, urged forward! still forward! by the restless pursuer of his fated race.

Wander whither you will, — take any direction, the most frequented or the most secluded, — at every and at all points do these lines of railway intercept your path. Each state, north, south, and west, is eagerly thrusting forth these iron arms, to knit, as it were, in a straiter embrace her neighbours; and I have not a doubt but, in a very short time, a man may journey from the St. Lawrence to the gulf of Mexico coastwise with as much facility as he now does from Boston to Washington, a distance of four hundred and fifty miles, which may be at this day performed within forty hours, out of which you pass a night in New York.

But to leave anticipations and imaginings, — which, by the way, is a forbearance hard of practice in a region where all things are on the whirl of speculative change, and where practical results outrun the projections of even the most visionary theorist, — and return to make such rapid survey of this interesting city as may be ventured on during a first visit of some twenty days. I feel, indeed, that but little can be really known in so short a time of a place containing two hundred and twenty thousand souls, and having in a rapid state of advancement various alterations and improvements, including nearly five thousand new buildings all immediately required: although there are persons gifted with such power of intuition, that, as I learn from their own showing, they are enabled in half the period to decide upon the condition of the whole state of Pennsylvania; to discover the wants of its capital, the defects of its institutions, the value of its commerce, the drift of its policy; to gauge its morals, become intimate with its society, and make out a correct estimate of its relative condition and prospects compared with the other great divisions of the Union, surveyed, I presume, with equal rapidity, judged with equal candour, and estimated with equal correctness.

Each in his degree: and so, in my way, good reader, I will endeavour to give you some notion of this capital of old Penn's Sylvania; but if your own imagination come not to the help of my outline, I fear, after all my painstaking, your notion of the subject will be only a faintish one.

Philadelphia is built upon a peninsula formed by two rivers, the Delaware and the Schuylkill, having a long graduated rise from each, the highest point being about the centre of the city. It is laid out in squares, and the streets run in parallel lines of two and three miles in length, retaining the same names throughout, only divided by Market-street into north, and south: with the exception of this dividing street, those running east and west are named after trees, flowers, and fruits, — as chestnut, walnut, peach, &c.; and those parallel with the rivers, first, Front-street, or that facing the water; next, Second-street, third, fourth, fifth, &c. distinguished as, divided by Market-street, into South-second, North-second, &c.; a simplicity of arrangement which is unique, and renders the stranger's course an exceeding easy one: all he has to do is, first, to run down the latitude of his street by any of the great avenues, and, having fairly struck it, steer north or south, as may be, till he hits upon the friendly number.

The side-walks throughout are broad and well-ordered, neatly paved with brick, and generally bordered by rows of healthful trees of different kinds, affording in hot weather a most welcome shade, and giving to the houses an air of freshness and repose rarely to be met with in a populous city.

The dwellings are chiefly of brick, of a good colour, very neatly pointed; and nothing can be more tasteful than their fitting-up externally. The windows are furnished with latticed shutters; these, when not closed, fold back on either hand against the wall, and being painted green, and kept with much care and freshness, would invest humbler dwellings with an attractive air, especially in the eyes of an Englishman, accustomed to the dingy aspect of our city residences, which look as though the owners had resolved on making them as forbidding as possible without, in order to enhance the excelling comforts within.

Now the houses of Philadelphia are as clean and neat in all the detail of the exterior, as they are well-ordered and admirably furnished. The mountings of the rails and doors are either of polished silver plating or brass, and kept as bright as care can make them. The solid hall-door, in hot weather, is superseded by one of green lattice-work, similar to the window-shutters, which answers the purpose of keeping out every intrusive stranger, except the air, — air being at such seasons, as most strangers are at all times, especially welcome to Philadelphia, which is about the hottest place I know of in the autumn; the halls are commonly flagged with fine white marble, are spacious, lofty, and well fitted-up.

The houses average three stories, but in the best streets, those of the first class are run up to five, and even six, and are of great depth: indeed, I should say, the inhabitants of this city generally enjoy greater space in their lodgings than is afforded to those of any other large capital. Where population increases rapidly rents are necessarily high; and a good house in Philadelphia costs about as much, independent of taxation, as a dwelling of the same class in London.

Besides the great market, which gives its name to the dividing line of the city, and runs through its whole breadth, there are several others, less extensive perhaps, but all alike under cover, well adapted to the purpose, and boasting a due proportion of the abundance of good things, which, profusely displayed on all sides, give ready evidence of the agricultural wealth of the neighbourhood.

Numbers of the best market-farmers for vegetables, poultry, butter, &c. are Germans, who, although most earnest in enriching the country by their labour, yet cling with strange tenacity to the customs and language of "Fader-land." Their costume and manner yet continues as distinct and recognizable as was the appearance of their progenitors on landing here some eighty years back, for the colony from which they are chiefly derived had existence about the middle of the eighteenth century; and many of these men, yet speaking no word of English, are of the third generation. They have German magistrates, an interpreter in courts when they act as jurors, German newspapers, &c.; and are the stoutest, if not the promptest, asserters of democracy.

They are usually found a little in arrear on the subject of all passing events; and at election times, or on occasions of extraordinary stir, when a man is striving to render them *au courant* with late occurrences, they will now and then interrupt their informant with, "Bud why de teufel doesn't Vashington come down to de Nord and bud it all to rights?"

The public buildings are here of a more ambitious style of architecture than any of the other cities can boast, and some of them are built in exceeding good taste; but the one which had most interest in my eyes was the old State-house, wherein the "Declaration of Independence" was signed. The Senate-chamber is, I fancy, little changed since that period; and contained, when I was last within it, models for various public works: amongst others, several for a heroic statue of Washington, about to be erected, somewhat late in the day to be sure, by the city; others for the new college, now building, according to the will of the late S. Girard, and intended to assist in perpetuating his name and wealth to all posterity.

Such appears to have been the great object of the will of this worthy citizen, and there is every prospect of its fully answering the purpose, since it has already set the whole community by the ears, and promises to prove as prolific of evils as the strong box of Miss Pandora, without having even Hope at the bottom.

This man, who has been so much eulogized dead, seems, as well as I could glean amongst his contemporaries, to have been anything but estimable in his living character. He is universally described as having been tricky, overreaching, and litigious in his dealings as a merchant; an unfeeling relation, an exacting, ungrateful, and forgetful master; and a selfish, cold-hearted man: unoccupied with any generous sympathy, public or private, throughout a long life, devoted to one purpose with sleepless energy, and to one purpose only—making and hoarding money; which, living, he contrived, as far as in him lay, to render as little beneficial to any as possible, and, dying, disposed of to his own personal glorification, but to the vexation of the community, amongst which he appeared to have lived unhonoured, and certainly died unregretted!

I am aware that "de mortuis nil nisi bonum" has usually been applied to cases similar to the above; "nil nisi *justem*" I think a sounder reading where a man is held up as a public example, and deem that the selection of a church or a college for a monument should not be permitted to shield the base from animadversion, or call for honours to the worthless.

THE THEATRES—WALNUT
AND CHESTNUT:

So called were the houses at which I first acted here, situated in the two fine streets bearing the same names.

The Walnut is a summer theatre, and the least fashionable; and here it was my fortune to make my *début* to the Philadelphians with good success: a French company occupied at the same time the Chestnut, where, after a seven nights' engagement at the other house, I succeeded them; the proprietors being the same at both.

These houses are large, handsome buildings, marble-fronted, having ample and well-arranged vomitories; and are not stuck into some obscure alley, as most of our theatres are, but standing in the finest streets of the city, and every way easy of approach: within, they are fitted up plainly, but conveniently, and very cleanly and well kept. I prefer the Chestnut, as smaller, and having a pit—as I think all pits ought to be—nearly on a level with the front of the stage, instead of being sunk deep below, looking, when filled, like a huge dark pool, covered with upturned faces.

A crowded audience here presents as large a proportion of pretty, attractive women as are anywhere to be seen; and the male part is singularly respectable and attentive. Here again I must protest against the charge of insensibility being laid at their doors; that is, as far as my own feeling and experience goes.

If by applause, a constant clapping of palms or hammering of sticks is only meant, interspersed with cries of "Bravo!" I admit they are deficient; but if an evident anxiety to lose no word or look of the artist, an evident abstraction from everything but the scene, with demonstrations of admiration discriminating and well applied, may be accepted as sufficient marks of approval, then has the actor no cause of complaint.

With the tragedian, who strains after what in stage parlance are called *points*, and calculates on being interrupted by loud clapping before the sense of the sentence be complete, or else wants breath to finish it, a Philadelphian audience might prove a slippery dependence, since they come evidently to hear the author as well as see the actor, and are "attentive, that they may hear."

For myself, the unreserved laughter in which they indulged I found abundant applause, and in well-filled houses the best assurance that they were pleased. The company here was a very good one, and the pieces as well gotten up as anywhere in the States.

I paid frequent visits to this charming city, and shall have occasion again to refer to it. My first impressions are here set down, and favourable as these were, a more intimate knowledge only served to confirm them.

JOURNEY TO BOSTON

THE EAST RIVER.—HURL-GATE.— THE SOUND.—POINT JUDITH.— NEWPORT HARBOUR.—PROVIDENCE

On Saturday morning, at 7 A.M. Sept. 28th, quitted Philadelphia; arrived in New York at 2 P.M.; and transferring my baggage from the steamer on the North River to the one about to depart for Providence, and whose wharf lay upon the East River, I had a couple of hours' leisure, which I employed in writing home, for the packet of the 1st of October; and at five o'clock P.M. left the city, in the noblest steam-vessel I had yet seen.

The view of Brooklyn, the Navy Yard, and this part of the harbour, is very attractive from the point of departure; and the numerous little steamers, actively plying to and fro at the various ferries, give an unceasing air of bustle to the scene. I was greatly charmed by our sail up this passage into the Sound dividing Long Island from the continent, which it flanks and protects for a distance of one hundred miles.

The banks on either side do not vary a great deal in elevation, but are of a slightly undulating character, beautifully wooded, and sprinkled with the attractive-looking villas of the country. Mr. Cooper's graphic description of Hurl-gate, in his novel of the "Red Rover," led me to look out for it with an interest which the reality did not repay, although the tide was in a favourable state. I confess, however, I think that my imagination rather outran discretion than that the whirlpool lacked grandeur: that it was not to be encountered without some peril we had very good evidence; for, on a rocky islet to the southward of the worst part of the fall, a large schooner lay hove up on her beam-ends, with all her spars aloft and her sails half furled, as she had been abandoned by her crew. Our pilot informed me that the accident had occurred the day previous, and was by no means a rare example, the downward passage at the last of the ebb requiring great care and experience.

Our powerful engines forced the vessel through the dark eddies, apparently without difficulty; and in a little while this long looked-for wonder was forgotten.

I remained on deck until after midnight; for there was a bright moon and a calm clear sky, and the Sound was sprinkled with craft of all kinds.

I must not omit to notice supper, or tea, — for it was both, and an excellent meal it was, — served about eight o'clock upon two parallel tables, which ran the whole length of the cabin, at least one hundred and eighty feet; and to which sat down about one hundred persons of all ranks, — the richest merchants, the most eminent statesmen, and the humblest mechanic who chose to pay for a cabin fare, as most of these persons who travel do. I was seated with an exceeding lady-like and well-bred woman on my left hand, and on my right sat a man who, although decently dressed, was evidently a working operative of the humblest class; yet was there nothing in either his manner or appearance to annoy the most refined female: he asked for what he wanted respectfully, performed any little attention he could courteously, and evinced better breeding and less selfishness than I have witnessed at some public dinners at home, where the admission of such a person would have been deemed derogatory.

I do not mean by this description to infer that a crowded table of this kind is as agreeable as a party whose habits, education, and sympathies, being on a level, render intercourse a matter of mutual pleasure: what I would show is, that in this mingling of classes, which is inevitable in travelling here, there is nothing to disgust or debase man or woman, however exclusive; for it would really be impossible to feed a like multitude, of any rank or country, with slighter breaches of decency or decorum, or throw persons so wholly dissimilar together with less personal inconvenience either to one class or another.

I had been accustomed to see this set down as one of the chief nuisances of travelling in this country, and the consequences greatly exaggerated: things must have improved rapidly; since, as far as I have hitherto gone, I protest I prefer the steam-boat arrangements here to our own, and would back them to be considered less objectionable by any candid traveller who had fairly tested both.

During the night it blew fresh, and the vessel pitched a little, the consequence of which movement was evident in the desertion of the upper deck in the morning. I had noticed it, the evening previous, occupied by sundry little groups reading or chatting, and with more than one couple of merry promenaders: I now made its circuit, meeting with but one adventurer, a lively-looking old gentleman, of whom I inquired where all our passengers were vanished to.

"Most of them in bed yet," said the old gentleman, "or keeping out of the way in one hole or another. If there's any wind or sea, you always find the deck pretty clear till we get round Point Judith. Once let us get to the other side that hill yonder, and you'll see the swarm begin to muster pretty smart."

I had often heard "Point Judith" mentioned by the New-Yorkers, as the Cockney voyager talks of Sea-reach, or the buoy at the Nore; and here it was close under our lee, — a long, low point of land, with a lighthouse upon it.

We soon after opened the entrance to the fine harbour of Newport, and, as my informant predicted, the deck gradually recovered its population: some came up because they felt, and others because they were told, we had passed Point Judith.

It was about seven o'clock A.M. that we ran alongside the wharf at Newport to land passengers. The appearance of the town, rising boldly from the water's edge, was imposing enough; but trade, judging from the deserted state of the wharves, is now inconsiderable, although formerly of much importance.

After a delay of a quarter of an hour, we once more got under weigh; and one of the chief advantages of a steamer is the ease and facility with which this important movement is effected: nowhere is the management of these immense bodies, in my thinking, so perfect: the commanding position of the wheel, clear of all obstruction, and under the hand of the pilot, whose finger also directs the machinery below, through the medium of a few well-arranged bells, — the absence of all bawling and shouting, and the being independent of transmitted directions, gives these craft facilities which make their movements appear like inspiration.

This system I found prevailing all through the States; and, as far as possible, it would be well to adopt it here. The arrangement of the wheel, or steering apparatus, if I remember rightly, was fully and technically described by Captain Hall. I do not know whether it has in any case been adopted; but if it were enforced upon our crowded rivers, there would, I feel assured, be fewer accidents.

The fogs of the Sound, in this passage, — a highway as much travelled as the Clyde, — and indeed on all the great American rivers, are only to be paralleled by a London specimen about Christmas, in addition to the former being more frequent; yet accidents arising from running foul are of very rare occurrence, although the desire to drive along is yet stronger than with ourselves.

The river up to Providence is of a breadth and character to command the voyager's attention, but offers little in detail to repay him for it. With the exception of the time devoted to breakfast, which a supply of newly-caught fish, taken on board at Newport, rendered a positive treat to me, I paced the upper deck, according to my custom, until we arrived at Providence, a very thriving place, seated on a commanding ridge, and already having, as viewed from the river, an air and aspect quite city-like.

Here we found a line of coaches drawn up upon the wharf, awaiting our arrival. I had already secured a ticket for the Mail Pilot: and in a few minutes the luggage was packed on; the passengers, four in number, were packed in; and away we went, rolling and pitching, at the heels of as likely a team of four dark bays as I would wish to sit behind. At our first halt, I left the inside to the occupation of my companions, — a handsome girl, with, "I guess," her lover, and a rough specimen of a Western hunter or trader, who had already dubbed my younger companion Captain and myself Major, and invited us both to "liquor with him." I declined, but *the Captain*, to his evident satisfaction, frankly accepted his offer; and whilst I mounted the box, and the horses were changing, they entered the house together.

This is a courtesy the traveller to the South will find constantly proffered to him by a class of honest souls, whose good-fellowship sometimes exceeds their discretion; and I had been told it was not at all times possible to decline the offer without risking insult. I discovered by experience this to be one of the numerous imaginary grievances conjured up to affright the innocent. In this, as in all other points, I have never departed from my own habits; and although often in remote parts of the Union strongly urged "to liquor," have always found my declaration that it was a custom which disagreed with me, an excuse admitted without hesitation or ill-humour.

In this, my first experiment, indeed, I had to deal with the most punctilious specimen I ever afterwards encountered; for when, some two hours after I had declined his request, I called for a glass of lemonade, my friend popped his head out of the coach-window, calling out with a most beseeching air —

"Well but, Major, I say; stop till I get out: you'll drink *that* with me any how, won't you?"

He was in the bar-room at my heels in a twinkling, and I need hardly say we emptied our glasses together very cordially, although their contents would, I fancy, in my friend's opinion, have assimilated best in a mixed state; for, giving his *sling* a knowing twist as I swallowed my excellent lemonade, he observed:

"Now that's a liquor I never could bring myself to try nohow, though I'm sometimes rather speculatin' in drink, when I'm travellin' or out on a frolic. Poorish stuff, I calculate: but *you* hav'nt got the dyspepsy, have you, Major?"

I assured my friend that I was perfectly free from dyspepsia, and that it was because I desired to continue so that I avoided any stronger drink before dinner.

We were now summoned to our places, my companion declaring—

"It is past my logic how lemon and water can prevent dyspepsy better than brandy and water;" adding, with a look half comic, half serious—

"But I suppose everybody will go for the Temperance-ticket soon, and I shall be forced to clear out of all my spirits; for I never can drink by myself, if I'm forced to take to the milk and water line for company."

Our road was a tolerably good one as roads go here, and the horses excellent. We arrived in Boston about half-past three, having performed forty miles in five hours, all stoppages included; and the whole distance from Philadelphia, being three hundred and twenty miles, in thirty-two hours and a half, including about three hours passed in New York. Quick as this travelling is, they contemplate, when the railroad to Providence shall be opened, by the aid of that and an improved steam-boat, to deduct eight or nine hours from the time between this and New York.

Alighting at the Tremont hotel, I found dinner over, as on Sunday they accommodate the hour of dining to the time of church service: I was, however, quickly provided with a good meal, which a keen breeze, a long ride, and a long fast enabled me to do good justice to. In the afternoon, *malgré* a cutting east wind, which was anything but agreeable after the hot weather I had been living in, I took a long walk about the town, accompanied by an old friend of mine and a constitutional grumbler, who yet joined with me in declaring that a first impression of Boston could hardly fail pleasing any man who could be pleased by a near view of a city, well and substantially built, as it is undoubtedly nobly situated.

BOSTON

The approach to Boston, either by sea or land, gives to it an extremely bold and picturesque character. It is spread over a series of lofty heights, nearly insulated, and is surrounded by a marshy level running from the highlands on the main, to which the city is united by a very narrow isthmus to the southward.

The lofty dome of its State-house, and the numerous spires and towers of its churches, rising between two and three hundred feet above the surrounding level of either land or sea, combine to produce a *coup d'œil* more imposing than is presented by either New York or Philadelphia.

The streets of the city generally are narrow and irregular, following the windings of the lofty hills over which it is spread, and having more the air of an old English county-town than any place I have yet seen in the country.

Its wharfs are spacious and well constructed, and it is not without surprise that one views the evidently rapid growth of these best evidences of prosperous commerce. I observed in my walks lines of substantial granite-built warehouses and quays, newly redeemed from the water: all were in occupation; tiers of vessels of every kind thronged them; and the inner harbour was thick with masts.

The most modern quarter of the city lies to the west, surrounding the park, or common, as it is termed, — an ancient reserve of some sixty acres, the property of the citizens, beautifully situated and tastefully laid out. It is bordered on the lower side by a mall of venerable-looking elms; has a pretty pond of water under a rising ground near its centre, the remains of an English fort; and open to the front is the Charles River.

On three sides, this common is flanked by very fine streets, having houses of the largest class, well built, and kept with a right English spirit as far as regards the scrupulous cleanliness of the entrances, areas, and windows. The English are a window-cleaning race, and nowhere have I observed this habit so closely inherited as here. Overlooking this common, too, is the State-house; and, on a line with it, the mansion of its patriot founder, Mr. Hancock, a venerable stone-built edifice, raised upon a terrace withdrawn a few yards from the line of the present street. The generous character of its first owner has made this house an object of great interest, and it is to be hoped the citizens will look carefully to its preservation as a worthy fellow to Fanieul Hall, for by no one was the "cradle of Liberty"[3] more carefully tended than by the owner of "Hancock House."

Here, as in the other great cities of the Union, upon a close survey, I found the prevailing impression on my mind to be surprise at the apparent rapidity of increase made manifest in the great number of buildings either just completed or in progress. If the possession of inexhaustible supplies of the finest granite, marble, and all other material, be accompanied with taste and spirit in their use, the future buildings of this city will have an air of grandeur and stability superior to those of any other in the States.

To reach the surrounding country in any direction from the peninsula the city occupies, one of its great bridges must be crossed. Of these there are six, besides the Western Avenue as it is called, a dam of vast extent; and they form the peculiarities of this place, to a stranger, most curious, and, in truth, most pleasing. By day, they form agreeable walks or rides, offering a variety of charming views; and, if crossed on a dark night, when their interminable lines of lamps are beheld radiating, as it were, from one centre, and multiplied by reflection on the surrounding waters, the effect is perfectly magical. The stars show dimly in comparison: and casting your eyes downward, it appears as though you beheld another and a brighter sky glittering beneath your feet.

The great dam rises about five feet above the tide, is provided with enormous flood-gates, and in length is something over a mile and a half. The length of the other bridges varies from two thousand five hundred to one thousand four hundred feet.

Crossing at any one of these points, you gain the open heights upon the main. Here you are first struck by the aspect of the soil, everywhere having huge masses of dark rock protruded above its surface. The country is said to be poor: of this I cannot judge, but I know it to be beautiful. It is everywhere undulating, and often broken in the wildest and most tropical manner. Like the interior of Herefordshire, it is cut up in all directions by rural lanes, bordered by stone walls and high hedges, and dotted thickly with handsome houses, whose verandahs of bright green, and whitened walls, show well amidst the luxuriant foliage by which they are commonly surrounded.

About five miles from the city are a couple of delightful pieces of water, called Jamaica and Fresh-ponds; each bordered by wood, lawn, and meadow, naturally disposed in the most attractive manner. At the last-named pond, — which sounds unworthily on my ear when applied to a piece of water covering a surface of two hundred and fifty acres, — I passed an afternoon during the period of my first visit here.

We sailed about, exploring every harbour of the little sea, caught our fish for dinner, and by the hotel were furnished with a well-broiled chicken and a good glass of champagne, with ice worthy of being dissolved in such liquor. I fell premeditatedly in love with the place; and D— —, who was on the look-out for a location, and something hard to please withal, had already selected a site for building: but, alas! even Paradise, before the mission of St. Patrick, had serpents; and the delightful copses and rich meadows of Fresh-pond are, it appears, the haunts especially favoured by the incarnation of all Egyptian plagues, musquitoes.

During the winter this is a great resort of the lovers of *bandy* and *skating*; and from this ample reservoir is taken that transparent ice which gladdens the eyes and cools the throat of the dust-dried traveller throughout this part of the State. Nor is its grateful service confined to these limits; for cargoes of it are, during the spring, regularly shipped to the Havannah, New Orleans, Mobile, &c.; and, — for where will enterprise find limits? — this very season has a shipment of three hundred tons of the congealed waters of this pond of Massachusetts been consigned to Calcutta. Ice floating on the Ganges! How old Gunga will shiver and shake his ears when the first crystal offering is dropped on his hot bosom!

Wild as the idea may at first appear of keeping such a commodity for a voyage of probably a hundred days in such latitudes, I am informed the speculator is assured, that with an ordinary run, enough of his cargo may be landed to pay a good freight.[4]

Near to this pond lies another favourite spot of mine, "Mount Auburn;" a tract of woodland, bordering on Charles River, appropriated and consecrated as a cemetery, on the plan of "Pere la Chaise," but having natural attributes for such a purpose infinitely superior. It is covered by a thick growth of the finest forest-trees, of singular variety; and presents a surface, now gently undulating in hill and dale, now broken into deep ravines, or towered over by bold rocky elevations; and, intersecting the whole space from north to south, runs a natural terrace, having a surface so well and evenly levelled that one almost doubts its being other than the work of art.

It takes its name from a lofty eminence, which, rising high over the surrounding level, commands as fine a view as any spot in the vicinity. Winding and well-kept avenues intersect the ground in all directions, giving it an appearance of much greater extent than it in reality possesses, and rendering the most secluded spot easy of access to those who desire to

"Choose their ground,

And take their rest."

The ostentatious mausoleum may be placed by a broad carriage avenue, where its hollow walls will reverberate to every passing triumph of the tomb; the quiet and the lowly can build their humbler dwelling in some secluded nook, bordered by a narrow path the foot of affection alone will seek to tread, and where no heavier sound will ever echo!

The perpetual right of sepulture may be purchased of the company whose property the place is; and already a number of monuments, in marble and granite, betoken the favour with which this place of "everlasting rest" is viewed. Most of these monuments are of a simple, unassuming character, and some of them gracefully appropriate.

A wooden fence encircles the cemetery, and a lofty gateway leads into it, of Egyptian fashion, but of the like American material, which, it is to be presumed, will speedily be superseded by suitable erections of the fine dark granite found here in abundance.

This spot, if presided over by anything like taste, must become, in a very few years, one of the places one might reasonably make a pilgrimage to look upon; so lavish has Nature been in its adornment, and so admirably are its accessories fitted to its present purpose.

Boston and its neighbourhood possess, in the eyes of a British subject, a number of sites of singular historical interest.

On Hancock's Wharf that tea-party was held which cost Britain ten millions of gold, and reft from the empire one quarter of the globe. The lines of the American army at Cambridge are still to be readily traced throughout their whole extent; the forts at the extremities, north and south, are yet perfect in form as when designed by the engineer.

Across the peninsula, to the west of the isthmus, may be traced the British lines and the broad deep fosse which, filled by the tide, insulated the city these were projected to defend: their remains testify to the care and labour bestowed upon their completion.

Bunker's Hill and the Breeds, where the first determined stand was made against the British army, is commanded from the steeples and many house-tops of the city.

If the defenders of these miserable lines knew that they were observed by their kindred on this day, they took, at least, especial care that the lookers-on should have no cause to blush for their lack of manhood. Under cover of a hastily thrown-up breastwork, of which no trace remains, did those hardy yeomen abide and repulse several assaults of a regular and well-officered force; nor was it until their last charge of ammunition was delivered that they turned from the defences their courage alone had made good. The result proved how few charges of theirs were flung away; these men knew the value of their ammunition, they were excellent shots, and the word was constantly passed amongst them to "take sure aim."

On Bunker's Hill a national monument is in progress, which, when completed, will form an obelisk of fine granite, according to the published plan, thirty feet square at the base, two hundred and twenty feet high, and fifteen feet square at the summit. After considerable progress had been made in this most durable memorial, the funds ran out and the work stood still; however, the reproach of its remaining unfinished is now likely to be speedily removed, for during this last year, I believe, the necessary sum has been raised, and the national monument of Massachusetts put *en train* for completion.

Below this celebrated hill lies one of the most complete and extensive navy-yards in the States. At the period of my visit its dry dock was occupied by a pet ship of the American navy, "the Constitution," or, as this fine frigate is familiarly called, "Old Ironsides." She was stripped down to her kelson outside and in, for the purpose of undergoing a repair that will make her, to all intents, a new ship.

She is what would now be called a small frigate, but one of the prettiest models possible as high as the bends; above, she tumbles in a little too much to please the eye. Nor did her gun-deck appear to me particularly roomy for her burthen.

She was logged nearly eleven feet during the whole of the period she was last afloat, yet is said to have sailed faster than anything she met; this defect the builders have now remedied, and expect that, on a straight keel, she will prove the fastest ship afloat.

I also went on board a seventy-four, employed as a receiving ship; "a whapper! of her size," low between decks, but with a floor like a barn, and the greatest beam I ever saw in a two-decker. Here were also on the stocks a three and a two decker, both to be rated as seventy-fours; the latter a model of beauty.

From the roof of the house covering this ship I enjoyed the finest panoramic view imaginable. Boston, its long bridges, and the great dam connecting the blue hills of the main with the peninsulas of Boston, and that on which the populous village of Charleston stands, all lay beneath the eye on the land side; whilst looking seaward, the inner and outer harbours, together with their numerous islands, stretched away far beyond the ken; and, were these islands only wooded, no harbour in the world would excel this in beauty: at present, though grand, from its great extent it looks bleak and naked, so completely have the islands and the surrounding heights been denuded of wood.

I like this view better than either the one from the dome of the State-house or that from the summit of Mount Auburn: a few glances from this point affords one a good practical notion both of the city and the populous environs, which may be said to form a part of it, besides being in itself a varied and beautiful picture, viewed, as I first saw it, on the afternoon of a calm clear day.

FOOTNOTES:

[3] Fanieul Hall, so called, the old Town Hall, — a spot dedicated by the Bostonians to the recollections of their country's first struggle for independence, and greatly venerated.

[4] This calculation was more than realised, the loss not exceeding one-fourth on the whole cargo shipped. The grateful epicures of Calcutta made an offering of a splendid cup to the merchant, in return for his spirited speculation, which I believe he has this year (1835) repeated.

STATE PRISON

Whilst here, I visited the state-prison, the first I had seen where the Auburn system is pursued; that is, solitary night-cells, silence, and labour in gangs. The building itself is a fine one, having nearly four hundred cells, enclosed within external walls, round which run galleries that command a view of the interior of every cell without disturbing or annoying the confined; the whole covered by a common roof of the strongest kind, lighted and ventilated in the best manner.

The merits of this plan will be fairly set forth long before this trifle meets the public eye, a commission being now in progress throughout these States for the purpose of relieving England from the stigma of having no means of employment in her prisons less brutalizing than the tread-mill.

I here saw about two hundred convicts actively employed at various trades, preparing granite for building, doing smiths' work, making shoes, brushes, &c.; all very clean, but certainly not looking very healthy.

A single overseer went the rounds of each building or department, and kept the hive in motion, without a word spoken, unless in reference to the task in hand. Whilst passing through the masons' shed, I noticed two persons make inquiries of the superintendent: their questions were to the point, given in few words, but with an air perfectly free and unrestrained, and were replied to in the like manner.

Upon the value of this system as a preventive of crime, according to my view of human nature, I may be allowed to express a doubt, as well as of its applicability to the condition of Great Britain; but viewing it in the abstract, without such reference, I confess no philanthropic object ever struck me as so completely illustrative of the principles of true benevolence. This was, in fact, returning good for evil, in the most Christian sense of the word; "chastening as a father chasteneth." It would appear that a convict must be unnaturally hardened not to quit this abode a better man. Let him arrive here, however outcast, vile, ignorant, knowing no honest calling, broken in health and savage in spirit, here he will find teachers, masters, physicians, all provided for him by the community whose laws he has violated. His spirit is soothed, his health is recruited, his ignorance enlightened: he is made master of a sufficient calling; and, when restored to society, is able to contrast the value of the meal earned by the honest sweat of his brow with the bitter fruit of idleness and crime.

Such is the result contemplated by the benevolent promoters of the prison system of this country, which everywhere has societies of voluntary philanthropists who watch over and study to improve it. One is ashamed, after this, to avow a doubt of its success in practice, since it almost amounts to an admission that man is indeed the brute our European legislators appear to think him.

The subject is, at least, one that demands from England a rigid inquiry, when we call to mind what a den of debasement, what a sink of soul and body, a prison yet is amongst the most civilized and humane people in the world.

TREMONT HOTEL

My last, though not least, lion of Boston is the "Tremont House," which being, in my opinion, the very best of the best class of large hotels in the Union, I shall select as a specimen.

With externals I have little to do, although the architecture of this fine building might well claim a particular description: its frontage is nearly two hundred feet, with two wings about one hundred each in depth: it is three stories high in front above the basement, and the wings are each of four stories: the number of rooms, its proprietor informed me, amount to two hundred, independent of kitchens, cellars, and other offices: it contains hot and cold baths, and is, in fact, wanting in nothing essential to the character of a well-contrived hotel.

The curious part of the affair, however, to a European, and more especially to an Englishman, is the internal arrangement of such a huge institution, the machinery by which it is so well and so quietly regulated.

Let the reader reflect, that here are two public tables daily, one for men resident in the house, together with many gentlemen of the city, who regularly dine here; the other for ladies, or families who have not private apartments: of the latter there are a dozen, consisting of two or more chambers attached to each parlour; these are seldom unoccupied, and have also to be provided for: add to all this an occasional dinner or supper to large public parties, and he will then be enabled to appreciate the difficulties and do justice to the system which works as I shall presently describe.

At half-past seven A.M. the crash of a gong rattles through the remotest galleries, to rouse the sleepers: this you may hear or not, just as you choose; but sound it does, and loudly. Again, at eight, it proclaims breakfast on the public tables: as I never made my appearance at this meal, I cannot be expected to tell how it may be attended. The lover of a late *déjeûner* may either order his servant to provide one in his own room, or at any hour, up to noon, direct it to be served in the common hall: it will, in either case, consist of whatever he may desire that is in the house.

At three o'clock, dinner is served in a well-proportioned, well-lighted room, seventy feet long by thirty-one wide, occupied by two parallel tables, perfectly appointed, and provided with every delicacy of the season, well dressed and in great abundance,—the French cooking the best in the country,—this *par parenthèse*. Meantime, the attendance is very sufficient for a man not in a "devouring rage," and the wines of every kind really unexceptionable to any reasonable *gourmet*.

At this same hour, let it be borne in mind, the same play is playing in what is called the ladies' dining-room, where they sit surrounded by their husbands, fathers, brothers, or lovers, as may be; and surely having no meaner table-service. As for the possessors of an apartment, these persons order dinner for as many as they please, at what hour they please, and in what style they please, the which is duly provided in their respective parlours.

In the public rooms tea is served at six, and supper at nine o'clock; it being yet a marvel to me, first, how all these elaborate meals are so admirably got up, and next, how the plague these good people find appetite to come to time with a regularity no less surprising.

It was a constant subject of no little amusement to me to observe a few of the knowing hands hanging about, as feeding-time drew near, their ears on the prick and their eyes on the door, which is thrown open at the first bellow of the gong.

As to the indecent pushing and driving, so amusingly described by some travellers, I never saw a symptom of it in any hotel I visited throughout the country: on the contrary, the absence of extraordinary bustle and confusion, where such numbers have to be provided for, is not the least striking part of the affair; and only to be accounted for by supposing that the habit of living thus together, and being in some sort accountable to one another, renders individuals more considerate and courteous than they can afford to be when congregated to feed amongst us.

I confess that, at first, a dinner of a hundred, or a hundred and fifty persons, on a hot day, alarmed me; but, the strangeness got over, I rather liked this mode of living, and, as a stranger in a new country, would certainly prefer it to the solitary mum-chance dinner of a coffee-room.

By eleven o'clock at night the hive is hushed, and the house as quiet as any well-ordered citizen's proper dwelling. The servants in this establishment were all Irish lads; and a civiller or better-conducted set of boys, as far as the guests were concerned, I never saw, or would desire to be waited on by. The bar was also well conducted, under the care of an obliging and very active person; and the proprietor, Mr. Boydon, or his father, constantly on the spot, both most active in all matters conducive to the ease and comfort of the visitors.

This city abounds in charitable institutions, and nowhere have more princely contributions been made for philanthropic purposes,—witness the recent gift of Colonel Perkins of a mansion, valued at thirty thousand dollars, as a permanent asylum for the blind; one of those institutions most interesting in themselves, and which confer dignity and honour upon the age and upon human nature.

The Bostonians are said to be proud of their literary character, and boast a number of societies whose object it is to justify their claim to this honourable distinction. The only one I can speak of from personal observation is the Athenæum, an excellently-supplied reading-room; having attached to it a library of thirty thousand volumes, a valuable collection of coins and medals, a gallery for the exhibition of pictures, and lecture-rooms well furnished with the necessary apparatus for philosophical and practical illustration.

This institution is provided for by subscription: the principal portion of the mansion it occupies being the free gift of the same open hand which so munificently endowed the asylum for the blind.

The private literary society here is said to be very superior to that of any other city of the States, and by no means small. Of society so called I nothing know, never having had the honour of being admitted of the community, or indeed having made any attempts upon their proper realm beyond an occasional rude foray on the border, uncontinued, and consequently little noted.

Private intercourse is gay and agreeable, and less restrained by the exclusive pretension to dress and fashion which prevails in society both at New York and Philadelphia; whilst, if attractive women are less numerous here than in those cities, beauty is by no means rare; indeed Boston boasts of one family whose personal attractions might serve to sustain the pretensions of a larger population.

THE TREMONT THEATRE

In the same street, and immediately opposite the great hotel, is the Tremont Theatre, certainly the most elegant exterior in the country, and with a very well-proportioned, but not well-arranged *salle*, or audience part.

I commenced here on Monday the 30th of September, three days after closing at Philadelphia, to a well-filled house, composed, however, chiefly of men, as on my *début* at New York. My welcome was cordial and kind in the extreme; but the audience, although attentive, appeared exceedingly cold. On a first night I did not heed this much, especially as report assured me they were very well pleased; but throughout the week this coldness appeared to me to increase rather than diminish, and so much was I affected by it, that, notwithstanding the houses were very good, I, on the last day of my first engagement of six nights, declined positively to renew it, as was the custom in such cases, and as, in fact, the manager and myself had contemplated: on this night, however, the aspect of affairs brightened up amazingly; the house was crowded; a brilliant show of ladies graced the boxes; the performances were a repetition of two pieces which had been previously acted, and from first to last the mirth was electric; the good people appeared, by common consent, to abandon themselves to the fun of the scene, and laughed *à gorge deployée*. At the fall of the curtain, after, in obedience to the call of the house, I had made my bow, the manager announced my re-engagement; and from this night forth I never met a merrier or a pleasanter audience.

It was quite in accordance with the character ascribed to the New-Englanders that they should coolly and thoroughly examine and understand the novelty presented for their judgment, and that, being satisfied and pleased, they should no longer set limits to the demonstration of their feelings.

In matters of graver import they have always evinced the like deliberate judgment and apparent coldness of bearing; but beneath this prudential outward veil they have feelings capable of the highest degree of excitement and the most enduring enthusiasm.

I do not agree with those who describe the Yankee as a naturally cold-blooded, selfish being. From both the creed and the sumptuary regulations of the rigid moral censors from whom they sprung, they have inherited the practice of a close self-observance and a strict attention to conventional form, which gives a frigid restraint to their air that nevertheless does not sink far beneath the surface.

A densely-populated and ungrateful soil has kept alive and quickened their natural gifts of intelligence and enterprise, whilst the shifts poverty imposes upon young adventure may possibly at times have impelled prudence to degenerate into cunning. But look at their history as a community; they have been found ever ready to make the most generous sacrifices for the commonwealth. In their domestic relations they are proverbial as the kindest husbands and most indulgent fathers; whilst as friends they are found to be, if reasonably wary, at least steadfast, and to be relied on to the uttermost of their professions.

I can readily understand a stranger, having any share of sensibility, not liking a people whose observances are so peculiar and so decidedly marked; but I do think it impossible for an impartial person to spend any time in the country, or have any close intercourse with the community, without learning to respect and admire them, *malgré* their calculating prudence, and the many prejudices inseparable from a system of education even to this day sufficiently narrow and sectarian.

As far as my personal experience is worthy of consideration, I must declare that some of the kindest, gentlest, and most hospitable friends I had, and, I trust I may add, have, in the Union, were natives of New-England, or, as they say here, "real Yankee, born and raised within sight of the State-house of Bosting."

JOURNAL

Oct. 20th, New York. — Began my second engagement here, — the weather divine. Procured a very good hack at Tattersal's, and daily "skir the country round." The environs of this city possess more variety of scenery than one would suppose from a cursory glance at the country, which appears tame and unbroken. The river views are most attractive to me.

Rode to the race-course on Long Island, this being the period of the "Fall Meeting," as it is termed. The assemblage thin on the first day — Appointments of the negro jockeys more picturesque than race-like, — ill-fitted jackets, trousers dirty, and loose, or stocking-net pantaloons ditto, but tight, with Wellingtons over or under, according to the taste of the rider; or shoes without stockings, or stockings without shoes, as weight may be required or rejected. They sit well forward on to the withers of the horses; do not seem over steady in their saddles, but cling like monkeys, their whole sleight-of-hand appears to consist of a dead pull; and their mode of running, with their time for lying back or making play, seems to be entirely governed by their masters, who, on a mile-course, they must frequently pass in heats, and who appear ever on the alert to direct them.

After the running, which was indifferent, went to see "Paul Pry," a trotting-horse of Mr. M'Leod's, now in training to do a match of eighteen miles in the hour.[5] With the exception of a few scratches on one of his legs, he looked in slapping order; a powerful grey horse, just sixteen hands, with a fine countenance, and appearing to be nearly, if not quite, thorough-bred.

Second day. — Witnessed a good race, which a little mare, called Trifle, won in two four-mile heats. She had, on a former occasion, run four heats, or twenty miles, over the central course at Baltimore, and was beaten by one of her present competitors, a fine mare called Black Maria. Trifle is very little, but powerfully put together, and exceedingly handsome; her only drawback being a pair of mulish-looking ears. She has uncommon speed, and is one of the steadiest and smoothest gallopers I ever saw go over turf.

I, at the start, took a great fancy to the little pet, and backed her even against the other two horses for a dozen of gloves with my friend Mr. C— — n. By the close of the second heat our bet had increased ninefold, — Next morning received a box containing nine dozen of French gloves. It will be my duty henceforth to back Trifle.

October 29th. — The city yet crowded with strangers; every hotel full.

Find out that I am No. 1. in this enormous house; the first time I ever could boast such an honour, and now am by no means certain that it is worth the labour it imposes, since it leads me a dance to the third story: however, it is an excellent room, very large, and removed from the bustle below; the sound of the dustman-like bell, which calls the house to meals, barely reaches my ear. I often catch myself parodying poor Maturin's lines, which I have applied to this unpoetical grievance, and concluded most impotently —

----"Bell echoes bell,

Meal follows meal,

Till the ear aches for the last welcome summons

That tolls an end to the day's cookery."

At this time there cannot be far short of one hundred and fifty persons dining daily in the public room: did I desire to dine at it, however, the hospitality of my friends I find would render this impracticable.

November 3rd. — Dined at Harlaem, a pretty village eight miles from the city, but daily drawing closer to it. Here a certain Mrs. Bradshaw fries chickens in a *sauce tartarre,* to the which could pen of mine do justice, "I guess" I know folk "our side" the water who would be stealing across to Harlaem some fine day to dine. We had tarapins too, of whose excellence most unfortunates in Europe, happily for their poor wives and innocent children, are ignorant.

On our way home halted at Cato's, and discussed the comparative merits of hail-storm and julep, demonstrating our arguments by the practical experiments of this distinguished spirituous professor.

The day deliciously genial, and the night like a fine harvest-moon at home. Of a verity this American autumn, or fall, as they call it, is a most delicate season.

Friday, 8th. — Up with the lark, and, accompanied by Captain D— —n, got on board the steamer for Philadelphia, *viâ* Amboy.

The morning was clear, with a warm sun just tempered by a breeze balmy and soft: the packet was crowded, and our passage across the harbour a pleasure to remember. We were soon, however, to have all the happy recollections of this journey miserably blotted out by one of the most fearful accidents I ever beheld.

At Amboy we took the railroad; and every one was delighted to find that the locomotives were now in operation, anticipating a quick and pleasant ride to Bordentown. For a time all went well: various surmises were made as to our rate; some calculated it at twenty miles in the hour; D— —n and the Belgian minister, Baron de B— —r, were disputing the point, watch in hand, when an alarm was given from the rear: our attention was quickly arrested by loud cries to "stop the engine," coming from the windows of every carriage in the train.

On the halt being accomplished, the carriages were deserted in a moment; for it was discovered that one of those in the rear had been overturned in consequence of the axle breaking,—its occupants' fate as yet unknown.

I was soon on the spot, and what a scene was here to witness! Out of twenty-four persons only one had escaped unhurt. One man was dead, another dying, and five others had fractures, more or less serious; a couple of ladies (sisters) dreadfully wounded; the children of one of them, two little girls, with broken limbs.

Never were sufferers more patient; one of them was a surgeon, a fine young fellow, who immediately set about doing the best his skill could accomplish for those most desperately hurt. D— —n and I volunteered as his assistants; and with such splints as the shattered panels of the carriage supplied, the fractured limbs were bound up.

It was a melancholy task; but this gallant fellow stuck to it until he saw such of his patients as it was possible to remove disposed of in one of the baggage-cars, emptied for this purpose. I had, in the course of his task, frequently observed him pause, as though either faint, or finding some difficulty in the act of stooping, which was constantly required; but it was not until he had seen the last of his fellow-sufferers disposed of to his best ability that he examined his own condition, when it was discovered that two of his ribs were broken.

It was full three hours before the wounded could be removed from the sandy bank on which they had been stretched; and it was an afflicting thing to see them lying here, bloody and disfigured, exposed to the glare of a hot sun, without the possibility of procuring them shelter; for we were some miles from the nearest village when the accident occurred.

The ex-president, Mr. Quincy Adams, was in the carriage immediately attached to the one overturned: by his direction an inquest was held upon the deceased before we departed; and, this being concluded, the train once more moved forward, but with a character mournfully altered since our first departure.

We found the steam-boat yet in waiting at Bordentown; and, bearing with us those of the wounded who could proceed so far, we reached Philadelphia at a late hour in the afternoon, with such a freight as I trust may never again visit its wharves.

Saturday. — Called to inquire after such of our wounded fellow-passengers as we could trace. The lady so severely hurt pronounced out of all danger; and her dear baby still living, with hopes of saving it. A man with numerous fractures, who had been left behind, report says, is relieved by death from all farther suffering.

This is the first serious accident that has occurred upon this line, which appears to be most carefully conducted; one of the active proprietors or more — the Messrs. Stevens, men of great prudence and practical skill — being constantly upon the road, and personally supervising every department connected with both boats and railway.

Sunday, 10th. — At six A.M. departed for Baltimore, *viâ* the Delaware and Newcastle railroad: the day was cloudless, and as warm as it is in England in June. I often, on these bright days, think of my good folk in Kent, — clouds and fog without, and sea-coal fire within: no bad substitute for a sun, by the way, after all; especially after one has had a sniff of the anthracite coal used in the close stoves here, an atmosphere which dread of freezing only could reconcile me to.

FOOTNOTE:

[5] Which he shortly after won with ease, and was backed on the ground to perform nineteen, and twenty. No takers.

BALTIMORE

The day upon which I first approached this city would have given a charm even to desolation. It was on the tenth of November; the air elastic, but bland as on a fine June morning at home; the temperature was about the same too, but attended with a clearness of atmosphere in all quarters that seldom falls out within our islands.

The passage down the Elk river is quite beautiful: the shores on either hand are bold and undulating; the country finely wooded; the banks indented by numerous bays and inlets, whose jutting capes so intersect each other that in several reaches the voyager is, as it were, completely land-locked, and might imagine himself coasting about some pretty lake.

We neared the well-closed harbour amidst a fleet of some hundred and fifty sail, of all sizes and of every variety of rig, from the simple two-sailed heavy sloop to that perfection of naval architecture, the Clipper schooner of Baltimore, with her long tapering masts raking over her taffrail, and her symmetrical hull fairly leaping out of water, as though she moved from wave to wave by a succession of graceful bounds rather than held her course by cleaving a pathway through them, as did her more cumbrous fellows.

The eye was charmed and the heart elevated by these unequivocal evidences of thriving commerce sweeping towards the city; which rises gradually, as it spreads over the face of the irregular hill it occupies. Several domes of considerable magnitude, a tall column or two, with various towers and spires, rendered conspicuous from the nature of the site, invest it with an air of much importance, and have gained for it the title of the City of Monuments.

The main street, like that of Boston, has very much the look of an English county-town; and the air of the shops is wholly English. I wandered about here guided by curiosity and caprice, — the only cicerone I ever desire, — and saw most things worthy note. I attended service at the cathedral, where I heard mass admirably performed, for in this choir are several voices of a very high order.

The interior of the church is good; the altar most worthily fitted up; and the general effect would be imposing were it not marred by the introduction of regular lines of exceedingly comfortable but most uncatholic-looking pews, with the which, I confess, I felt so vexed, that I could have found in my heart, Heaven pardon me! to have wished them fairly floating in the bay, only for the delicate creatures who sat within them, on whose transparent brows and soft dark eyes it was impossible to look and breathe a wish or harbour a thought of evil.

I next mounted the Washington column, as it is called, and beheld a sunset from its top that would have well recompensed a poet or painter for a journey over "the broa-a-d At-álantic," as poor Incledon used to emphasize it.

This is a noble column and splendidly put together, of workmanship and material calculated to endure,—lasting, unimpeachable by time or change, as is the fame of the patriot to whose virtues it is well inscribed; but the statue itself is bad, ineffective, and in no situation or distance I could discover at all like the great original, whose personal characteristics were nevertheless striking, and well adapted for the artist.

The inverted bee-hive too, which is overturned on the head of the capital, for the purpose, as it were, of hoisting the figure a little higher, is in bad taste, and detracts from the plainness of the column, which, if divested of both bee-hive and figure, would be an object worthy to commemorate the citizen Washington, in whose character simplicity gave lustre to the grandeur with which it was happily blended; softening and chastening it, and making him, even in the sternest times, more loved than feared.

I rode hard for a few hours to the north and west of the city, accompanied by a Scotch friend; in the course of which ride we dived down some wooded glens, and crossed some rock-strewn brooks, that called to his memory the brawling waters of his own rugged land,—so constantly, at all times and in all places, is the wanderer's mind prepared to veer homeward.

I have sometimes smiled at the total absence of similarity between the distant original and the subject that has served to challenge comparison. In this case, however, there was, in my mind, good ground enough for the recollection: at one spot, in particular, we broke from a thickly-wooded hill side that we had for some time been blindly threading, and found ourselves just over a clear pebbled stream, skirted on the opposite bank by a fair fresh meadow, itself bounded again by a wooded height yet more stony and steep than that by which we sought to descend: on our right, in an angle of the meadow, stood a farmhouse, roughly built of grey-stone and lime, surrounded by numerous offices; and, lower down the brook, a mill of similar character.

After a long look upon this pretty sequestered spot, we descended to the bed of the stream, and found a railroad already skirting its course.

Passing the mill by a bridle-path, we here saw the bed of our little brook, fallen far beneath, tossing, raging, and whirling its way amongst great masses, and tumbling over the rocky ledges dividing smooth beds of close black gneiss. Yet a little lower, we struck a road leading over a bridge, by which we re-crossed the now important current; and hence the upward view was as glen-like, gloomy, and wild as Scottish imagination could desire.

BALTIMORE

JOURNAL CONTINUED

Monday, 11th. — Find other Richmonds in the field, the Kembles being announced also, for to-night, at the Holiday Theatre, under the management of Mr. De Camp: I occupying "Front Street," with what is termed the regular Baltimore company. My front will prove in the rear, I fear.

This *untoward* meeting was purely accidental; a thing not desired or premeditated by either party: my interest and inclination making it desirable that I should give these attractive objects to the rest of the world, what sailors term, "a wide berth." Shame that I should say so, and a lady concerned too!

The Front Street. — A huge theatre, nearly as large as Covent-Garden. At night, I found there was indeed ample space "and verge enough." My clients, however, were uproariously merry, and made up for half an audience by bestowing upon the performance a double allowance of applause.

Tuesday, 12th — At 'em again! — "the Holiday" against "the Front!" I have discovered that the *people* are with *us*; "the Holiday" being considered the aristocratic house, and "the Front," being, indeed, the work of an opposition composed of the sturdy democracy of the good city.

The manager says that last night our side was taken by surprise, but that now our forces are afoot. The worst of my case is, that I am compelled, *malgré bon-gré*, to laugh at my "beggarly account of empty boxes:" my tragic rivals may, at least, have the satisfaction of lowering upon their empty pit. But the *people* are for us, consequently the right is with us; *ergo*, we must prevail.

Eight o'clock P.M. — A narrower selvage round the vast area of our *parterre*. "Front Street" for ever!

Wednesday, 12th. — I, this night at least, had the satisfaction of seeing my antagonists; for in the side-box I spied Messrs. Kemble and De Camp laughing to my teeth. I would have forgiven this, and joined with the wags, had my forces been assembled; but the musters on our side I find are not yet quite complete.

Tuesday, 18th. — The struggle continued until yesterday without either party being able to claim an absolute victory; nor is it for me now to record a triumph, since I left the allies yet camping on the field, whilst on their part they must at least admit that I marched off with all the honours of war.

This day returned to Philadelphia — weather yet unbroken. Reached Mr. Head's in time to come in with the dinner.

Wednesday, Nov. 20th. — Took a long walk round the city; the weather fine. About midday Chestnut-street assumed quite a lively and very attractive appearance, for it was filled with shopping-parties of well-dressed women, and presented a sprinkling of carriages neatly appointed and exceedingly well horsed.

Satisfied that I am correct in my judgment, when I assert that this population has the happiness to possess an unusual share of handsome girls. They walk with a freer air and more elastic step than their fair rivals of New York; have clear brunette complexions, and eyes of great beauty.

The theatre very full, and the dress-boxes containing a large proportion of ladies.

21st. — On horseback early; crossed the Schuylkill, over the Manayunk bridge, and back by the right bank of the river. The piers of a viaduct, about to be thrown from the opposite heights by the Lancaster Rail-road Company, already much elevated since my first visit here in September. Highly beneficial to the community, no doubt; but destructive of the repose and seclusion of this charming scene. The sweetest spots, and such as one would most desire to conserve, seem to be always the places peculiarly selected for these useful but most unpicturesque invasions.

23rd. — Visited the dock-yard in company with Lieutenant I— —d. A three-decker, classed according to law as a seventy-four, almost ready to be sent off the stocks—a noble ship. A frigate is housed close by her, but looks a mere toy when one views it immediately after having contemplated the proportions of the Pennsylvania. This dockyard is smaller, and in appearance inferior every way to that of Boston.

27th. — Having exhausted all the rides in the immediate neighbourhood, I this day determined upon widening my circle; so went, accompanied by K— —r, about fifteen miles up the Delaware by the Bristol road.

On the way-side we halted to look upon a mansion, made memorable for ever by one of those wild atrocities, the details of which indeed appear, upon review, fitter for the pages of romance than for a journal of every-day life, yet too striking to be heard and forgotten, or passed by without comment. I must only premise, that the affair I am about to describe is of recent occurrence, and strictly true in all its horrible details.

THE TEMPERANCE HOUSE

Within these three years the house in question was inhabited by its builder, a respectable citizen, together with his wife, a woman of much intelligence, and possessed of considerable beauty, though no longer young. They had for many years kept a creditable academy; but had, a short time before the commencement of this relation, retired with ample means from the exercise of their honourable profession, built this house, and with an only child, a handsome girl of sixteen, here dwelt, as far as their neighbours could judge, contented and happy. It is certain that they were well considered and respected by all who knew anything of them.

One afternoon, whilst the master was busied in his garden before the house, a passing wayfarer halted by his fence, and besought some refreshment. The accent of the stranger was foreign, and his aspect and whole appearance, although haggard and miserably needy, still bore evidence of better days, as his address did of gentle condition.

After a moment's questioning, Mr. C—— asked the hungered and weary traveller to enter his house; and, with the hospitable promptitude of country life, a comfortable meal was set before him.

Before another hour had elapsed, so strongly did the stranger's story of himself interest the kind nature of his host, this act of common charity was succeeded by an invitation to him to remain for a few days as the guest of the house, which was thankfully accepted.

Senhor Mina, for this was the guest's name, was, as he said, a political exile, and having strong claims of a pecuniary kind upon the American government, he was on his way to the capital to prosecute them; when, through a total failure of his resources, he became exposed to the misery and want from which this providential chance had so happily rescued him. His appearance at this point arose from his inability to pay his fare on board the steam-boat; where some altercation taking place between him and the captain, who charged him with a design to cheat, it ended in his being summarily set ashore to make the best of his way to the end of his journey.

The senhor was a scholar, was intelligent, and, what was better, interesting, having visited many lands, and encountered many of the adventurous perils of war and travel. He was here a penniless soldier in "the land of the brave" — a friendless exile for liberty in the "home of the free." He talked well; and by his enthusiastic discourses in favour of equality and independence, — topics which possess a charm for most American ears, — he quickly gained an interest in the best feelings of his honest host. He sang as all Spaniards sing, and touched the guitar as only Spaniards can; and with this artillery won yet more suddenly the love of his host's frail wife.

Time passed rapidly in a little circle so happily constituted to banish tedium: nor was business wanting to occupy a due share, for the senhor despatched many letters; and, having established a correspondence with the foreign-office, the necessity for his own presence at the seat of government next became manifest. This was no sooner made known to Mr. C— — than ample means were placed at Senhor Mina's disposal; when, with the best wishes of the whole family, he took a short farewell of Pennsylvania.

The absence of the interesting stranger was signalized by a change in the habits and condition of this household as sudden as that which had attended his first introduction to it. Mrs. C— — grew gradually fretful, restless, and anxious; which might well be, for her husband was on a sudden laid up with sickness, and their only child studiously shunned their society, locking herself within her chamber, or moping about the grounds she had so lately bounded over in the buoyancy of health and happy youth.

The sequel was not long in arriving: the sick man daily grew worse and weaker; and his wife, as was perfectly natural, daily grew more wretched and impatient. She was assiduous to a jealous degree in the performance of her duties and close attendance on her husband's bed; she mixed his medicines, prepared his food and such diluents as were considered best calculated to allay the fever that for ever burned him up. With his hand within her's, she watched his last agonies, which were protracted and extreme; and received from his lips grateful acknowledgments of her unwearied kindness, and his dying blessing.

So far all went unsuspectedly and well: for one month the widow lived unseen and retired, as became a sorrowing woman; but about the end of that period, to the great surprise of the neighbourhood, she was made again a bride by the grateful stranger, Senhor Mina.

And now it was that men began to shake their heads and find their tongues; comments upon the shameless precipitancy of this wedding were everywhere heard, mixed up with strange surmises, and suspicions too horrible to remain long suppressed.

Curious inquiries were next made amongst the domestics, and one servant girl quickly called to mind having noticed a sediment in the remains of a basin of soup prepared by her mistress for the sick man, which having been thrown to the poultry, together with some of the rice, these had all since withered and died; nay, a hardy hog even, whose portion had been small, with difficulty weathered an attack of sickness which had quickly followed.

A legal inquiry was next demanded by the roused public, upon which such strong evidence appeared as to render the exhumation of the body necessary: the contents of the stomach were yet in a condition to admit of chemical analyzation, and the exhibition of a large portion of arsenic was by these means proven past doubt.

The unconscious senhor — with whom, during this part of the process, they had prevented the miserable woman holding any communication — was meantime busily prosecuting his affairs, whatever they were, amidst the gaieties of Washington. One night, upon his return from a public ball, he was arrested by an officer who had just reached his quarters with a criminal warrant, taken back to the scene of his ingratitude, and, together with the partner of his crime, put upon trial for the murder of his benefactor.

The guilt of both parties was established, I believe, beyond a doubt; but some legal loophole was found by which the woman was permitted to elude the capital punishment, and condemned to live. The ungrateful guest was sentenced to be hanged: shortly before the time of execution he made full confession of his having planned and instigated the poisoning of his unsuspecting host, and died the death of an assassin.

Here is a suite of horrors, plainly and briefly set down, sufficient to supply stuff for any murder-loving three-volume novelist; yet is there one other, and that not least, to be added; for it appeared in the progress of the trial, and time in the ordinary course confirmed this evidence, that the poor child, the daughter of the murderess, had fallen a victim to the lust of this devil, Mina.

The fate of the girl and her infant I could not rightly learn; all that was known, indeed, being her removal to some distant part of the continent. The mother, it was believed, yet resided within the walls her guilt has made for ever infamous.

The house is always pointed out to the passing stranger, and was, when I saw it, no unfit monument of its owner's crime, and the curse which so quickly followed on it. Its fences were thrown down, its outhouses in ruin, the paths about it overgrown with filthy weeds; and the latticed window-shutters, once gay as green paint could make them, now dirty and broken, were left to swing loose from every wall. Still, evidences of its being inhabited were exhibited about the yard, where a dog and a few fowls lay basking; and suspended from the branch of a blighted tree, standing near the fallen entrance-gate, hung an ill-inscribed sign, bearing the inscription "*Temperance House*" in large characters.

A singular change, — the abode of the grossest lust, and the scene of the foulest murder, perhaps, ever combined in the full catalogue of crime, changed into a temple to Temperance.

JOURNAL

Sunday, December 1st. — A little cloudy, but mild and pleasant. We have up to this date no severe weather; and, indeed, with the exception of now and then a day not colder than some which we experienced in September, have had no remembrancer of the approach of frost: but I fancy old father Winter "'bides his time," and will not spare us when his icy wings are once locsed upon the north-east wind.

Rode to German Town, and down the ravine of the Wisihissing. A stranger, looking over the continuous level which is presented to his view on a first glance at the country surrounding Philadelphia, has many pleasant surprises in store, if he be of an errant habit and much given to exploration; since there are several ravines of singular wildness in this vicinity, having bridle-paths connecting them with the different roads, and a great deal of broken country, whose variety well repays the adventurous equestrian.

This is a mode of proceeding I would counsel every traveller to follow who desires to become well acquainted with the general character of a country, as but little of this can be known from a hasty drive along the common line of road. Never let the idea of being badly mounted deter a man from this experiment; but let him send for the best hack that the place may afford, or, what is a better plan, go and see after one.

In America, although all the nags thus procured may not prove the smoothest goers in the world, they will uniformly be found strong and well up to their work. Only let the stranger acquire the habit of getting into saddle with promptitude on arriving at a strange place, and more may be seen of its neighbourhood, and known of its condition, by this means, in a morning foray or two, than a month of idling will compass.

Saturday, 14th. — Back again to Baltimore to act in Front-street the same night.

A clear cold morning until about midday, when it became overcast, with some rain and wind, which, just as we cleared the Elk river, was exchanged for snow. Not an inch of our way did we see after this: the boat was frequently stopped, and soundings carefully made; our speed was reduced to the slowest possible pace, and every precaution taken that prudence could suggest to the experience of our captain. Night came on, however, and we had the pleasant prospect of passing it in the bay of the Chesapeake, or on one of the shoals, or shores, about us, when happily our look-out got a momentary glimpse of Fort M'Henry, which we were about to pass to the southward. Had we done so, we must in a short time have grounded in the Patapsco, there to rest for the coming clear weather: as it was, a short time saw us snug in harbour, although we could hardly see ourselves when we got there.

I was too late for Front-street, a circumstance which I did not regret, remembering its situation and the state of the weather, but consoled myself readily over a canvass-back duck and a tumbler of Monongahela, — when old, equal, if mixed with hot water, even to Innishtowen; at least I remember I thought so on this occasion.

Retired early to my room, intending to read for an hour, having observed a cheery-looking fire in it whilst changing my wet things. It was exceedingly cold without; the snow fell thick, and the sight of a grate full of cinders, glowing like lumps of iron at red heat, was especially enlivening. I sat down to read, but in a few minutes found my eyes become strangely dim: after a vain attempt to clear them by ablution, I resigned my book, gave way to the headache and weariness, which grew worse every minute, and got into my bed, concluding these unpleasant symptoms were occasioned by previous cold and exposure to the weather.

I lay down, but to rest was impossible; my temples throbbed, the veins became swollen and tense, whilst my breathing grew short and difficult: getting at last a little alarmed, and, indeed, fearing a fainting fit, I rose to ring for my servant; but not finding the bell, opened my chamber-door with the intention of seeking some assistance.

I had not proceeded many steps down the passage before I felt my illness abate, in a manner quite as sudden and strange as its advance had been; my sight became clear, my pulse grew regular, my breathing natural; and after a momentary pause, almost of doubt at this rapid restoration to health and ease, I retraced my steps to my chamber, feeling glad that I had not communicated a false alarm in a house where two or three sudden deaths, from what was called cholera, had already predisposed the inmates to be nervous.

On re-entering my room, the cause of my late symptoms became manifest in the first breath I inhaled of the atmosphere; even as it now was, comparatively purified by a current of fresh air, the gaseous smell continued disagreeable and distressing.

I sent for the fireman of the hotel, — that is, the person so called who lights and looks after the hundred fires going in one of these establishments: he was a countryman and a staunch personal friend; and, after hearing my story and removing the anthracite coal, he pledged himself never to burn anything but wood in my chamber for the time to come.

I next questioned my friend as to whether he had ever before known any person as severely affected from the same cause. He said he had heard gentlemen complain now and again, "But the cowld soon makes them get used to it," said Pat; adding, that most persons left a little of the window open if the weather permitted.

This was my first and last experiment with this coal, which is nevertheless burned almost universally in the north, though they have abundance of fine Nova Scotia coal, that appears little inferior to the best Lancashire. Liverpool coal is a good deal used in New York; but the ladies give the preference uniformly to the anthracite, which does not yield much dust or black smoke, and consequently preserves for a longer period both furniture and dress: it also renders a room quickly and equally warm without requiring attendance, when once lighted, burning constantly with a red heat, and fiercely or otherwise in proportion to the draft, which all the stoves here permit to be regulated at will.

Nevertheless, I think all its advantages are nothing when weighed against the injurious effect the atmosphere it generates must have upon the health of those constantly within its influence.

It may, with great advantage, be used for hall-stoves, for heating air-pipes, or in situations where there is a ready circulation of air; but ought not, I think, to be continued in the drawing-rooms of families or in the chambers of the studious.

Sunday, 15th. — The snow lying about a foot deep in the streets, but in places drifted to a great height: numbers of make-shift sleighs already jingling about the town, Baltimore having precedence of the northern cities this year in an amusement not often enjoyed here.

I had a trial of the sleigh for a couple of hours; and in company with a fat friend was bumped over the gutters through the soft snow, — for on it we could not be said to ride, — whilst every inequality of the streets was made evident to our bones.

This is a species of amusement into which the Northerns enter with a spirit of positive enthusiasm: man, woman, and child all talk of, and look forward to, the arrival of sleighing-time as a season of the highest festivity. In New York, I am told, the first heavy fall of snow brings even business to a stand-still, and the whole population is seen whirling over the streets in every description of vehicle that can be lifted off its wheels and lodged upon runners.

The regular fancy sleighs I have frequently examined: they are tastefully and comfortably built, and fitted up with all sorts of furs, — skins of bear and buffalo, and various other beasts; are lined and betasseled in a way that renders them quite beautiful; and might defy the recognition of their nearest of kin.

18th. — The snow has vanished wholly, and the weather is again mild as spring: the Southerners yet lingering here upon the confines of the north are, however, alarmed by this early demonstration of the absence of winter so far south, and daily set off for their yet sunny abodes in Georgia, the Carolinas, Alabama, or Louisiana.

Our excellent table is gradually thinning off; and King David's labour, as grand carver, is daily abridged. We this day had a haunch of Virginia venison, with fat an inch and half deep, the flavour equal to anything I ever ate: it is the first fat venison I have seen in the country. Canvass-back still in abundance, and not to be wearied of. This, I find, is the true place to eat these rare birds: their case is well understood here, and they are treated to a nicety.

Saturday, 21st. — Back to Philadelphia, on my way to New York — will pass this night in the City of Squares, and Sunday — the day positively warm; observed, however, a thin flaking of ice stealing over the shaded surface of the Elk river.

Monday, 23rd. — Once more in New York, *viâ* the Delaware and Raritan. Although on Sunday it was feared that these rivers would be closed with ice, we had only a little coating of Jack Frost to break through, suffering no detention, and found the bay perfectly free; arriving here about three o'clock.

27th. — Walked to the top of Broadway, which has lost much of its crowd, but is yet quite bustling enough to be a very lively and pleasant lounge.

Went into the Episcopalian church near the Park, the graves of Montgomery and Emmett being the chief attraction: the monuments erected to their memories stand outside, close upon the street. Just as I turned out of the gate, after having read the inscription upon the monument of the latter, I was joined by R— —t, who gave me an interesting account of the last meeting of the devoted brothers.

Thomas Emmett being at Rotterdam, after his release from Fort George, on his way to the United States, chanced to be in waiting for his letters at the post-office, when a man stepping from the crowd threw himself into his arms with exclamations of glad recognition: it was his brother Robert, just arrived from Paris, and attending here on a like errand.

"And from whence come you?" demanded Robert, the first congratulations being past.

"Just escaped from poor Ireland," replied the senior brother; adding, "and whither are you now bound?"

"Just escaping to poor Ireland," was the reply.

The meeting was a short one; Robert would listen to no word of accompanying his family in their exile. He declared his only desire was either to procure for his country even justice, and freedom from neglect and oppression, or for himself a grave, and oblivion of her people's sufferings and degradation.

The brothers parted here, never again to meet. Robert quickly found the fate he courted, and sleeps beneath the soil he died for, — mistakingly it may be, but neither unwept, unpitied, nor unsung.

The senior pursued his more prudent course, and landed with his wife and children in this city, unknown, and having slight recommendation beyond his misfortunes and his country; these, however, proved all-sufficient to procure for him the sympathy and respect of the citizens from whom he sought adoption. He rested amongst them, became one of them, and lived to see his children standing with the best and most esteemed of the country.

In the fulness of his honours Thomas Addis Emmett died, and on the most conspicuous part of Broadway stands the obelisk of marble reared in honour of his memory, and bearing testimony to the high talent and the many virtues of the Irish exile, the banished rebel, or the unsuccessful patriot; for the terms are yet unhappily considered by some as synonymous, and may be selected by each according to his political creed. By his family and associates, however, he appears to have been truly beloved, and by all men to have been viewed as an upright citizen and a most able counsel; his eloquence at the bar being still the theme of frequent enthusiastic eulogium.

This night went to a dance at the hospitable house of Mr. C— —ne, the first occasion which afforded me a view of the New York belles in society. The party was not large, but there were several very pretty women, and waltzing and music alternated in charming succession: there were two ladies who sang with infinite taste and sweetness, and we kept it up until rather a late hour for a sober country. My impression of the New York women is, that they are frank, lively, and intelligent, with much gentleness in their manners and address: in short, that these were very amiable and attractive specimens of their sex and country.

20th. — Went to look over the Opera-house, which has been built here very suddenly by subscription. It is about the size of the Lyceum; arranged after the French fashion, having stalls, a *parterre*, and *balcon* below; and above, two circles of private boxes, the property of subscribers. Some of these are fitted up in a style of extravagance I never saw attempted elsewhere. There has been a sort of rivalry exercised on this head, and it has been pursued with that regardlessness of cost which distinguishes a trading community where their *amour propre* is in question.

Silk velvets, damask, and gilt furniture form the material within many; and, as the parties consult only their own taste, the colours of these are various as their proprietors' fancies. I do not find the *ensemble* bad, however; whilst the shape and mounting of the *salle* are both unexceptionable.

This effort, however creditable to the good taste of the city, is premature, and must be doomed to more failures than one before it permanently succeeds. A refined taste for the best kind of music is not consequent upon the erection of an opera-house, nor is it a feeling to be created at will. Even in the metropolis of England, with a capital so disproportionate, and possessing such superior facilities for the attainment of novelty, did the continuance of this refined amusement depend solely upon the love of good music, it would quickly die, if not be forgotten.

From time to time, a small, but efficient and really good Italian troop, will, beyond doubt, find liberal encouragement in the great northern cities, and also in New Orleans, provided they make a short stay in each; but, rapidly as events progress here, I will undertake to predict that a century must elapse before even New York can sustain a permanent operatic establishment.

JOURNAL CONTINUED

NEW YEAR'S DAY IN NEW YORK

With an unclouded sky, and a sun as bright and genial as we would desire on a May morning, the first day of January 1834 makes its bow to the New York public; and in no place does this same day meet heartier welcome, or witness better cheer.

On this day, from an early hour, every door in New York is open, and all the good things possessed by the inmates paraded in lavish profusion. The shops and banks alone are closed: Mammon for this day sees his altars in one spot on earth deserted. Meantime every sort of vehicle is put in requisition; and if a man owns but a single acquaintance in the wide city, he on this day sets forth in kind heart to seek and shake him by the hand.

On this day all family bickerings are made up; fancied or real wrongs admitted, explained, and forgiven. The first twenty-four hours of the new year in New York is a right *Trève de Dieu*, during which foes cease from strife, the long divided are re-united, and friendly compacts renewed and drawn closer: even Avarice, more wary of approach than the hare, on this day forgets to bolt his door, or calculate the cost of bidding welcome to his visitor.

The stranger is also made sensible of the benevolent influence of this kindly day, if I may draw any inference from my own case. At an early hour a gentleman of whom I had a slight knowledge entered my room, accompanied by an elderly person I had never before seen, and who, on being named, excused himself for adopting such a frank mode of making my acquaintance, which he was pleased to add he much desired, and at once requested me to fall in with the custom of the day, whose privilege he had thus availed himself of, and accompany him on a visit to his family.

I was the last man on earth likely to decline an offer made in such a spirit; so, entering his carriage which was in waiting, we drove to his house in Broadway, where, after being presented to a very amiable lady, his wife, and a pretty, gentle-looking young girl, his daughter, I partook of a sumptuous luncheon, drank a glass of champagne, and, on the arrival of other visitors, made my bow, well pleased with my visit.

My host now begged me to make a few calls with him, explaining, as we drove along, the strict observances paid to this day throughout the State, and tracing the excellent custom to the early Dutch colonists.

I paid several calls in company with my new friend, at each place met a hearty welcome, and witnessed the same abundant preparation; but to lunch at each was, with the best intentions possible, quite out of the question. After a considerable round, my companion suggested that I might possibly have some compliments to make on my own account, and so leaving me, begged me to consider his carriage perfectly at my disposal.

This was very kind, but I at the time knew only two or three families; and indeed, on being left to myself in solitary state, where every carriage that whirled by was filled with merry stranger faces, my courage oozed away. So, leaving a card or two, and making a couple of hurried visits, I returned to my hotel, to think over the many beneficial effects likely to grow out of such a charitable custom, and to wish for its continued observance.

We have days enough of division in each year, and should indeed welcome and cherish one which inculcates peace and good-will to all; a day on which little coolnesses are explained away, past kindnesses confirmed, and injuries consigned to oblivion.

At night, the theatre was filled to suffocation by a joyous throng, although this portion of the season is not propitious to theatricals; but on to-day, as though no house must be left unvisited by any of its ordinary frequenters, the Park came in for a full participation in the benefit of this honoured custom.

Friday, 3rd. — The prevailing topics of the new year are the President and his *quondam* chum, Major Jack Downing;[6] the agitation of the community on the Bank question becoming daily more violent, as the limitation placed on credit embarrasses trade by narrowing its resources. I observe, however, that, in the midst of much wordy violence, the bulk of the people appear confident that matters will, to use a coinage of their own, "*eventuate* for their ultimate benefit." Meanwhile, the government and the laws appear equally omnipotent; and although much embarrassment is unquestionably felt in the money-market, and all stock become unseasonably low for the sellers, yet is the country generally admitted to be very prosperous, and perfectly able to meet this shock without any permanent or ruinous difficulty. We shall see.

Went to Mrs. H——'s box at the opera, — the "Donna del Lago," for Bordogni's benefit: a very pretty woman, very well instructed; but with a little pipe, in which sweetness cannot make up for want of force. Fanti, a really good actress, and, although with a veiled voice, a capital singer, is not so much considered, I discover, as Bordogni.

The house was quite filled, the boxes rejoicing in a display of pretty faces few *salles d'opéra* might be admitted to rival. The prevailing head-dress exceedingly showy and fanciful, a little too much so perhaps: — but these are doings which, after all, change with each season; therefore fashion can alone be arbiter. On the subject of beauty I speak fearlessly, all men, having clear eyesight, being, upon this point, admitted as competent witnesses. The *parterre*, too, was occupied by a few parties of well-dressed women; but its prevailing character, stalls included, was sombre and great-coatish, — not quite up to the pit of the King's Theatre; — there was more applause though, therefore I presume more enjoyment, which is the main object after all. At the close of the performance several delicate bouquets, together with a pretty coronal or two of choice flowers, were showered on the stage in compliment to the fair *bénéficière*.

Wednesday, 12th. — Winter has at length arrived in person, and his active bridge-maker is laying for him a firm icy path across the waters. It was reported yesterday that the passage between Staten Island and New Jersey was no longer open, Amboy Creek being thickly frozen from Newark Bay to the Raritan. On reaching the steamboat this morning, I found that the report was a correct one, and that our only practicable passage lay through the Narrows and round the south end of Staten Island. The occasion thus presented of a winter view of the bay quite reconciled me to this more exposed and circuitous route, as it, in truth, amply compensated for it.

It was just seven A.M. when I reached the dock where the boat lay, to all appearance firmly imbedded in thick ice; the river, I perceived, was still pretty clear. Punctual as usual, the bell ceased to clang; the paddle-wheels were vigorously applied; and in a few moments we burst our bonds, thrusting the thick flakes of ice aside, and darting into the clear river free from all farther impediment.

There were very few passengers, and I had the promenade deck to my exclusive use. Although day had not long broke, the clearness and purity of the atmosphere gave to the most distant parts of the landscape an outline cold and distinct, and brought all objects apparently much nearer to each other, and to the looker-on, than they had ever before appeared. The city of Jersey, the woods of Hoboken, and the far-off bluffs of the Palisadoes, were each seen to stand separated and alone; not blended together into one harmonizing mass, as, through the medium of a rich warm atmosphere, I had hitherto viewed them. The effect was for a moment to render this scene, which frequent observation had made familiar, quite strange to me; and at the same time to invest its now separate portions with new and peculiar attractions.

The yet quiet city soon dropped astern; and on a good plan of its streets one might have traced the earliest and most notable of its sections, if not the particular houses, by the thin spiral lines of smoke which curled distinctly high above the chimneys from which they escaped.

We held our course close along the east side of Staten Island; and as we shot by the quarantine establishment, with its hospital and many offices, the sun rose, without one attendant cloud, over the forest heights of Brooklyn, burnishing, as with gold, every window and weathercock opposed to its radiance.

The drooping boughs of the graceful willow tribes, and all the neighbouring shrubs, which only a moment before I had shivered to look upon, bent down, as they appeared, beneath a load of ungenial icicles, were now, as though touched by some enchanter's wand, sparkling and brilliant, reminding one of the diamond-growing trees of young Aladdin's cave.

The Narrows were next passed, but the view seaward was bleak and cheerless: the Neversink hills for the first time appearing to me worthy such a high-sounding distinction. Not a symptom of frost was here, although the wind had ceased to stir the waters of the bay, and to the sun alone was left the task of opposing the advance of the ice-king. Sol, though with diminished powers, had made a glorious rally on this day; for not a thicket or creek within sight but rejoiced in his cheering rays, and gladly owned his supremacy.

The smoothness of the sea enabled our boat to make rapid way; and by a little after ten o'clock we were landed at Amboy, where we found the train awaiting our arrival. As we left our first stage, Hights-town, an accident occurred similar to the one I had, on my last trip southward, seen attended by such fearful consequences. We were proceeding, luckily at a moderate rate, when the axle of the engine-tender broke in two: the car occupied by myself and three others led the van, yet the first intimation we got of the break-down of our tender was our running foul of it with a bump that fairly unshipped us all, pitching the occupiers of the hind-seats head-on into the laps of those *vis-à-vis* to them. Happily, this was the worst of the present mischance: the engine was speedily arrested, a sound axle drawn from the near car to replace the one fractured, myself and the others belonging to the carriage thus hauled out of the line were stowed in, as supernumeraries, elsewhere, and, after a delay, of some forty minutes, off we bowled again.

Halting for a few moments at Bordentown, where the Delaware steamer waits when the river is practicable, it now spread away below us in a solid mass; and we pursued our journey by the railroad provided for such seasons so far as it was at this time completed, that is, for some eight or nine miles farther on. This point achieved, we discovered a group of the clumsy-looking stage-coaches of the country, to the number of twelve, each having a team of four horses, ready harnessed, standing amongst the trees below.

The cold was by this time extreme; bustle was the word, therefore, amongst all parties, — drivers, porters, and passengers; and in a quarter of an hour the transfer was completed, the luggage packed, the people arranged, and the caravan in motion. The place had quite a wild, lone, forest air; and it was a curious scene to view the bustle, and hear the noise, so uncongenial to the spot, and no less so to observe the coaches wheeling about amongst the trees as each Jehu sought to make the best of his way into the lane at a little distance.

Miserably uncomfortable as the driver's seat is before these machines, I, as usual where the course was strange to me, requested leave to share it with him. I had cast about to select a team; and was soon seated, well rolled in broadcloth and bear-skin, behind four dark bays that might have done credit to a better judgment.

We soon got into a very narrow lane, through which lay the first few miles. In this the ruts, or track, as it is here called, was over a foot deep: on either side grew trees, thick and low-branched; therefore my companion and I had as much as we could do to avoid broken heads and keep the track. I looked impatiently, after practising this dodging exercise some time, for the great road which the driver told me was "a bit further ahead;" and at last we broke from our leafy shelter into it, but with little advantage that I could discover; for, though our heads were in less peril, our necks, I considered, required more especial looking after than ever. We certainly had here wider space, and a free choice of ruts or tracks, for there were several; but not one of them less profound than those we had hitherto ploughed through. In one or two places, the road was deeply trenched in every direction, and the edges of these cuts so glazed with new-formed ice that I expected my friend who was pilot would pass the box and back out. But no such thing, faith! he steered round all impediments as coolly as the wind that whistled through the half-frozen reins he held.

Finding one place in the road quite impassable, he cast his eyes about him for a moment, and chose the best part of the right bank; when, gathering up his leaders, he first vexed them a little with the whip, and then, putting them fairly at it, gained its summit, drove along for a hundred yards, crashing through a thick cover of shrubs growing breast-high, when having thus turned the impracticable bit of highway, he coolly dropped down into it again. On looking back, I saw each team taking in succession the line we had thus led over.

This was all performed clumsily enough, as far as appearance went, I allow; but cleverly and confidently, though with leaders hardly within calling distance: and four snaffle-bits, and a pig-whip, being the only means of dictation and control possessed by the coachman. The more I see of these queer Whips the better I like them: it assuredly is impossible to conceive anything more uncoachmanlike than their outward man; but they grapple with the constantly occurring difficulties of their strange work hardily and with superior intelligence.

I have seen a pass on the high-road between Albany and New York, where a descending driver perceiving that collision with a coming carriage was from the slippery condition of the hill unavoidable, and also being aware that such an event would be fatal to both parties, on the instant turned his horses to the near bank, and dashed down into the bed of the Mohawk, a descent of more than a hundred feet, as nearly perpendicular as may well be. His presence of mind and courage saved both his own passengers and those in the other vehicle, with the loss of his coach and one of his horses only. The man was publicly thanked and rewarded, and, I believe, yet waggons the same road.

One might almost back one of these crack hands to hunt a picked team of their own, a cross country, with the Melton hounds, coach and all; and if it was not for the *pace*, it would not be such a very bad bet either.

At Camden we quitted our vehicular mode of progressing, and took once more to the water, or rather to the ice, since it certainly ruled over the broad Delaware. In many places this was strong enough to sustain the weight of our little steamer's bow, and only gave way beneath repeated heavy blows of the iron-sheathed paddles.

After a hard fight we forced a path through all obstacles, and as the clock struck four were alongside the Chestnut-street wharf; having, notwithstanding the delays occasioned by our mishap and various changes, accomplished the hundred miles in exactly ten hours.

I was expected, found a dinner prepared for five o'clock, and, going at once to my chamber to dress, thought I had never seen the Mansion-house look to greater advantage. A well-warmed and carpeted corridor led to my snug little room, the window of which looking into the inner court, afforded one of the most attractive winter prospects imaginable, in the form of entire carcasses of several fat bucks all hanging in a comely row, and linked together by a festooning composed of turkey, woodcock, snipe, grouse, and ducks of several denominations. Although quartered here for a month to come, I felt fortified against any fear of famine by this single glance without; nor did my interior appear less inviting, cheered as this was by a brisk fire of hickory, several logs of which lay athwart my hearth, sustained by a couple of antique-looking brass dogs, blazing and crackling most uproariously: this is a fire I prefer even to one of Liverpool coal; and how it can ever be superseded by that quiet, unsocial, unearthly-looking and smelling, anthracite, I am at a loss to *guess*!

FOOTNOTE:

[6] Described as the officer commanding the Downingsville militia, a New-Englander, and a stanch adherent of the "Gineral's, so far as 'a decent hunk of the animal wint,' but entirely agin' the whole-hog system." Under this perfect assumption there appeared a series of really familiar epistles, either remonstrating with or speaking of the "Gineral," or, as the Major latterly styled the President, "the Govermint;" no less admirable for the political acumen they display than for a caustic drollery, which is enforced with shrewd Yankee humour, and in the singular phraseology current amongst 'Uncle Sam's' kindred. These letters have been collected, and are published both in America and in England; and although neither the purity of the politics or the dialect of the honest Major can be fully appreciated by strangers, his intrinsic wit and native humour will well repay the task of a perusal by all who admire originality of thought and expression.

THE DUTCH AND IRISH COLONIES
OF PENNSYLVANIA

Here are two colonies yet existing within this State,—samples of both indeed may be found within a few miles of Philadelphia,—and these constitute with me a never-failing source of interest and amusement. They are composed of Dutch and Irish, often located on adjoining townships, but keeping their borders as clearly defined as though the wall of China were drawn between them. No two bodies exist in nature more repellent; neither time, nor the necessities of traffic, which daily arise amongst a growing population, can induce a repeal of their tacit non-intercourse system, or render them even tolerant of each other. I have understood that Pat has on occasions of high festivity been known to extend his courtesy so far as to pay his German neighbours a call to inquire kindly whether "any gintlemen in the place might be inclined for a fight;" but this evidence of good-nature appears to have been neither understood nor reciprocated, and, proof against the blandishment, Mynheer was not even to be hammered into contact with "dem wilder Irisher."

It is a curious matter to observe the purity with which both people have conserved the dialect of their respective countries, and the integrity of their manners, costume, prejudices, nay, their very air, all of which they yet present fresh and characteristic as imported by their ancestors, although some of them are the third in descent from the first colonists. Differing in all other particulars, on this point of character their similarity is striking.

Amongst the Germans I have had families pointed out to me, whose fathers beheld the commencement of the war of Independence in Pennsylvania, yet who are at this day as ignorant of its language, extent, policy, or population, as was the worthy pastor of whom it is related, that, having been requested to communicate to his flock the want of supplies which existed in the American camp, he assured the authorities that he had done so, as well as described to them the exact state of affairs:

"I said to dem," he repeated in English, "Get op, min broders und mine zisters, und put dem paerd by die vagen, mit brood und corn; mit schaap's flesh und flesh of die groote bigs, und os flesh; und alles be brepare to go op de vay, mit oder goed mens, to sooply General Vashinton, who was fighting die Englishe Konig vor our peoples, und der lifes, und der liberdies, op-on dem banks of de Schuylkill, diese side of die Vestern Indies."

In his piggery of a residence and his palace of a barn, in his waggon, his oxen, his pipe, his person and physiognomy, the third in descent, from the worthies exhorted as above, remains unchanged. The cases upon which, as a juryman, he decides, he hears through the medium of an official interpreter; he has his own journal, which serves out his portion of politics to him in Low Dutch, and in the same language is printed such portions of the acts of the State legislature as may in any way relate to the section he inhabits; the only portion of the community, indeed, which he knows, or cares to know, anything about.

My honest countrymen of the same class, I can answer for being as slightly sophisticated as their colder neighbours: it is true, their tattered robes have been superseded by sufficient clothing, and a bit of good broadcloth for Sunday or Saint's day, and their protracted lenten fare exchanged for abundance of good meat, and bread, and "tay, galore, for the priest and the mistress;" but when politics or any stirring cause is offered to them, their feelings are found to be as excitable, and their temperament as fiery, as though still standing on the banks of the Suir or the Shannon.

On all occasions of rustic holiday they may yet be readily recognised by their slinging gait, the bit of a stick borne in the hollow of the hand, the inimitable shape and set of the hat, the love of top-coats in the men, and the abiding taste for red ribands and silk gowns amongst the women.

The inherent difference between the two people is never more strikingly perceived than when you have occasion to make any inquiry whilst passing through their villages. Pull up your horse by a group of little Dutchmen, in order to learn your way or ask any information, and the chance is they either run away, "upon instinct," or are screamed at to come within doors by their prudent mothers; upon which cry they scatter, like scared rabbits, for the warren, leaving you to *Try Turner* or any other shop within hail.

For myself, after a slight experience, I succeeded with my friends to admiration: the few sentences of indifferent Dutch which I yet conserved from my education amongst the Vee boors, at the Cape, served as a passport to their civility. Without this accomplishment, all strangers are suspected of being Irishers; and, as such, partake of the dislike and dread in which their more mercurial neighbours are held by this sober-sided and close-handed generation.

On the other hand, enter an Irish village, and by any chance see the young villains precipitated out of the common school: call to one of these, and a dozen will be under your horse's feet in a moment; prompt in their replies, even if ignorant of that you seek to learn; and ready and willing to show you any place or road they know anything, or nothing, about. I have frequently on these occasions, when asked to walk into their cabin by the old people, on hearing their accent, and seeing myself thus surrounded, almost doubted my being in the valley of Pennsylvania.

So little indeed does the accent of the Irish American, — who lives exclusively amongst his own people in the country parts, — differ from that of the settler of a year, that on occasions of closely-contested elections this leads to imposition on one hand and vexation on the other; and it is by no means uncommon for a man, whose father was born in the States, to be questioned as to his right of citizenship, and requested to bring proofs of a three years' residence.

I now passed another month in this city most agreeably, during which the weather was never unendurably cold: sharp frosts, but not a single fall of snow that continued over an hour or two, or lay longer on the ground. The majority of days I find noted in my journal as frosty but fine, many as mild, and some even are described as warm: there were few, indeed, during which exercise on horseback might not have been pleasantly taken. When February set in, and no snow had yet fallen, I heard much despair evinced on the diminished chances of a good sleighing-time; and, although an enemy to severe cold, I confess I had my own regrets at not being permitted to assist at a sleighing frolic, of which I received on all hands such glowing descriptions.

On the eighth of this month I looked with some anxiety for the continuance of mild weather, as the Delaware was, happily, once more open, and the line by way of that river and French-town resumed; a very important event, as far as both comfort and expedition were concerned. Indeed, a journey by land to Baltimore was an adventure by no means to be desired; the time of travel having varied during the last month from three to nine days, the distance being under a hundred miles. But the waters were up, the bridges down; one road was washed away, and another filled in with rocks, and roots of trees on their travels from the Alleghanies to the Atlantic, which rested there, abiding the next flood, without any fear of receiving a visit *ad interim* from M'Adam.

All, however, went well; the steamer was advertised to sail on the morning of the 9th: there were here several weather-bound Southerners, who, like myself, were anxious to proceed as easily as possible to the capital; and we congratulated each other on the prospect we had of accomplishing this by aid of steamboat and railroad, now once more available.

THE STEAMBOAT

DELAWARE.—NEWCASTLE.— RAILROAD.—FRENCH-TOWN.—ELK RIVER.—NORTH POINT.—BAY OF CHESAPEAKE.—BALTIMORE

Quitting one of these great seaports by the ordinary conveyance of steamboat, early on a fine winter morning, is at once an amusing and interesting event.

Hastily summoned by your servant, who, himself not over early, bustles up to your bedside with "Just five minutes after six o'clock, sir," you start from a slumber that has been for some time back uneasy enough, broken up by visions of steamboats, locomotives, canvass-back ducks, Nott's stoves, and crowded cabin-tables.

At the first shake out you jump, well aware how peremptory is the steamer's bell above all other *belles*,—make hasty toilet, and bustle into the hall, where a few half-burned candles yet outface the daylight; and here you find a dozen newly-awakened miserables like yourself, equipped for some steamer.

The waiter inquires if you would like a cup of coffee, which as a matter of course you accept; and, hurrying after him into the next room, you are yet in the act of blowing and sipping your Mocha, which for once you find sufficiently hot, when a friend pops his head in to say that the baggage-cart is off, and your latest second of time come. Remedy there is none; a delay of one minute is fatal, since no timekeeper is so punctual as an American steamer anywhere north of the Potomac.

Out you trudge, great-coated, muffled up in fur and shawl, to find the street silent and untrodden, except by a straggler or twain bending their steps hurriedly towards Chestnut. As you turn out of South-third into this great thoroughfare you observe an immediate change; the stragglers preceding you have mingled with the main current, and are quickly confounded amidst a confused jumble of men, women, and children, carts, coaches, and wheelbarrows, pressing in long columns of march down towards the Delaware.

In the distance may be seen, curling from below, wavy pillars of dense black smoke, intermingled with vicious-looking lines of thin whitish vapour, which rush through and tower high over the more sluggish smoke with a savage, hissing sound that almost drowns the bell, now tolling a last summons.

The wharf is gained: here lie the boats side by side, one going north, the other south: they are surrounded by a crowd, — friends making hasty adieus; porters, of all shades of colour, hurrying to and fro, aiding, scrambling, and squabbling, with the important air and ceaseless loquacity everywhere characteristic of the African race.

Amidst this motley throng the unoccupied and observant man will easily pick out many individuals of gaunt outline, a bilious aspect and a staid sober demeanour, each carrying a small valise, a carpet-bag, a long Boston coat or cloak, and steadily and deliberately making a straight course for the common bourne, unaided and unaiding, self-sustained, independent, and, each for himself alone.

At length, after a few last hasty bangs, the heavy bell clappers cease to move; the porters quit the luggage-cars and spring nimbly ashore; the independent gentlemen dispose of their *kits*, each after the fashion and on the spot he "judges" most convenient; the hissing sound of escaping steam suddenly stops, and this momentary silence is succeeded by the quick motion of the paddle-wheels.

The vicious-looking columns of white vapour melt away; wheeling majestically about, the huge boats steadily head towards their opposite courses, and, in the next moment, are rushing, like unslipped greyhounds, through the smooth waters of the Delaware.

And now occasionally arrive discoveries, at once whimsical and amusing to all save the sufferers. A lady with her children going South, for instance, finds out that her husband, or her carriage and horses, one or both, have gotten by mistake aboard the New York boat, and are off back again to the North: perhaps you get a glimpse of the miserable biped in question, like a waterman, looking one way and going the other. Without great care, these little accidents will occur, as I can vouch for; as the lines depart full drive at the same instant, stopping is out of the question; and the disunion of a day, at least, is the consequence of one moment's delay or mistake.

Our way lies downward, and the long line of quays is dashed by like lightning. You have just time to mark, well pleased, the early activity of the numerous little steamers plying to and fro between Camden and the city ferries. You cast perchance a rambling glance over those pretty villages, above which the ruddy hue of morning is serenely spreading, and, even as you gaze, behold them melt away in the river's haze.

The Navy-yard, with the huge wooden mansions built to shelter the "Pennsylvania" and a neighbour frigate, glide, as it were, hastily by; and nothing remains to break the monotony of the long level lines skirting the river, and hardly rising above it.

Of this prospect the eye soon becomes weary, and now is the time to look upon your fellow-passengers. You descend from the upper or promenade deck, which, if the morning be chilly, you have most likely held in sole occupation. On the next deck beneath, seated back to back upon long ranges of settees, you behold the female portion of the living freight; for, I take it for granted, this is the first direction of your regards, and a pleasant task it often turns out to be; for, as I have already said, and shall probably yet more strongly confirm hereafter, the average of female beauty in America is high, and but few women are without those always striking points, fine expressive brows and eyes, which, shaded by a tasteful bonnet, and accompanied by a certain coquettish air, leave little wanting to ensure the admiration of the passing stranger.

Having lounged about here for a turn or two, you find yourself reminded of a certain indispensable ceremony by a Stentor-lunged black, who most perseveringly vociferates, "Gentlemen who have not yet *paid*, will please step to the captain's office and settle their *passage*."

At your convenience you obey this gentle hint; securing at the same time a ticket for breakfast, now becoming a very important consideration, assailed by a good natural appetite, sharpened in the shrewd air of a clear, cold morning. At last, ring goes the bell; and the deck, already thinned of the more anxious, or more provident, of the party, becomes, at that magic tinkle, a desert.

On descending the stair, you perceive two long ranges of table thickly bestrewn with dishes containing beefsteak, ham, fish, chicken, game, *omelettes*,—together with hot rolls, cakes, and bread of every other form and denomination, with tea and coffee, borne about as called for; the whole arranged with an attention to neatness and propriety quite surprising when you consider the place, and the difficulties which are inseparable from having to cater and cook for such a multitude.

If you are not of an active habit, or if you object to remain stewing in the cabin for a time waiting on the event, you observe at a glance that, ample as the tables appear, every seat is occupied. Here is no reservation of places — possession is your only admitted right, and, were the President himself too late, he must sit out, or be admitted of the party on courtesy: of this, however, let me add, it never was my chance to perceive any lack. One of the black waiters, recognising you for a frequent passenger, is touched by your appealing glance, motions you to follow him, advancing at the same time a stool with an insinuating air between two goodhumoured-looking men, with "Please, make a little room for this gentleman."

A niche is readily conceded; and, casting an eye right, left, or straightforward, you can hardly fail to find something to your liking. The board is soon clear of the "Rapids," — a large family in most such places; and now you acquire ample space to prove your prowess in.

Having breakfasted, you once more mount the upper deck and breathe the pure air of heaven, unpolluted by that unpleasant gas which escapes from the iron coal burnt in the cabin stoves. Such at least was my constant habit: the natives, I observed, although accustomed to a climate whose vicissitudes are extreme, never appear voluntarily to face the cold, but for the most part, abide below, congregated in concentric circles, of which a red-hot stove, filled with that to me deadly abomination, anthracite coal, forms the centre.

Wrapping well up, I found, even in the severest season, no difficulty in facing the open air, and have more than once paced the upper deck for a passage of three or four hours without having my territory invaded, or at most only for a few minutes by some adventurous spirit, who invariably dived down after a shiver or two.

Here then, between your meals, you may promenade upon a noble deck fifty feet long, smoking your cigar, and eyeing the flitting forest or meadow, amidst dreamy reveries of William Penn's description of the populous tribes of the Delaware, and that first simple treaty which consigned to the unwarlike strangers a country and a home, a treaty which was a deed of disinheritance to the posterity of the donors, and of destruction to their nation, of whom, in their own land, their name has long been the sole memorial left.

In travelling, as I did much and alone, this was always the current set of my day-dreaming. I never could draw on fancy to the exclusion of the Red-man; but, on the contrary, constantly detected myself re-peopling every wood with the wild forms of the aborigines, and in each distant skiff that darted over the broad stream picturing the fragile canoe, and its plumed and painted occupant.

The town of Wilmington, the chief place of the little State of Delaware, shows very attractively from the river, with which it communicates by a navigable creek, and, together with the neighbouring springs of the Brandywine, is in high repute for the beauty of its scenery as well as for its general salubrity.

Arrived at Newcastle, an ancient but not very populous city,—which nevertheless possessed an interest in my eyes, from the circumstance of my having chosen to write about it long before I ever dreamed of seeing it,— you quit the steamer, and, seating yourself in one of the long line of railway cars awaiting you, are whisked over the intervening neck to French-town,— by courtesy so called, since the *town* is yet to be,—a distance of sixteen miles in about fifty minutes; and are there reshipped on the Elk river, down which you rush, at the usual rapid rate, amidst scenery that is really charming.

At the junction of the Susquehannah, the view up the two fine rivers, with the dividing headland, the numerous winding creeks, deep shady coves, and spacious bays, all well wooded and backed by a range of bold mountainous ridges, calls for unqualified admiration, and cannot be too often seen.

The vast bay of the Chesapeake now opens gradually out before you. On the right lie the Gunpowder and other rivers, famous as the favourite feeding-ground of the canvass-back; and here you find amusement in watching the innumerable flocks, or rather clouds, of every denomination of the duck tribe, which, disturbed by the noisy steamer, rise from the water in numbers that hide the sun.

Boats too, of a beautiful model and most *varmint* rig, now begin to thicken on the track, working up, close-hauled, into the eye of the wind, or going, right before it, with the foresail guy'd out on one side and mainsail on the other, showing an uncommon spread of canvass. Here and there, too, the masts of tall ships rise, as more gravely they seek their port, or win their way to the yet distant ocean, performing a voyage before they reach the sea.

North Point is next passed by; and the fate of poor Ross is yet occupying the mind, when the city-crowned hill begins to open on the view, and Baltimore, with all its domes, spires, and columns, stands forth in bold relief against the evening sky.

A bustle soon after commences on deck: the ladies draw closer their hoods and cloaks, and the men move to and fro, warned by the sable Mentor of the place, who paces the decks below and above with a ceaseless cry of "Ladies and gentle-*men* will be pleased to step forward, and point out their bag-*gage*."

A general loading of wheelbarrows is now the order of the hour; most of the waiters exercising the office of porters, and carrying with them their barrows. The landing-place gained, you are hailed by many voices ringing in a rich brogue, "Coach, your honour! Long life to ye! want a carriage?" and eager looks and ready uplifted fingers woo you for an assenting nod. Nowhere on this continent is the presence of Pat so immediately recognizable as in this good catholic city, where the office of Jarvey is nearly a monopoly amongst my poor countrymen, who appear to have left no tittle of their good-humour, eager importunity, and readiness of wit behind them.

Being once known, I felt at all my future landings quite at home here, as these honest fellows were to me particularly attentive. Driving to Barnum's hotel, the stranger may count on a hearty welcome from King David (whom Heaven long preserve!) and from his household much civility; and here, with capital fare, over a fire of wood, — never use anthracite in a close room, — will find, if he has been as observant as he ought, much to amuse and gratify him in a retrospective glance over a journey of some hundred miles, performed with little fatigue or inconvenience, between the chief cities of quaker Pennsylvania and catholic Maryland.

WASHINGTON

On arriving at Baltimore, I found that so woful was the condition of the road between this city and the capital, that, although the distance is but thirty-seven miles, and that there remained full three hours of daylight, still no regular stage would encounter, until morning, the perils of the road.

I thereon made an agreement with two gentlemen, — one of whom was an excellent and learned judge, on some State business; and the other a Philadelphia merchant, escorting his daughter, and a pretty young lady her friend, on a visit of pleasure to Washington, — that we would together engage an extra coach for our party; and, instead of starting at the monstrous hour of five in the morning, set out at half-past eight, when, with the advantage of a light load and good horses, we might reasonably hope to reach our destination before dark.

This was done accordingly: an extra, or exclusive carriage, to hold six inside, was contracted for with the proper authorities, and chartered to Washington city, to start between eight and nine next morning, for the sum of twenty-five dollars, or about six pounds sterling.

With the punctuality for which these people are distinguished throughout the States, our carriage drove up to Barnum's door at a few minutes after eight; and, breakfast being despatched, our party was seated fairly, with all the luggage built up on the permanent platform which graces the rear of these machines, within the time appointed: a very creditable event, when it is considered there were two young ladies of the party.

The air was mild as in May, and there being a goodly promise of sunshine, I resigned my share of the inside to my servant Sam, — the very pink of brown gentlemen in appearance, besides being a pattern of good-breeding; and seeing something unusually knowing in the look of our waggoner, mounted the box by his side, uneasy though it was; for never was anything worse contrived for comfort than the outside of a Yankee stage-coach, — except, perhaps, the inside of an English mail.

Mr. Tolly, whose acquaintance I now made, let me record, was the only driver I ever met in America who took up his leather, and packed his cattle together, with that artist-like air, the perfection of which is only to be seen in England.

The coachmen are not here, as with us, a distinct class, distinguished by peculiar costume, and by characteristics the result of careful education and exclusive habits; but might be taken for porters, drovers, or anything else indeed, — being men who have followed, and are ready again to follow, a dozen other vocations, as circumstances might require: they are nevertheless, generally, good drivers, and, uniformly, sober steady fellows.

Mr. Tolly, however, one might see at a glance — despite the disadvantages of his toggery, plant, and all his other appointments — was born to look over four pair of lively ears; and had Fortune only dropped him in any stable-loft between London and York, there would not have been a cooler hand or a neater whip on the North road.

About a mile from the city we came upon the country turnpike; and of this, as I now viewed it for the first time, any comprehensible description is out of the question, since I am possessed of no means of illustrating its condition to English senses; — a Cumberland fell, ploughed up at the end of a very wet November, would be the Bath road compared with this the only turnpike leading from one of the chief sea-board cities to the capital of the Union.

I looked along the river of mud with despair. Mr. Tolly will pronounce this impracticable after the night's rain, thinks I; but I was mightily mistaken in my man: without pausing to pick or choose, he cheered his leaders, planted his feet firmly, and charged gallantly into it.

The team was a capital one, and stuck to their dirty work like terriers. Some of the holes we scrambled safely by would, I seriously think, have swallowed coach and all up: the wheels were frequently buried up to the centre; and more than once we had three of our cattle down together all of-a-heap, but with whip and voice Mr. Tolly always managed to pick them out and put them on their legs again; indeed, as he said, if he could only see his leaders' heads well up, he felt "pretty certain the coach must come through, slick as soap."

Mr. Tolly and myself very soon grew exceedingly intimate; a false reading of his having at starting inspired him with a high opinion of my judgment, and stirred his blood and mettle, both of which were decidedly game.

Whilst smoking my cigar, and holding on by his side with as unconcerned an air as I could assume, I, in one of our pauses for breath, after a series of unusually heavy lurches, chanced to observe, by way of expressing my admiration, "This is a real *varmint* team you've got hold on, Mr. Tolly."

"How did you find that out, sir?" cries Tolly, biting off about a couple of ounces of 'baccy.

"Why, it's not hard to tell so much, after taking a good look at them, I guess," replied I.

"Well, that's rum any how! but, I guess, you're not far out for once," answers Mr. Tolly, with a knowing grin of satisfaction: "sure enough, they are all from Varmont;[7] and I am Varmont myself as holds 'em. All mountain boys, horses and driver—real Yankee flesh and blood; and they can't better them, I know, neither one nor t'other, this side the Potomac."[8]

I found my *hirgo* was thrown away, but did not attempt an explanation, and became in a little time satisfied that this odd interpretation of my compliment had answered an excellent purpose; for my companion became exceedingly communicative, and most indefatigable in his exertions. More plucky or more judicious coachmanship, or better material under leather, I never came across in all my journeyings. About half way we bade adieu to my Varmont friend, to my great regret.

Wearied with my rough seat, which the companionship of Mr. Tolly had alone rendered endurable so long, I now got inside; the Philadelphia gentleman succeeding to the vacancy on the box.

I did my best to draw my fair companions into a little chat, but found my *vis-à-vis*—the daughter of my successor outside—most impracticable; a monosyllable was the extent of her exertion: whilst her companion, who was a lively, intelligent-looking girl, and very pretty withal, was necessarily chilled by the taciturnity of her senior. I note this as being an unusual case, since, when once properly introduced, the ladies of America are uncommonly frank and chatty, and evince an evident desire to please and be amiable; which is creditable to themselves, and to strangers is both flattering and agreeable.

In the good old judge, whom I had the honour of meeting often after, I found one of the most amusing and intelligent companions a man could desire to rumble over a villanous road with, and for a couple of hours we made time light, when our day's journey had well-nigh terminated in an adventure that might have been attended with ugly consequences.

Although the road for this stage was something less bad, our driver was not a Tolly; in avoiding some Charybdis or other, he let his leaders slip down a bank about eight feet deep, whither, but for the good temper and steady backing of the wheel-horses, we should have followed: as it was, we managed to pick out our cattle, and got off with a couple of broken traces. These being duly cobbled, away we scrambled again, I resuming my seat on the box; the last occupant having become most heartily sick of his elevation.

About the end of nine hours' hard driving, the high dome of the Capitol showed near; and the city toll-gate, situated about a mile from this magnificent building, was opened. The prospect was, notwithstanding, yet sufficiently uncheery; a steep hill lay in front, having a road that looked like a river of black mud meandering about one side of it—the other side was seamed with various tracks made by the vehicles of bold explorers, who, like ourselves, had been doubtful about facing the regular road—the counsel of a well-mounted countryman, who reported that he had just passed the wrecks of two coaches on the turnpike, decided us to eschew it, and boldly try across country.

We all alighted, except the ladies; and acting as pioneers, pushed up the hill, breasting it stoutly. It was very well we took this route; for, having at last safely crowned it, we beheld on our right the two coaches that left Baltimore three hours before us, hopelessly pounded in the highway, regularly swamped within sight of port; for the Capitol was not over three or four hundred yards from them.

The passengers were all out, most of them assisting to unharness and unload, that, by combining both teams, they might extricate their vehicles one at a time.

Here, within the shadow of the Capitol, I was struck with the gloomy and unimproved condition of the surrounding country. Except our caravan, not a living thing moved within sight—all was desert, silent, and solitary as the prairies of Arkansas.

The great avenue once entered upon, the scene changed, and we rattled along briskly over a well Macadamized road. The judge we set down at the top of the Capitolinean hill, where his honourable brothers held their head-quarters; my other companions had rooms secured at Gadsby's, where we next halted; but to my inquiries here, I was answered, "All quite full." They advised me, at the same time, to try *Fuller*, which I thought waggish enough: however, after driving about a mile farther down the avenue, I found at Mr. Fuller's hotel rooms taken for me by a considerate friend, and had to congratulate myself now and henceforward on being the best-lodged errant *homo* in the capital of the United States.

The windows of my sitting-room, I perceived, commanded a view the whole extent of the avenue; but, for the present, I limited my speculation to the dinner that was soon placed before me, and which a fast of eleven hours had rendered a particularly desirable prospect.

FOOTNOTES:

[7] Varmont is a State famous for its wild mountain scenery, and having a breed of horses unequalled for hardihood, fine temper, and bottom: they are found all over the States, and are everywhere in high esteem.

[8] The river Potomac is held to be the dividing line between the northern and southern States.

THEATRE, WASHINGTON

I made my *début* professionally in the capital upon the 12th of February. The theatre here was a most miserable-looking place, the worst I met with in the country, ill-situated and difficult of access; but it was filled nightly by a very delightful audience; and nothing could be more pleasant than to witness the perfect *abandon* with which the gravest of the senate laughed over the diplomacy of the "Irish Ambassador." They found allusions and adopted sayings applicable to a crisis when party feelings were carried to extremity. The elaborate display of eloquence with which Sir Patrick seeks to *bother* the Spanish envoy was quoted as the very model of a speech for a non-committal orator, and recommended for the study of several gentlemen who were considered as aiming at this convenient position, very much to their amusement.

The pieces were ill mounted, and the company unworthy the capital, with the exception of two very pretty and very clever native actresses, Mesdames Willis and Chapman. The latter I had the satisfaction of seeing soon after transferred to New York, in which city she became a monstrous favourite, both in tragedy and comedy: a very great triumph for Mrs. Chapman—for she succeeded Miss F. Kemble in some of her best parts, and an excellent comic actress, a Mrs. Sharpe—acting on the same night Julia in "The Hunchback," and the Queen of Hearts in "High, Low, Jack, and Game," with a cleverness which rarely accompanies such versatility.

I have much pleasure in offering this just tribute to a very amiable person, who has, since my departure from the States, quitted the stage, on which, had she been fortunately situated, she would have had very few superiors.

I wonder there are not many more native actresses, since, I am sure, there is a great deal of latent talent in society here both for opera and the drama: the girls, too, are generally well educated; are pretty, have much expression, a naturally easy carriage, and great imitative powers. The latter talent is singularly common amongst them; and I have met, not one, but many young women, who would imitate the peculiarities of any actress or actor just then before the public with an accuracy and humour quite remarkable.

I acted here seven nights on this occasion, and visited the city again in May, when I passed three or four weeks most agreeably. I had the pleasure, too, during this last visit, of seeing the plans for a theatre worthy the audience, and which, I trust, has by this time been happily erected, as the greatest part of the fund needed was readily subscribed for; and the attempt can hardly fail amongst a people so decidedly theatrical, and who are, besides, really in absolute want of public amusements for the number of stray men turned loose here during the session, many of whom are without other home than the bar-room of an inn, or better means of keeping off *ennui* than gin-sling or the gaming-table.

I shall now throw together in this place the result of my "Impressions" as received during my separate visits.

The scenery in the neighbourhood is naturally as beautiful and varied as woods, rocks, and rivers, in all their most charming features, can combinedly render it. One of the finest of many noble prospects is, in my mind, that from the heights just over George Town. From this point the vast amphitheatre of city, valley, and river may be embraced at a glance, or followed out in detail, as time or inclination prompts.

Following the windings of the majestic Potomac below the bridge, — which, viewed from this elevation, looks like a couple of cables drawn across its channel, — the town of Alexandria is clearly seen: away, on the other side, Fort Washington may be made out; and, opposite to this, the ever-hallowed, Mount Vernon is visible; a glimpse in itself worthy a pilgrimage to every lover of that rare combination — virtue and true patriotism!

Turning from this direction, and setting your face towards the Capitol, you perceive extended in dotted lines, the thinly-furnished streets of the city: viewed from here, the meagre supply of buildings in proportion to its extent is made obvious; each separate house may be traced out; and, in their irregular and detached appearance, all design becomes confounded. It seemed to me as though some frolicsome fairy architect, whilst taking a flight with a sieveful of pretty houses, had suddenly betaken her to riddling them over this attractive site as she circled over the valley in her airy car.

One of my most favourite rides was to a secluded spot in this neighbourhood, of which I shall attempt some description, since I would, in the very fulness of my heart's charity, induce all succeeding wayfarers to visit it.

PIERCE'S GARDEN

At about four miles from the city, a gardener named Pierce has taken up his abode on the summit of a high and on all sides nearly precipitous hill, immediately surrounded by similar elevations, but separated from them by very deep ravines. Through one of these, encompassing two sides of the hill, rushes a clear, active little river, such as a trout-fisher would glory in, only that its banks in this neighbourhood are everywhere sentinelled by trees of willow, dog-wood, laburnum, &c. whose flowery arms entwined within each other shadow the clear water, and protect from the lure of the angler its finny inmates.

Across this ravine lies the ordinary path by which the future stranger, who is an amateur of Nature's painting, will seek to gain one of those fair scenes she has lavished much care upon.

No bridge connects the little domain with the busy world, from sight or sound of which it is isolated as absolutely as was the valley of Rasselas; but, slowly winding down an abrupt, thickly-shaded forest path, you at once break through this "leafy skreen" upon the ford, on the opposite side of which, a little to the right, lies the gate leading into the garden.

Pushing your horse boldly through the stream, — for, though noisy, the bottom has been cleared, and is not usually over knee-deep, — you dismount, and open the only barrier. Right above you stands a rude stone dwelling, stern and square of outline, and in no way suited or in keeping with the graceful trees and shrubs whose rich verdure shadow its rough walls. Towards this you press onward and upward, until the natural platform on which the dwelling is placed be gained; when the view of and from this spot will well reward you for a ride through a secluded forest country, the freshness and wildness of which have already pleased you, especially if you are, as I happily was on most of my visits here, accompanied by companions at once fair and intelligent.

Upon this little platform the grass is always of rare verdure for this country. Immediately in front of the dwelling four or five forest trees of the finest kind fling their branches athwart the entrance; and, a few yards removed, around the foot of a venerable elm, is spread a variegated carpet of daisies and other pretty flowers, whose colours the Persian loom might be proud to imitate for a prince's divan.

A few garden-seats are placed here and there for the ease of visitors; and here have I often sat whilst Mr. Pierce was arranging a bouquet, — an art, by the way, and no mean one, in which he excels, — and looking about on the well-sheltered spot, have thought of my poor old friend Michael Kelly's ballad, until I have fancied him "alive again," and breathing over the folds of his ample cravat,

"And I said, if there's peace to be found in this world,
A heart that is humble might look for it here!"

But there is no peace to be found in this world; so, after indulging a few wild fancies, that come quickly in such places, I quitted this, as I have done a hundred other like oases in life's desert, to wander again about the busy world and jostle with the worldly:

"We feel pangs at parting
From many a spot, where yet we may not loiter."

I did not bid adieu to this, however, before its tranquil and peace-giving features were impressed for ever upon my memory.

The wooded and well-rounded hills which encircle the garden, are placed at distances varying from half a mile to half a bow-shot right Sherwood measure: within this range two buildings only are to be seen; one a pretty, classic-looking dwelling, nestled under the brow of the hill to the eastward; the other, sunk low in the extreme western distance, a rude-looking stone-built water-mill, surrounded by all its healthful and picturesque appointments; adding to the rustic beauty of the scene, yet so far removed as in no way to disturb a feeling of absolute seclusion, if such should be the desire of the possessor of this little domain, which a moderate sum of money, laid out with good taste, might render surpassingly beautiful.

I observed that Mr. Pierce kept a few men constantly employed; and as he is a person of evident intelligence, neither unaware of the value of his possession, nor deaf to the admiration of his visitors, I trust it may become worth his while to complete by art what nature has so happily designed.

Flowers were to be procured here at a season very far advanced, and a high price was given for bouquets, the procuring which for ladies on the evening of a ball or party is a common act of gallantry; consequently there is much rivalry amongst the beaux in gleaning the rarest and most beautiful flowers.

This is a graceful and pretty fashion, and one not likely to grow out of use amongst women, which opens a market well worth the florist's notice.

If my voice could reach Mr. Pierce, two things I would seek to press upon his consideration: the first should be never to suffer himself to be persuaded to throw a bridge—above all, a wooden one—across that prettiest of fords; the other, that he would, out of humanity to the cattle, and out of consideration for the necks of his fair visitors, make the drive, so called, leading through the wood into the George-town road, just passable.

Meantime, until this be accomplished, let me caution all future explorers against venturing the approach by that route. The one by the race-course, and across the ford, is as good as need be; somewhat steep, a little difficult here and there, but in no way perilous.

I might have selected spots for detail in this neighbourhood, which in other eyes may have attractions, though different, quite as powerful; but this, somehow or other, won strangely upon my fancy, and grew to be my favourite resort when pursuing my accustomed rides. I paid to it many visits alone, and in company it became associated with some of the pleasantest hours I passed here; and thus comes it that the reader is afforded such an opportunity as a meagre sketch can give, of becoming acquainted with this secluded spot, once perhaps the summer bower of some native princely Sagamore, and now the location of Mr. Pierce, gardener and seedsman!

THE GARDEN, POETICAL
AND POLITICAL

I one day had the honour of accompanying a lady on a drive to make some calls in the environs, and a most agreeable drive it was. One of our visits turned out to me quite an adventure; and procured me the acquaintance of a character rarely encountered in these rule-of-three days, wherein humanity is clipped and trained upon the principles of old Dutch gardening,—no exuberances permitted, but all offshoots duly trimmed to the conventional cut, until individuality is destroyed, and one half of the world, like Pope's parterre, is made to reflect, as nearly as possible, the other.

We drove for some distance through an ill-tended but naturally pretty domain, alighting unnoticed at a house having an air of antiquity quite refreshing; three sides of the building were encompassed by a broad raised stoop, covered with a wide-spread veranda, whilst the walls were thickly coated with ivy, like the tower of an English village church.

We mounted the stoop, which commanded a vast extent of valley bounded by distant hills, only needing water to make a perfect prospect. A few moments after we had rested here, the mistress of the place made her approach, hoe in hand, for she had been tending her flowers in person. Such a dear old shepherdess of a woman I have not seen for many a day, with all the poetry and enthusiasm of nineteen, and a pastoral, simple, unworldlike air, worthy the golden age of the flower-wreathed sheep-crook.

She had an anecdote connected with every flower-bed;—her story of the ivy, so abundant, quite pleased me, as being interesting in itself, and made doubly so by her *naïve* mode of telling it.

It appeared that the plants were originally cultivated by Mr. Roscoe, on his place near Liverpool; that the shoots were gathered by the hands of that amiable and illustrious man, and sent, in fulfilment of a promise made, to Mr. Jefferson, for the adornment of Monticello.

The bearer of the plants, on arriving at Washington, could find no immediate means of forwarding them safely into Virginia; so placed them in the keeping of their present enthusiastic possessor, beneath whose careful tending,—for the trust has not been reclaimed,—the gift of friendship has flourished and increased, and will, I hope, remain fresh as her own spirit, and fadeless as is the fame of the first donor!

Her parterre afforded quite a summary of the history and habits of the departed great: here were stocks that had been cultivated by the hands of George Washington, and lilies growing from bulbs dug up by those of Thomas Jefferson, after each had cast aside the ungrateful cares of government and resumed those simpler and happier pursuits in which both delighted; and these flowers of theirs flourish yet in peace and beauty, side by side, and, fragile as they look, are perhaps more durably linked than the mighty Union over which these illustrious florists presided with views so widely different.

The fruit-trees were thick with blossoms, and the air was absolutely perfumed. I felt exceedingly loath to obey the summons of my fair guide when informed that the time of departure was arrived, and have seldom found a visit to appear so very short. The carriage being laden with the sweet-scented spoils, — or, rather let me say, gifts of our kind hostess, for nothing could exceed the free hand with which every shrub was rifled for us, — we made our adieus, and set forth to return to the city by a different road, paying a call at another cottage residence by the way.

Of these unpretending, but attractive-looking places, there are numbers in this neighbourhood; and if ever Washington rises to the importance fondly anticipated by its founders, no city ought to boast more charming environs.

Here is no end of sites for country dwellings, — valley and hill, river and rivulet, towering rocks and dark ravines abound in as wild a variety as heart could wish; with land and living both exceedingly cheap.

I saw one of the prettiest houses possible, with nearly a hundred acres of land, that had been purchased, a few months before, for five thousand dollars; and, during my stay here, a first-rate house, with stabling, &c. complete, as well situated as any in Washington, and as well built, sold for the same sum. At present, indeed, I should say land about here is of very little value: though admirably calculated for the residence of an independent class of gentry, here is no temptation for the planter or merchant; and but few in this country seek to live a life of leisure or retirement.

THE FALLS OF THE POTOMAC

On St. George's day, in company with Captain T— —ll, an engineer officer of high standing, and Mr. K— —r, I set out on horseback, at an early hour, to view the much talked of, but too rarely visited, Falls of the Potomac.

Our way lay along the tow-path of the Chesapeake and Ohio canal, planned to unite the Potomac river with the Ohio below Pittsburg,—one of the greatest works yet contemplated. Its length will be three hundred and forty miles: the locks are of stone, one hundred feet by fifteen; and the amount of lockage designed for the whole line is three thousand two hundred and fifteen feet. Piercing the Alleghany mountains, where the canal attains its highest level, a tunnel is planned, four miles and some yards in length.

For upwards of a hundred miles the line is already available; and in this distance are reckoned forty-four locks, and several noble aqueducts, in an ascent of a quarter of a mile.

For sixteen miles we followed this magnificent work, which as far as one of the uninitiated may judge, presents a promise of endurance worthy the best days of Rome: the width of the canal here varied, as my companion informed me, from eighty to seventy feet, and the depth from six to seven feet.

Independent of this work, in itself so interesting, the scenery is varied and striking. Upon our right lay the canal, to whose course all nature had been subdued,—the forest rooted up, the Potomac bestridden by an aqueduct eighteen hundred feet in length, beds of solid gneiss hewn out fathoms deep, valleys filled up and ramparted with granite against the assaults of the near river; everything on this hand was trimmed and levelled in a workmanlike manner: the labour of man was evident throughout, and the well-trained water stood still, or moved onward or backward, as directed by its master.

Close upon our left ran the Potomac, but so changed in character, that the stranger, who from the Capitol had traced the mazy windings of this mighty stream, whose deep indents and sluggish current show like a series of lakes stretching away till lost in distance, suddenly removed to this point, short of two miles, would hardly credit that the narrow, noisy mountain stream beside him was the same, the very fountain and feeder of the inland sea spreading below.

It was now dry, fine weather; no rain had fallen for some time; and the stream, pent within narrow limits, cowered beneath the wooded heights of the Virginia shore: but the condition of every unprotected level on our side spoke awfully of its force, when, backed by supplies from the mountains, it extends itself abroad, overthrowing trees and banks, and leaving their huge ruins to mark in undoubted characters the true limit of its sovereignty.

At this time it was in its most peaceful mood, and went on, now expanding placidly over an even bed, and now divided before some stubborn rock-founded islet, chafing as it were at being compelled to yield to an obstruction it had as yet failed to overcome.

Viewed at all points, the stream conducted by Nature outfaced, in my eyes, the neighbour work of her children; coursing onward, as it went, defying the hand of man, and rejoicing in its rude freedom.

About the most savage part of our ride, where the path was a wide rampart of stone without any parapet, bounded on one hand by the canal and the overhanging rocks through which it was cut, and on the other, at a precipitous depth of eighty feet, by the rocky bed of the river, we were threatened with a hurricane, or other outbreak of the elements, of the wildest kind.

It had become on a sudden unnaturally sultry: before us a cloud fell like a huge black curtain, until resting upon the lofty bluffs between which the river now ran, it was draped in folds down to the water; over this curtain broke a lurid silvery sort of light, making all things hideous; a heavy moaning sound as of wind was heard throughout the forest; the leaves shook rattling upon the surrounding shrubs, yet no air was perceptible even whilst going at a gallop. For a moment this strange sound would cease wholly, and then roar forth again, as though the pent tempest was striving close at hand for space and freedom of action.

Occasionally a vivid flash of lightning would stream from the impending cloud downward upon the river; and, in momentary expectation of a regular tornado, on we spurred to reach some shelter.

But after all, our fears were fruitless, or let me rather say our hopes, since we agreed that a hurricane chancing here would be a consummation singularly happy. It is certain no fitter scene could well have been selected for such an event, and indeed this was all that was needed to make the savage grandeur of the picture perfect.

Expectation had attained its height, when, after a few big splashes of rain, the sombre curtain drew gradually up, the sun looked forth once more, shining vividly, and the so lately gloomy waters below, again laughed and sparkled as they went bounding, gladly, over their rugged bed.

About midday we arrived at a house occupied by a person who attends one of the many locks on the canal; and by the ready aid of this worthy and his-pretty young helpmate, our horses and ourselves were well supplied with *vivres*, and otherwise cared for.

After we had discussed sundry rashers of ham, broiled chicken, and new-laid eggs, we were informed by our friend the lock-keeper, who had been examining the ford, that the frail bridge which had recently served to cross a branch of the stream to an island from whose southern side alone the Falls might be surveyed, was no longer in being.

What was to be done? was the whole purpose of our hard ride to be defeated by the dislocation of a few loose planks? Our cool pioneer even admitted that it seemed "mighty hard," and called his spouse to council; but from her we received small hope, as she at once decided that to cross so as to get anywhere within sight of the Falls was impossible.

We as stoutly declared our resolution to attempt fording the dividing current, and requested our host to point out the best probable place for this purpose.

This he at last agreed to do; adding that "he guessed, with more or less of a ducking, we might gratify our curiosity, though he could not help thinking it was mighty foolish."

The lady of the lock, more timid, or, as it turned out, more sage, remonstrated in vain. In the teeth of her advice and predictions, sufficiently alarming, we mounted our nags, and, under the good man's guidance, descended to the ford, by a very rough path; the din of the unseen torrent sounding in our ears.

On reaching the stream in question, we found it not over twenty yards across, with an apparently tolerable landing on the opposite side; so that, albeit it had a threatening sort of look, and bullied and blustered somewhat loudly, myself and Mr. K— —r decided *instanter* upon crossing. Our companion, a very tall and heavy man, mounted on a little thorough-bred steed none the stronger for the severe bucketting it had already gone through, we very wisely prevailed upon to await our return, and serve as our guide to the right landing when we should have to re-cross.

With all that eagerness with which men rush on novelty, especially when any obstacle is thrown in the way, we pushed forward, listening impatiently to the distant thunder of the Falls. Like all obstacles, we found these before us less in reality than in report, our chief difficulty lying in the strength of the current, flowing over an unequal bottom; but in no part was the water up to the horses' shoulders. We kept their noses well up stream, and, after a little floundering about, reached and mounted the sandy bank in no time, whence a short rough ride over the thickly-wooded islet, gave the wished-for sight to our eyes in all its gloomy grandeur; and never before do I remember having looked upon so wildly sublime a scene.

We dismounted; and, tying our horses to a tree, descended into the vast basin within whose rugged depths the river finds at all seasons ample space for its fury. Opposite to our stand the face of the black rock rose perpendicular for a hundred and fifty feet; and over its brow waved a grove of lofty trees and graceful flowering shrubs, forming together a plume befitting such a crest, and worthy to float above such a *mêlée*.

Along in front of our position, and only a few yards off, the river was precipitated from a ledge of rock, three huge masses of which towered high over it, lying athwart the line of the torrent at apparently equal distances, as though Nature had designed to bridge this fearful caldron, but, having raised these piers had rested, content with this evidence of her power, and so left the work unfinished.

Through the intervals of these piers then, if they may be so denominated, the water was impelled in three distinct columns of foam with inconceivable impetuosity; then, after forming many vortices, frightful to contemplate steadily, whirled boiling away beneath the boldly jutting table-rock, which afforded us sound footing amidst a din that of necessity made admiration dumb, since to hear your own voice or any other person's was quite out of the question.

Oh what a pit of Acheron was here! I would have given a million a-year to have had Martin with me, pencil in hand, looking upwards upon the centre one of those three terrible piers. What a throne would it have made in his hands for the arch enemy of man! How his fancy would have imaged the lost angel forth, standing there in his might armed for hopeless combat, shadowed grandly out amidst the silvery vapours curling round him, whilst up through the raging whirlpools drove the countless columns of hell in battle array; what tossing of co-mingled plumes and waves above the thick squadrons of horse, who, with flowing manes and fiery nostrils, would be seen breaking through and riding over the foaming torrent, all shadowed forth in a dim reality he knows so well to deal with, and which, in his creations, leaves the fancy, already startled by that it can define, afraid to guess at all which yet remains only half told!

We wandered here, from point to point, unable to express our bewilderment and delight otherwise than by pantomimic gestures more amusing than intelligible; and then, in consideration of the lone condition of our excellent comrade, began to crawl and climb our way back to the shade where we had left the horses.

The table-rocks were everywhere worn into circular basins of greater or less dimensions; when the floods of spring and autumn subside, these pools are left well stocked with pike, trout, and other sorts of fish; the water was at this time exceedingly low, and a long continuance of premature heat had shortened the allowance of the denizens of these pools; our near neighbourhood, therefore, deprived as they were of the means of retreat or concealment, caused a great sensation amongst them, and much rushing, and floundering, and darting to and fro.

We joined cordially in commiserating the fate of these unlucky *détenus*, who, as the summer advances, must, to say the least of it, become most uncomfortably warm about the middle of the day. K— —r wasted, as I considered, much time in sentimentalizing over their probable fate, for I found that he loitered behind by every basin which contained a larger specimen than usual.

After a rather prolonged halt, I was preparing to *row* my friend for his vexatious display of philanthropy, when he came to me with his right arm soaked up to the shoulder, grievously lamenting his having failed, by an untimous slip, in securing a fellow of at least nine or ten pounds' weight.

"What the devil!" exclaimed I, "is it possible that you contemplated scrambling your way back to give this finny gentleman the freedom of the river?"

"Not at all, my dear fellow," replied my sensitive friend; "I merely contemplated carrying him to Washington, and giving him the freedom of the boiler. The Baron would have rejoiced in him; he was a fish for the Czar himself! Besides, it would have been an act of charity to the poor devil of a fish, the consummation of whose horrid fate is alarmingly nigh, since there is not over six inches of water on the rock, and that already as close as may be upon ninety-four degrees. That one dip has parboiled my right arm; I must plunge it in the first running water to cool it."

I enjoyed a good laugh at K— —'s hot-bath fishing, but did not dream of the thorough cooling in store for my charitable piscator.

On we dashed, full of excitement and high spirits, and hit the stream at a point very little below where we had before landed. Captain T— —ll was still on his post; and with less of precaution than we had used at crossing, in dashed K— —r some yards in advance of me, although I being mounted on a more powerful horse, had before taken the first of the current whilst my friend rode on my quarter, thus mutually sustaining each other.

Whilst I was yet upon the bank, K— —'s nag lost his footing, and turned fairly head over heels in the very middle of the passage, at the shortest possible notice. The first intimation I got of the event was missing my man, and in his stead perceiving four bright shoes glancing in the sun above the broken water. In a moment, however, he emerged to day once more; and after a second dive or so, gained good bottom, losing only a few ounces of blood from a broken nose. I led his horse safely ashore; and the brute, though the least hurt, was by far the most frightened, for he shook like a negro in an ague fit.

As for K— —r, he bore his mishap with a *sangfroid* and good-humour that were admirable: the only regret I heard from him was, that Sir Charles Vaughan's ball should come off on this night, since his appearance was marred past present help; and indeed, notwithstanding applications of whisky, cold water, vinegar, &c. which our friends of the lock supplied, the nose was growing of a most unseemly size.

The lock-man expressed much regret; whilst his good lady, I fancied, was not very sorry to have her predictions fulfilled at so cheap a rate. I ventured to hint to my friend something about retributive justice, alluding to his fishy longings amongst the pools; but he rejected the application with indignation, insisting upon it that his desire to secure that fine fish was founded in the purest charity.

We lost no time in setting out for home by a shorter route; and after a hard, hot ride, got back to the city in good time to dress for dinner, at which I was sorry to find my philanthropic fisherman did not make his appearance. This was the only drawback upon the pleasure with which I contemplated our day's work; indeed I had special cause to regret the mishap, since it was for my gratification alone K— —r was led to push over this unlucky stream, he having before visited the Falls. However, I do not forget his amiability upon this and many other similar occasions, and hereby pledge myself to swim across a broader current, either with him, or for him, on any day between this and the year of our Lord 1850.

Early hours being the mode here, about nine o'clock drove to Sir Charles Vaughan's, who, in honour of St. George's-day, gave a ball, to which all the beauties in the capital were bidden. I found the guests on this occasion less numerous than at one I had attended early in the season, during my first visit here. The scene was already brilliant as light, and life, and youth could make it; the music, consisting of a harp and four other instruments, was exceedingly good; the women were well-dressed and pretty, and danced with infinite grace and spirit.

The *tournure* of an American girl is generally very good; she excels in the dance, and one sees that she enjoys it with all her heart. In England I have rarely felt moved to dance; on the other hand, in France and America, so electric is evident unrestrained enjoyment, I have found it sometimes difficult to repress the inclination within becoming bounds.

About midnight supper was announced; and let it not be forgotten, since it was of an order worthy the country represented, and our excellent minister's character for hospitality. After this the party thinned rapidly, and by half-past one o'clock the ball-room was silent. I lighted my cigar, and took my accustomed walk up the great avenue to the Capitol hill, thence surveyed for a moment the silent city, and back to my quarters at Fuller's, making a distance of full three miles; and so concluded a busy and right pleasant four-and-twenty hours.

IMPRESSIONS OF WASHINGTON SOCIETY, PUBLIC AND PRIVATE

I attended several large assemblies at Washington, and must here, after a second visit, and so much experience as my opportunities afforded, enter my protest against the sweeping ridicule it has pleased some writers to cast upon these doings here; since I saw none of those outrageously unpresentable women, or coarsely habited and ungainly men, so amusingly arrayed by some of my more observant predecessors. I can only account for it by referring to the rapid changes ever taking place here, and to which I have alluded in my introduction to these "Impressions."

The ordinary observances of good society are, I should say, fully understood and fully practised at these public gatherings, and not more of the ridiculous presented than might be observed at any similar assemblage in England, if half so much; since here I have commonly found that persons who have no other claims to advance save money or a seat in the legislature, very wisely avoid *reunions*, where they could neither look to receive nor bestow pleasure.

It is quite true that many of these members, all of whom are by rank eligible to society, may be met with, who are more rusty of bearing than most of those within St. Stephen's; but I will answer for this latter assembly outfacing them in samples of rudeness, ill-breeding, and true vulgarity: for it is a striking characteristic of the American, that, if not conventionally polished perhaps, you will rarely find him either rude or discourteous; whilst amongst those who, in the nature of the government, are elevated from a comparatively obscure condition to place and power, although refinement cannot be inserted as an addendum to the official diploma, the aspirant usually adopts with his appointment a quiet formal strain of ceremony, which protects himself, and can never give offence to any.

In the absence of that ease and self-possession which can only be acquired by long habitual intercourse with well-bred persons, this surely is the wisest course that could be adopted, and a hundred degrees above that fidgety, jackdaw-like assumption of *nonchalance* with which the ill-bred amongst ourselves seek to cover their innate vulgarity.

At all these assemblies, as elsewhere, great real attention is paid to women; and I vow I have, in this respect, seen more ill-breeding, and selfish rudeness, at a fashionable rout in England, than could be met with, at any decent crush, from Natchetoches to Marble-head. Beyond these points within the States I speak not, since without them the land is strange to me.

No levee of the President's has occurred during my sojourn here; but I learn that in the true spirit of democracy, the doors on these occasions are open to every citizen without distinction of rank or costume; consequently the assemblage at such times may be oddly compounded enough.

As for private society in Washington, although limited, it can in no place be conducted in a manner more agreeable, or extended to the stranger with more unostentatious freedom. Once presented to a family, and the house is thenceforward open to you. From twelve o'clock until two, the inmates either visit or receive visitors: between these hours, the question, "Are the ladies at home?" being answered in the affirmative, you walk into the drawing-room without farther form; and, joining the circle, or enjoying a *tête-à-tête*, as it may happen, remain just so long as you receive or can impart amusement.

Again, after six, if you are so disposed, you sally forth to visit. If the family you seek be at home, you find its members forming a little group or groups, according to the number present, each after their age and inclination; and politics, dress, or scandal are discussed: or, if the night be serene, — and what lovely nights have I witnessed here, even at this early season! (May) — you make a little party to the covered stoup, or balcony, extended along the back-front of most houses; and here a song, a romp, a waltz, or a quiet still talk, while away hours of life, unheeded until passed, but never to be recalled without pleasure. About eleven the guests generally depart, and by midnight the great avenue of this city is hardly disturbed by a foot-fall; not a sound comes on the ear except the short, fierce wrangle of packs of vagrant curs crossing each other's hunting-ground, which they are as tenacious of as the Indians are of their prairies.

At this hour I used often, after returning from a party, such as is described above, to put on my morning-gown and slippers, and light my pipe, then sallying forth, have strolled from Fuller's to the Capitol; and climbing its bold hill, have looked down along the sleeping city, speculating upon its possible destinies until my fancies waxed threadbare, and then quietly returned, making a distance of nearly three miles, without encountering an individual or hearing the sound of a human voice.

At set balls even, the first hour of morning generally sees ample space on the, till then, crowded floor; and the most ardent pleasure-lovers rarely overleap the second by many minutes.

The consequence of this excellent plan is, that, although the ladies are weak in numbers, they are always, to use an expressive sporting phrase, ready to come again; rising, the morning after a dance, unwearied and elastic in mind and body. I hope, for the sake of my American friends, it will be very long before these healthful hours are changed to those which custom has made fashionable in England; hours that soon fade the roses even on their most genial soil, the cheeks of the fair girls of Britain, blighting the healthful and the young, and withering the aged and the weak.

Much of the population of Washington is migratory; and, during a long session, samples may be found here of all classes, from every part of the Union, whether represented or not. There are, however, generally resident a few old Southern families, who, together with the foreign ministers and their suites, form the nucleus of a permanent society, where the polish of Europe is grafted upon the simple and frank courtesy of the best of America. Were it not in violation of a rule I have imposed upon myself as imperative, I could name families here whose simple yet refined manners would do honour to any community, and from an intercourse with whom the most fastidious conventionalist would return satisfied.

IMPRESSIONS OF ALEXANDRIA

A BLANK DAY

My worthy manager had often pressed me to accompany him on one of our off-nights to Alexandria, which he assured me boasted a very pretty theatre, and a population, if not generally theatrical, still capable of filling the house for two or three nights upon an extraordinary occasion. Such he was pleased to consider the present; and although I suggested the probability that most of the play-loving Alexandrians had most likely, during the late very lovely nights, visited the Washington theatre, Mr. Jefferson argued, there yet existed a sufficient body, of the unsatisfied curious, to repay us for our short trip. A steam-boat, he said, would take down him and his troop, bag and baggage, in a couple of hours; and, as I was fond of riding, it was for me but a pleasant canter.

As it was my intention to pass a few hours at this city, whose spires might be seen any fine day from George-town heights, and close to which lived a gentleman whom I had promised to visit, I decided with the manager upon making trial of our popularity by convening on a certain evening a public meeting of its inhabitants; our object being similar to that of most conveners of public meetings, viz. to amuse the lieges and benefit ourselves.

The town was advertised of our intended purpose, the night appointed, and all the usual blowing of trumpets duly done, when on the forenoon of a lovely day, accompanied by Captain R— —y of the navy, I traversed the interminable-looking bridge uniting the district of Columbia with Virginia, and entered the *Old Dominion*, as the natives love to distinguish their State.

The road was excellent, bordered with turf nearly the whole way, and commanding extensive and varied views of the Potomac, together with George-town and the Capitol. I often halted and turned my horse's head to look upon this picture, for such it truly was. Nothing, in fact, can be more panoramic than the aspect of these cities, lying in one of the best-defined and most beautiful of natural amphitheatres, and flanked by the grandest of rivers. At the distance of five or six miles all the meannesses of the city are lost sight of, and the extreme ends, so widely apart, and so worthily bounded, by the Capitol on the north and the President's mansion, with the surrounding offices belonging to the state department, on the south, combined with the dock-yard and a few other large public buildings in the middle distance, give to the metropolis of America an aspect no way unworthy of its high destiny.

Arrived at Shooter's Hill, the seat of Mr. D— —y, we were encountered with a welcome characteristic of a Virginian gentleman on his own soil, and worthy the descendant of an Irishman.

Here then we dined, took our *tisan de champagne glacée* upon the well-shaded gallery fronting the river, and in due time I mounted, and rode down to the city, to make my toilet and receive the Alexandrians. The first I soon effected, and the last I should have rejoiced to have also done; but they would not be received—"the more we waited, the more they would not come."

I took possession of the stage, the only portion of the house occupied, where, eyed by half a dozen curious negroes, who were evidently amateurs, and by their good-humoured air ready to become admirers, I awaited the appearance of the audience. In lieu of these, some half-hour after the time of beginning, Mr. Jefferson made his appearance *solus*, with an expression half comic, half vexed.

"It's no go, my good friend," said I.

"They're not come *yet*" said Mr. J.

"Nor are they on the road, Mr. Jefferson."

"They're a long way off, I guess, if they are," said he.

"And won't arrive in time, that's clear. Hadn't you better postpone the business *sine die*?"

"We've nothing else left for it, I fear," said Mr. J., taking a last careful survey of the well-lighted solitary *salle*: adding, "We must dismiss."

"That ceremony will be quite superfluous," observed I, "unless as far as we ourselves are concerned, and our sable friends here."

I had observed that the two or three little knots occupying the intervals of the side-scenes were evidently interested observers of our debate, and grieved and disappointed by the result. I should have liked to have put them all into the front, and then have acted to them, could one have insured their not being intruded on by any stray white-man. As it was, Mr. Jefferson begged me to consider myself at perfect liberty.

"It's provoking too," added my good-humoured manager, who was quite a philosopher in his vocation; "for it's a pretty theatre, isn't it?"

"It is a very pretty theatre," responded I. And so it was, exceedingly so. It had been built when the place flourished, and the community was prosperous and could afford to be merry. Now, trade having decayed, and money ceased to circulate, the blood has also grown stagnant amongst this once gay people: the fire is out and the drama's spirit fled.

Mr. Jefferson, however, had a much more summary mode of accounting for our desolate state; for, on my suggesting that his bills might have been ill distributed or his notice insufficient, — being rather desirous thus to find a loophole for my vanity to creep out of, — he convinced me that all points of 'vantage had been most provokingly well cared for.

"What the plague can be the reason they won't come for *once*, at least, Mr. J.? One would be less surprised at their not answering to a second summons."

Jefferson shook his head, in a fashion that expressed more than even Puff designed Lord Burleigh's shake to convey:[9] adding, by way of commentary,

"The Bank question, sir! all the Bank question!"

I waited for no more, feeling that this was indeed an explanation sufficiently satisfactory; since, for some time, it served to account fully for every possible event, moral and physical, — the depression of the markets, the failure of the fruit-crop, the non-arrival of the packets, the sinking of stock, and the flooding of the Ohio.

Joining my friends at the hotel, — an exceedingly good one, by the way, — we were soon once more in saddle; and, lighted by as beautiful a moon as ever silvered the smooth surface of the Potomac, off I dashed with them, for Washington at a slapping pace, in no way regretting my having visited Alexandria or my premature return, since my day had been most delightfully passed: and my not having a *soirée* of my own, enabled me to assist at one given by a very charming and intelligent person, to which I was bidden, but in consequence of my engagement to Mr. J. had no hopes of attending.

FOOTNOTE:

[9] See "The Critic."

THE FANCY BALL

This species of entertainment, so common in Europe, is in a great measure a novelty in the States; for although in New York and Philadelphia *materiel* may be procured in abundance,—and there is no lack of either wealth or spirit to put it in requisition,—yet the society is too much divided to admit of numbers, and variety, sufficient to relieve the groups from sameness and consequent insipidity. At Washington, I believe, there had never been more than two or three attempts made; when, therefore, Senator W— —e, of Florida, issued cards for a "Fancy Ball," with little more than a week's notice, the whole of the visiting community was thrown into confusion, and, indeed, despair. A rush was at once made upon the *materiel*; the candidates were many, the supplies few; and all were eager to monopolise as far as was possible.

In twenty-four hours after the summons had gone forth, not a plume of feathers, a wreath of flowers, or a scarf or ribbon *couleur de rose* or *flamme d'enfer*, could have been purchased in the city of Washington.

It was most amusing to assist at the consultations of the ladies: not a portfolio but what was rummaged, not a pencil but what was in requisition copying or inventing authorities for all sorts of real and imaginary costume.

Every man who either possessed, or was supposed possessed of, an iota of taste, suddenly found himself greatly increased in importance. The position of these virtuosi became enviable in the extreme: they ran or walked about the streets with an air of well-pleased mystery, their hands filled with delicate-looking triangular billets; they entered the residences of the most admired belles without knocking; they were consulted, caressed, listened to anxiously, smiled upon gratefully: in short, for three or four days, their influence seemed only limited by their discretion; they moved "air-borne, exalted above vulgar men."

But all human happiness is transient at best, and even the sovereignty of taste could not endure for ever. As the costume became settled, the fair clients fell off; the portfolios were returned with "thanks;" the drawings, so lately pronounced "perfect loves," and gazed upon as though worthy the creation of a Rubens, were now to be found doubled up in the card-rack, or transfixed by two or three pins on the cushion of a work-table; the three-cornered missives circulated in other channels; and the man of Taste found ample leisure once more to speak to a friend in the avenue, or fall quietly into the ranks at a dinner-party.

Nevertheless, up to the last hour, the ladies continued, if words might have been trusted, in absolute despair; and in truth, when one examined into the resources at their command, the case seemed desperate enough. To be sure, Baltimore was near, and was soon under contribution; even Philadelphia and New York were lightly visited, more than one belle having sent thus far for a dress. Some of these, by the way, were, like the Chevalier de Grammont's, swamped on the road, to the mortification of the fair expectants.

Three or four gentlemen joined company in getting up a diplomatic group, which my friend Kenny's little comedy of "The Irish Ambassador" had here made very popular. Of this group I formed a part; and being honoured by the company of an embassy from a new quarter, in the portly person of "His Excellency minister extraordinary, and Plenipotentiary, from the Dry Tortugas," together with his Secretary of legation and suite, our equipages, as we left Fuller's, made rather a formidable show.

Many other well-dressed groups of men were known to us as being prepared, and it was for the ladies only I felt any fear of a lame conclusion. But what will not the ingenuity of woman effect when inclination prompts and pleasure leads the way!

I entered the reception-room, quite sorrowing for one or two of my personal friends, whose regret at being so miserably unprovided up to the last hour had met sympathy from my credulous simplicity, when, lo! here I found these fair sly things set forth in character, all plumed "like estridges."

We made our bows to the lady patroness, a very charming person, habited as Isabel de Croye, and attended by a suite of well-chosen characters, very tastefully gotten up. Here were girls so unquestionably Greek, that any good Christian would willingly have ransomed them without suspicion of their country or quality; together with Turkish maidens, whose appearance would have dazzled and deceived even the argus-eyed guardians of the Imperial serai.

I was struck with the great variety of Asiatic costume present, of the richest and most perfect kind, both male and female: a couple of women, with fine black eyes and features of remarkable classic beauty, wore the costume of Tripolitan ladies of the highest rank, and it would be difficult to conceive anything richer or more strikingly picturesque. The Mediterranean is the favourite cruising ground of the American navy; and from this abundant wardrobe, of the most becoming costumes, every ship imports specimens for their friends at home. On this occasion these had been laid under requisition to excellent purpose.

There were two attempts only, as far as I remember, to embody character, as is more usual in masquerade; but these were both remarkable for their excellence. The most striking in appearance was a young officer of the United States' army, habited as an Osage warrior, painted and plumed with startling truth. Surrounded by all that was presumed to be strange and bewildering, never for a moment did the well-trained young warrior forget what was due to himself or his tribe: he looked on with the most imperturbable *sangfroid*, moved about with the ease and self-possession of one to whom all he mingled with had been a matter of common usage; heard jests, questions, or friendly explanations with the most unmoved gravity, replying by an occasional "Ou, ou!" or a slow bend of his head: his patience was indeed worthy the most tried of the race he represented, for never did he lose it or forget himself for a moment. He was a very fine young man, and the features of his face appeared to have been moulded to his present purpose.

The other was a Yankee young man, as he described himself, "jist come away south, to see about;" and who, "noticin' that all kinds o' queer men was comin' in here without payin' nothin', thought he'd best jist step in tu, and make one among the lot."

And of a certainty he did make the queerest specimen I ever met in this or any other lot. The supporter of this character was young Mr. W— —r. The total change in his appearance was effected by a certain set of the hat and a mode of placing it on the head quite characteristic, together with an odd hanging on of the coat and vest, which gave them the look of having belonged to some one else, and as likely to fit any one as the present wearer.

I had seen the original of this picture in the north, I had also witnessed it admirably represented by Messrs. Hill and Hacket, the rival Yankees of the American stage; but neither of them, I think, were so minutely perfect or so whimsical as this new actor. The abstraction was complete; and the odd questions, guesses, complicated relations, full of drollery and wholly applicable to the present scene and the actors engaged in it, were replete with humour, exhibiting a compound of vulgar assurance, simplicity, and native shrewdness, not surpassed by any assumption I have ever witnessed.

Although quite intimate with this gentleman, I stood for a while listening to him where he stood grinning amidst a group who were quizzing and questioning him, and for a short time imagined it was some veritable rustic they held immeshed. It was not until after I had learned who it was, that I succeeded in recognising a person who had been sitting with me that very morning.

A few of the gravest of the senators alone had been privileged by the host to appear *en habit de ville*, and these paid for their privilege before they got clear off. Their potent seignorships, in truth, soon found themselves exceedingly ill at ease here: jostled by lawless pirates, lassoed by wild Guachos, and plundered of their loose cash by irresistible broom and orange girls, they were fain to make an early retreat, with as good a grace as might be assumed, under circumstances so subversive of all due gravity.

If enjoyment be the object of such meetings, nothing could be more absolutely attained than it was at this little fancy ball; for a scene of higher festivity and good-humour no man could desire to assist at. It had, however, the sin to account for of keeping its fair patronesses together some two hours later than any other *fête* I witnessed in this most wisely merry capital.

On reaching Fuller's, accompanied by a joyous knot of diplomatists, it was discovered to be over three hours past midnight; a novelty in etiquette which it was decided *nem. con.* would have "plenty of precedents *after*."

LIONS OF WASHINGTON

THE INDIAN CABINET.—HOUSE OF LEGISLATURE.—SENATE.— LADIES.—SENATORS.—PRESIDENT

The principal lions of Washington, after the legislative chambers, are the Navy-yard, the President's mansion, the National Exhibition, connected with the patent-office, containing specimens of mechanical inventions either original or considered such by their industrious projectors, and lastly the offices for the department of State.

In the latter was a chamber which to me offered more attractions than all the other objects put together: it contained a collection of original portraits of the most distinguished amongst the aborigines, allied with or opposed to the States.

This is an object well worthy the care of government, and, it is to be hoped, one that will be persevered in, for yet but a few years, and here will be the only memento left of the Red-man within the land. Something is due to the memory of these savage warriors and legislators; this tribute serves to render them a sort of poetical justice, and wins a sympathy for their fate, through their portraits, which might have been withheld from themselves, — at least, judging of those I have seen, drunken, dirty, and debased.

Here, indeed, they show gallantly out, the untameable children of the forest, the lords of the lake and of the river, some of them absolutely handsome, their costume being in the highest degree chivalric; many, unluckily, are clad in a mixed fashion, half Indian, half American, — grotesque, but unbecoming when compared with the gaudily turbaned and kilted Creek, or the plumed and painted Winnebago, who, leaning on his rifle beneath a forest tree, and listening with a keen, unwearying aspect for the coming tread of his foe or his prey, looks like a being never born to wear harness or own a master.

A few of the chiefs are painted in the full-dress uniform of the American army, but are not for an instant to be mistaken; although Red Jacket, the great orator and warrior, and one or two others have features exceedingly resembling some of the Provençal *noblesse* of France: the common expression is, however, almost uniformly characteristic of their nature, cold, crafty, and cruel; I hardly found one face in which I could have looked for either mercy or compunction—always excepting the women, of whom here are a few specimens. It would be but gallant to add to the number, if there are many such amongst the tribes; for the features of these are pretty, their expression truly feminine and gentle, with the most dove-like, loveable eyes in nature.

I, some time after this, found a very fine work in course of publication at Philadelphia, containing coloured prints, large folio size, made from these and other original sources; with accurate biographical notices of the most important amongst the chiefs, and a detailed account of their history and habits. The author is Colonel M'Kenny, for many years resident Indian agent, living amongst and with the people he describes; and combining with these opportunities education, intelligence, and much enthusiasm on the subject. In this work will be given correct translations of their highly expressive but unpronounceable appellations; and as much justice done to their characters, as, I can answer for it, has been already rendered to their outward form and features.

The courtesy which distinguishes officials of every rank in this country makes a visit to this, or any public place, not only a matter of pleasure but of profit to the stranger; since one rarely returns without some anecdote or information connected with the object visited, given in an off-hand agreeable manner, which is in itself a gratification. I have never been a sight-hunter in Europe, and this not from indolence or lack of laudable curiosity, I believe; but simply through considering the forms and difficulties that hedge in most places and persons worthy observance, more than equivalent to the gratification to be won from a sight of them. The case is different here: there is no unnecessary fuss or form; the highest public servants are left to protect themselves from impertinent intrusion; and to the stranger, all places that may be considered public property are perfectly accessible, without any tax being levied on his pride, his patience, or his purse,—matters which might be amended in England, greatly to the advancement of our national character, and in these reforming days not unworthy consideration.

I was a good deal amused looking over the various costly gifts which have been, from time to time, presented by foreign potentates to the distinguished public servants of America, all of which are here collected; the law not permitting those on whom they were bestowed to retain them, although yielding to the custom which has rendered such marks of courtly approbation customary amongst the great ones of Europe.

I could not help smiling as I fancied the disgorgement of all the *cadeaux* exchanged between ministers and generals, and treaty-makers and breakers, since 1812, an epoch fruitful of such courtesies. Why, it would pay off the national debt of the general government of this country, and leave a surplus for watering the streets of the capital, if the legislature did not find fault with the appropriation, and continue to prefer being blinded, as they are at present, rather than purchase a few water-carts for the corporation, which it seems is too impoverished to afford any outlay on its own account.

There was nothing that puzzled me more, on a first view of the matter, than the utter indifference with which the Americans look upon the exceedingly unworthy condition of their capital, when considered in relation with the magnitude, the greatness, and prosperous condition of their common country. During months of every session, the roads leading through the district of Columbia are all but impassable: independent of the discomfort and delay consequent upon their condition, hardly a season passes without some member or other being injured more or less by overturns, which are things of common occurrence; yet, only let government insert one extra item in the budget to be applied to the service of this their common property, and all parties from all quarters of the Union unite to reject the supply.

I heard of a curious instance of this jealousy of poor Columbia whilst on my last visit here. The great avenue, or principal street, leading from the President's house to the Capitol, had recently been redeemed from mud according to the plans of M'Adam; but the exposure of the situation, and the nature of the material employed, rendered the improvement rather questionable: every breeze that now blew filled the atmosphere with thick clouds of dust charged with particles of mica, which really made it a hazardous matter to venture forth on a gusty day, unless in a closed carriage, when tired of sitting at home, suffocated with heat, or smothered with dust by the wind, which ought to have borne health and comfort on its wings instead of this eighth plague.

Every one complained, all suffered; members, senators, the President, and the cabinet, all were having dust flung in their eyes, at a period when the commonwealth required that they should all be most especially keen and clearsighted. The Potomac, meantime, swept by them, clear and cool, and the classic Tiber could with difficulty be kept out of their houses. The Romans would have made their Tiber useful on such an occasion, and the ready remedy at length suggested itself to the half-smothered senators. The sum of a few hundred dollars was promptly voted to abate the evil, in conjunction with the Tiber, whose contribution was here on demand. The bill was, however, rejected on its farther course: the dust continued to rise, the people saved their dollars, their representatives continued blind, and the banks of the Tiber remained undrawn on.

If you venture an observation upon this obvious absence of all decent pride in their capital, as being somewhat singular in a people who seem wrapt in their country, and solicitous that it should show worthily in the world's eyes, the case is admitted, and accounted for readily enough, but by no means creditably, in my mind.

The members from Louisiana or Maine will tell you that they cannot satisfactorily account to their constituents for voting sums of money to adorn or render convenient a city these may never see, and for whose very existence they have no care.

The man from the great western valley will shrug up his shoulders at your observation, admit its truth, but add, that the idea of the continuance of Washington, as the metropolis of the Union, and seat of the general government, is a ridicule, since this ought clearly to wait upon the tide of population, and be situated west of the Alleghanies.

Neither of these answers are worthy the country or the American people: the citizen voters of these distant states should be reminded that the district of Columbia is their common property, and Washington the capital of their great Union, representing them in the eyes of strangers, and from whose present condition the least prejudiced European will find it difficult to avoid drawing injurious conclusions.

Without internal resources, and entirely dependent upon the government, it would be worthy their national grandeur to make this district a type of that grandeur; and its city, as far as all public buildings and general conveniences might be concerned, second to none in the world.

Presuming even its occupation to be temporary, and that, at no distant period, it will be deserted, left again to the dominion of nature, to be once more incorporated with the forest,—why, a Russian boyard has raised as fine a city, to lodge his royal mistress in for one night, and set it on fire to light her home on the next after!

Were it of a certainty to be deserted in ten years, I would, were I a representative about to be sent to it, say to my clients: "As for Washington, let us build, beautify, and render it habitable and convenient, so that, when hereafter the European traveller seeks its ruins in the forest, he shall never doubt but that he looks upon the site once honoured as the capital of the American people."

I have, when in conversation with intelligent friends here, delivered similar sentiments, and they have smiled at them without admitting their justice or applicability: I now set them down for their further amusement, not because I imagine they will be a tittle the more regarded, but simply because such were my "Impressions" of Washington.

I went several times to the senate-chamber and the hall of the representatives; but was not fortunate enough to hear a debate in the latter, or find any very important topic under discussion. Speeches I never found much attraction in anywhere, unless deeply interested in the subject of them; and those of the American assembly are rather made to be read than to be listened to. The arguments, thus delivered in Washington, are in fact directed to, and intended for, the constituents of the party, to whom they are directly forwarded in the shape of most formidable-looking pamphlets, no matter to what distance, post-free, serving as an exposition of the author's sentiments, and an evidence of his industry.

In the senate I had the happiness to hear a slight matter debated, in which Messrs. Clay and Forsyth took part; and I was struck with the force and fluency of the one, and the gentlemanlike tone and quiet self-possession of the other. Mr. Henry Clay reminded me strongly of Brougham, when the latter happens to be in one of his mildest moods; — the same facility of words and happy adaptation of them; the same bold, confident air, as though assured of his auditory and of himself; and withal, a touch of sly caustic humour, conveyed in look and in manner, that an adversary might well feel heedful of awakening.

Mr. Webster, another of the thunderers of the senate, was in his place on the occasion I allude to, but did not rise, which I was exceedingly anxious he should do, for I had already heard him speak at Boston, and never remember to have been more impressed. The cast, and setting on, of his head is grand, quite antique, his features massive and regular, yet in their expression, and in the calm repose of his deep-set black eyes, there is a strong resemblance to the native Indian, with whose blood, I believe, the great orator claims close affinity.

Mr. Van Buren's manner I thought highly characteristic of his political character, — cool, courteous; with a tone quiet but persuasive, a voice low-pitched, but singularly effective from the clearness of his enunciation and well-chosen emphasis. He bestows an undivided attention to the matter before the house becoming his situation.

As vice-president, this gentleman is chairman of the senate; a situation at this time of peculiar delicacy, considering his position as the proclaimed director of the measures of General Jackson's cabinet, and heir to his party and his power. His filling this chair with so little reproach under assaults and provocations which it required the greatest good temper and good sense to encounter or turn aside, I consider no slight evidence of that wisdom and political sagacity for which his party give him credit, and which have acquired for him amongst his admirers the familiar cognomen of the Little Magician.

The ladies, however, formed the chief attraction of the senate-chamber. Occupying a sort of passage or gallery on a level with and circling round two-thirds of the floor, here they sit, listening to their favourite speaker wherever he may be engaged, either before the President's chair boldly advancing the common interest, or behind some fair politician's, timidly seeking to advance his own, and hence, deal forth their award in well-pleased smiles, in due proportion to the eloquence of the speaker, public or private.

This is a custom the advantages of which I am sorry to find are about to be tested in England. Shame that a man should ever have to express regret that one other muster-place had been invented for a *reunion* of pretty faces! But such is my honest impression, and with me honesty is paramount; — a quality which must serve to balance my discourteous opinion, and restore me to the sex's favour. Then again, I am not of the Commons' House, or likely to be; and do not choose, perhaps, that the members should divide with me that part of my audience I value most, and would desire if possible to monopolize.

Why then, it may be asked, are these your only reasons? In reply permit me to say, I have a reserve of minor importance, but which may be added as a make-weight to my graver argument, — I do not think the place will become them, or that the habit of hearing debates will improve them. I had as soon see a woman a dragoon as a politician: not a Hussar; for I have seen a lady of our land make a very dashing hussar, without forfeiting one charm as a woman. No: I mean a "Heavy," with jackboots and cuirass, helmet and horse-hair; and to this condition will the novelty of the thing, if it becomes a fashion, possibly degrade our gentle, retiring, womanly women.

Let me here, however, declare, that it does not appear to have had this fatal effect upon the American ladies, since I never found one amongst them who thought about talking politics, unless it was with some snob who was too stupid to talk any nonsense less dull. But then they are born to the manner, and very few of them resident in the capital. It is only a novelty, therefore, enjoyed once or twice; then yawned over, voted tiresome, and forgotten.

On the other hand, our ladies, who would be most likely to monopolize the house, are in town for the whole session, eager for new excitement, and prepared to die martyrs to anything that may become the rage: then again, although I will answer for their capability of remaining silent during a debate, unless they are differently constituted from their fair kinswomen, t'other side the Atlantic, yet is there a coming and going, a rustling of silk and pulling off of gloves, a glancing of sparkling rings and yet more sparkling eyes, anything but promoters of attention or order in the house; besides the danger of a faint or two during a crush or a row amongst the members, — the latter, if one may rely upon the journals, a thing of nightly recurrence now.

I have many other good reasons to advance, but as they chiefly apply to the younger members, I think it useless to add them; indeed, my object in saying so much is rather to justify my expressed opinion, than from either the desire or hope of seeing an order so likely to prove agreeable to the Commons' House rescinded.

Politics have rarely run higher, or assumed an aspect more startling to a European, than during my residence in the States; and though it is not my intention to deal largely with a subject which every brother scribbler, who spends his six months here, arranges to his great ease and perfect satisfaction, yet, whenever I think my object of making the people known may be advanced by giving a smack of their politics, I shall do so with perfect freedom, considering this as ground on which the best friends may differ without any impeachment of good feeling or sound judgment.

The assumption of a new power by the President in the removal of the national fund, upon his own responsibility, from the United States Bank, and in violation of the terms of their unexpired charter, deranged for a time the credit of the community, and convulsed the land from one extremity to the other. During this panic, remonstrances and prayers for redress poured in from one party; whilst addresses, laudatory and congratulatory, were duly gotten up by the other.

The sea-board cities, together with every trading community, crowded the capital with deputations, praying the President to restore the monies and heal the national credit, until their importunities became so frequent, so personal, and led to such undignified altercations between these delegates and the chief of the government, that the gates of the palace were fairly closed against them; and, as the Whig journals expressed it, "for the first time, the Republic beheld the doors of the chief magistrate barred upon delegates charged to pour out the sufferings of the people, to remonstrate against their causes, and to awaken their author to a sense of his tyranny and injustice."

In senate and congress the tone assumed by this party against government, and the violence of the language used, become really startling to the ears of the subject of a monarchy: for instance, Mr. Webster, in a recent speech, drew a parallel between Sylla and the President, or *Dictator*, as he styled him, of the States, by no means disadvantageous to the Roman; showing how the tyrant of old first excited the populace, by the basest flattery, to overturn the restrictive power of the senate; which done, and his lawless will being left without a check, he turned upon his restless, ignorant allies, and slaughtering them by thousands, succeeded in prostrating their liberties and the freedom of his country: the speaker adding,

"I fear the worst fate of Rome is hanging over us; whether that of Sylla be in store for our despot, I know not. Should he, however, abdicate at the end of three years (Sylla's term), he will be hunted by the cries of a guilty conscience and by the curses of an outraged people, more intolerable than the pangs which tortured in his last moment the Roman tyrant!"

In anticipation of another speaker's assault, a journalist says,

"We may, when he delivers his sentiments, — which will be indeed the reflex of public opinion, — look to behold the fur fly off the back of the treacherous old usurper, our implacable tyrant," &c. &c.

On the other hand, the adulation of the administration exhausts panegyric in the President's praise: his qualities are proclaimed to be superhuman, his intuitive wisdom and farsightedness approaching to omniscience; by this party he, indeed, is all but deified. The vice-president proclaims that he shall consider it honour enough to have it known that he held a place in his counsels. Members of the legislature, of sound age and high character, dispute in their places within the house their seniority of standing as "true *soldiers* of the General's administration;" an odd title, by the way, independent of the strangeness of the avowal, for a representative of the people.

The assumption of the act of responsibility, and its exercise, it is argued by this party, have been decisive as to the conservation of the *morale* of the country, without which their liberties were held by a tenure liable to be quickly subverted, and the blood, and toil, and treasure of their predecessors spent in vain; that the integrity of their institutions was by this act assured, and the continuance of the people's happiness and prosperity based upon marble, unimpeachable and to endure for ever!

In every society, in all places, and at all times, this subject is all-absorbent amongst the men. Observing with pity a very intelligent friend arrested in the lobby of a drawing-room which was occupied by a whole bevy of beauty, and there undergo a buttoning of half an hour before he could shake off his worrier, I inquired with a compassionate air, just as he made his escape, "whether he would not be glad when the present ferment was over, and this eternal spectre laid in the sea of oblivion?"

"No, indeed," replied my friend coolly; "since it would only vanish to be succeeded by some other, in reality not quite so important perhaps, but which, for lack of a better, would be made to the full as absorbing of one's time and patience."

And this is strictly true: whatever subject may turn up is laid hold on, tooth and nail, by the *Ins* and *Outs* of the day, who, dividing upon it, lift banners, and under the chosen war-cry, be it "Masonry," "Indian treaties," or "Bank charter," fairly fight it out; a condition of turmoil, which, viewed on the surface, may appear anything but desirable to a man who loves his ease and quiet, and troubles himself with nothing less than with affairs of state, but which constitutes one of the personal taxes men must pay who look to govern themselves, or who desire to fancy that they do so.

It is a matter of great regret to me that there occurred no levee whilst I was in Washington; because, had one taken place, I should have enjoyed the honour of a closer view of the venerable chief of the States than I could snatch from seeing him pass two or three times on the avenue. Not but that there are facilities enough afforded for a presentation to one who is never denied when disengaged from his public duties; facilities which it may be very right and proper for the American citizen to avail himself of, but which good taste might suggest to the stranger, especially the Englishman, it would be more becoming in him to forego: as it is, I have frequently, in travelling, heard Europeans talking with the most offensive familiarity of having called upon the President, who at home would have stood hat-in-hand in their county magistrate's office, waiting for an interview with the great man.

As viewed on horseback, the General is a fine soldierly, well-preserved old gentleman, with a pale wrinkled countenance, and a keen clear eye, restless and searching. His seat is an uncommonly good one, his hand apparently light, and his carriage easy and horseman-like; circumstances, though trifling in themselves, not so general here as to escape observation.

His personal friends, of whom I know many most intimately, speak of him with great regard, and describe him politically as one whose singleness of purpose and integrity of mind, in all that relates to his country, can never be fairly impeached upon any tenable ground. With these friends, without regard to rank or station, he lives at all times on the most familiar terms. When in his neighbourhood, they visit him as they have ever done, without finding the slightest increase of form; and, over his cigar, the President canvasses the events and receives the opinions of the day with all the frankness of an indifferent party, neither affecting nor enforcing mystery or restraint.

His address is described as being naturally fluent, pleasing, and gentlemanlike: this I have from a source on which I can confidently rely; for both the wife and sister of an English officer of high rank, themselves women of remarkable refinement of mind and manners, observed to me, in speaking of the President, that they had seldom met a person possessed of more native courtesy or a more dignified deportment.

To another of the great ones of the land I had an introduction, which, as it is characteristic of the man, I will here relate. One afternoon, about dusk, being on my way to a family party at the house occupied by the late Secretary of the Navy, Mr. Southard, I thought I had run down my distance, and began an inspection of the outward appearance of the houses, all puzzlingly alike, when a couple of men, lounging round a corner, single file, smoking their cigars, chanced to cross my track. Addressing the rearmost, I inquired, "Pray, sir, do you chance to know which of the houses opposite is Mr. Southard's, the senator from New Jersey?"

"I do know where Mr. Southard's house is," replied the stranger, eyeing me as I fancied somewhat curiously; "though it is not exactly opposite. But surely you and I have met before now, — more than once too, or I am greatly mistaken?"

"That is more than probable, sir," replied I, "if you are fond of a play. My name is Power, Mr. Power of the theatre."

"I thought so," cried the stranger, holding out his hand; adding cordially, "My name, sir, is Clay, Henry Clay, of the senate; and I am glad, Mr. Power, that we are now personally acquainted."

I need hardly say, I joined in expressing the pleasure I derived from any chance which had procured me this honour, begging that I might not detain him longer.

"But stop, Mr. Power," said the orator; — "touching Mr. Southard's; — you observe yonder long-sided fellow propping up the post-office down below; only that he is waiting for me, I'd accompany you to the house; which, however, you can't miss if you'll observe that it's the very last of the next square but one."

With many thanks for his politeness, I here parted from Mr. Clay, to pursue my way according to his instructions, whilst he passed forward to join the tall gentleman, who waited for him at some distance near the public building which he had humorously described him as propping.

An accidental interview of this kind, however brief, will do more to prejudice the judgment for or against a man, than a much longer and more ceremonious intercourse. I confess my impressions on this occasion were all in Mr. Clay's favour; they were confirmatory of the *bonhommie* and playful humour ascribed to him by his friends and admirers, who are to be found throughout every part of the country.

The very day following this little incident I bade adieu to Washington, after a second prolonged visit. I had here encountered and mixed with persons from every State of the Union, and became thus in possession of the means of making comparisons, and drawing conclusions, such as no other single city, or perhaps any period less generally exciting, could have supplied.

I quitted it gratefully impressed in favour both of its private society and of the kind and hospitable character of its citizens generally. I had, whilst here, without delivering a letter, received unlooked-for attentions and kindnesses from persons the most distinguished for character and talent: attentions which I am as hopeless of ever being able to return, as I am incapable of ever being desirous to forget.

BOSTON

JOURNEY ACROSS THE ALLEGHANY MOUNTAINS.—PITTSBURG

The season continued to wear away without any severe demonstration; and by the 19th of February, the day on which I reached New York on my way from Washington to Boston, I found the first boat advertised for the passage, just open, to Providence,—a piece of good luck, by hitting which I was saved a land journey of two hundred miles.

We were detained by a fog in the Sound for a few hours, but reached Providence by three o'clock P.M. next day, and were just ten hours going the forty miles between that place and Boston; one extra bad bit of about three miles took an excellent team exactly two hours to pull through it. I could not conceive the possibility of this road, which I had seen three months before in a very fair condition, being so utterly washed out; but the heavy snows of these Northern States would penetrate ways of adamant, and will for ever exclude them from attaining the perfection of a well-kept turnpike.

A little after one o'clock A.M. I was rattled up to the door of the Tremont; where, late as the hour was, I found friends waiting up for me, and experienced what at all times is a pleasure, but more especially after such a cold jolting,—a warm welcome.

I was now a resident of this city for a month, during which time I enjoyed a continued series of the most friendly attentions. I found three or four men, who, like myself, were fond of riding, and together we rambled over the whole of the surrounding country; and a beautiful country it is, with its island-gemmed bay and gaily-painted country seats. One of these, the house of Colonel Thomas Perkins, is seated within grounds well kept and tastefully laid out, with a very extensive range of noble hot-houses, within which, at this season and in this latitude, the fruit and flowers of the tropics were to be found in their freshest bloom and beauty. I think these grounds are more agreeably broken, offer a greater variety of soil, and command a finer prospect of land and sea, than any place I ever visited of equal dimensions.

We wanted nothing, on many of the fine open mornings we now had, but a pack of good foxhounds: the land is better cleared than it is farther south, the covers smaller, with fewer swamps, and no fencing that might not be crept round or got over by even a moderate-going man.

I had heard a good many amusing anecdotes of the infinite respect with which the country people of New England view and address persons of their own grade, and the utter disregard of decent ceremony which they evince towards all others: there appeared something so whimsically exaggerated in these stories, that I never had received them as veritable history; and when the Duke of Saxe Weimar told of the coachman's inquiring "Are you the man going to Portland? because, if you are, I'm the gentleman that's a going to drive you," I set it down for a good joke, illustrative, perchance, of a *brusquerie* of manner which did exist, but not in itself strictly true. I have, however, during my present sojourn here, received good corroborative evidence of its being a veracious report.

I went out on one occasion to partake of a fine black bear, that had been killed at a house famous for the plenty, the quality, and cooking of game. There were eight or nine men of the party, some of whom had ridden out on horseback: in going over a rail-fence close to the house we were to dine at, the horse I rode struck both hind feet and cast his shoes: as soon as I got into the yard, where some of the party had already dismounted, I inquired for the ostler. A good-humoured, active-looking fellow immediately made his appearance, with whom, being desirous to have my nag's feet looked after before we set out on our return, I was led into the following dialogue.

"Pray, have you a smithy in this neighbourhood?"

"We've gotten a blacksmith or two, I guess."

"At what distance is the nearest blacksmith's forge?"

"Well, I don't 'no; there is a shop about half a mile maybe, or ther'bouts."

"Can you have this horse taken down there to get the two hind shoes put on?"

"Guess not, 'cept I car' him down myself."

"Well, will you carry him down yourself?"

"Well, you see, I can't tell about that nohow at present. Guess I will, if I can tho', by an' by."

"But why can't you say whether you will or will not? I'll pay you for your trouble. Have you any objection to taking the horse down?"

"Oh no! not at all, by no means. I've no objection nohow to obleege you, if, you see, I can find some other gentleman to look after my horses whiles I go."

My companions, who had been enjoying this cross-examination of my equivocal friend, now laughed outright, and heartily did I join in the guffaw: they were to "the manner born," and it was my puzzled expression that so tickled them; to me, after the first surprise was over, the whole thing was indescribably droll. I caught instantly "another gentleman," an idler about the public-house door, who, for a shilling, found the cast shoes, and undertook to do for the horses whilst the first gentleman, of the stable, led my nag away to the forge.

This was a very fair specimen, but we were to be favoured with another and a better. Mr. T. P——s, a son of the Colonel's, one of the foremost citizens of this State, was driven out in his English landau, with certain delicacies not to be expected where we dined. As the coachman, who was a servant of the old Colonel's, drew up by the inn-door, he was immediately recognised, and saluted most cordially by the landlord; who, addressing him by his name,—Jenkins, or whatever it was,—hoped he was quite well, and was "uncommon glad to see him." During this ceremony, Mr. P——s had alighted; and, in order to be particularly civil, observed with great good-humour to the landlord,

"Ah, my friend, what you remember Jenkins, do you?"

"Why yes, I guess I ought," replied our host of the game; "I've know'd Muster Jenkins long enough, seein' he's the *gentleman* as used to drive old Tom P——'s coach."

The fact was, the man knew the Colonel—or old Tom P——s, as he styled him—quite well, but had forgotten Mr. P——s, who had been much in Europe, and was, moreover, put quite out of his latitude by the English landau Mr. Jenkins was driving: he guessed, I suppose, that this *gentleman* had hired a new master, and had consequently turned off the family of his old one.

Odd as all this sounds, the strangest part of the matter is, that there appears no disrespect, nor churlishness of manner, conveyed or implied by this reversal of conventional distinctions. I can at least answer for the ostler, who required some other *gentleman* as *aide*, turning out on this, and on other occasions, a most assiduously civil fellow; and as for our host, he served up the steaks of his bear as though it might never have danced to any but the "genteelest o' tunes," and himself have been its instructor.

He certainly gave us, in a plain but comfortable way, the best game dinner possible, including trout and codling of the finest flavour. Let me add, that I liked the bear vastly; and, after assisting to pick his ribs, carried away the skin which had once covered them, — not the least delicate portion of this bruin, by the way, for it was the blackest and richest fur, of the kind, I ever saw.

I quitted this hospitable city on the 10th of March, and remained in New York until the 20th, when I departed for Pittsburg *viâ* Philadelphia; although, from the little I had seen of stageing, I would have given a trifle to have been off the engagement, which I had made without contemplating the difficulties to be expected in a stage journey of three hundred miles over the Alleghanies at this early season. I had latterly, however, heard enough of the condition of this route, or line as it is called; but the intelligence was of a colour anything but cheering.

At Philadelphia I took my place for Pittsburg, in the "Good Intent line," professing to carry only six inside; but this excellent intention of the worthy proprietors must be consigned to the commissioners of pavement in a certain unmentionable place, since it was never fulfilled. We commenced our journey with seven, the book-keeper making it a favour that we should take in one gentleman who was greatly pressed for time. I perceived, as we started, another person get outside, which made us eight.

We were very soon transferred to the Columbia rail-road, which was in progress and now travelled upon for about twenty-one miles: along this I was rolled over the viaduct whose commencement I had noted, and, I believe, regretted. According to Mitchell's description, it crosses the Schuylkill at a place called Peter's Island; is one thousand and forty-five feet long and forty-one wide, being thirty feet above water-mark. Of the elevation, when I crossed on this occasion, we had an excellent opportunity of forming an opinion; for, except a pathway in the centre, the spaces between the beams had not yet been filled in, so that we looked through on to the water running beneath: the workmen were hard at it covering over and filling up; but it was passable in its present state, and therefore, "Go a-head was the word:" — there's no time lost here, i'faith! Immediately on crossing this viaduct, you come on an inclined plane two thousand eight hundred and five feet long: this struck me as being admirably contrived.

I was very sorry when we were once again to be re-packed in our stage. Though one gets accustomed to anything in time, I never exactly brought myself to view these frequent transfers as a part of travelling to be rejoiced in. Our system of running a coach through a journey is not yet adopted here; they still stick to the old plan,—every proprietor his own vehicle; consequently you are for ever trundling from one to another, to your own great discomfiture, and to the destruction of any but the toughest sort of trunks.

I forget how often we changed coach on this journey; indeed, I fancy that, during the third night out, I might have effected a transfer or two in my sleep; but I recollect that they were vexatiously frequent, and would have been more grievous had the weather been less generally fair.

My fellow passengers were, luckily, with one exception, thin spare fellows, all citizens of the frontier State of Illinois; the fat subject was a countryman of my own, who had been for many years a resident at Pittsburg, and was a merry, contented son of Erin as ever jolted over these rough roads, which he informed me he did once at least in every season.

We soon shook into shape: the condition of the turnpike, after the woful accounts I had received, appeared to me exceedingly passable; indeed, it was infinitely better than any part of the one between Washington and Baltimore, or than the Boston and Providence turnpike, as I had last experienced it. The country through which we rode was under excellent cultivation; the barns attached to the roadside houses were all large, brick-built, and in the very neatest condition. The approach to Lancaster, a fine town about forty miles from Philadelphia, was very beautiful, and bespoke the people rich in agricultural wealth. I have seldom seen a finer valley, or one under more careful cultivation.

The next large place we arrived at was Harrisburg, the capital of the State of Pennsylvania: it was midnight when we reached it; but I immediately walked to look at the State-house, where the legislature assembles, and about which are ranged the public offices.

The mass appeared large; and the effect of the buildings with their lofty classic porticos, viewed under the influence of a fine starlight night, was imposing enough: the situation is well chosen, appearing like a natural elevation in the midst of a plain, and overlooking the waters of the Susquehannah, above whose banks the city is built.

One always feels something like disappointment on entering one of these capitals, although previously aware that the site is selected with regard only to the general convenience of the community, and without reference to the probabilities of its ever becoming important for its trade or of monstrous size. A European accustomed to seek in the capital of a country the highest specimens of its excellence in art, and the utmost of its refinement in literature, and indeed, in all which relates to society, is necessarily hard to reconcile to these small rustic cities, whose population is doubled by villages he has only heard named for the first time whilst journeying on his way to the Liliputian mistress of them all. As places of meeting for the legislature, I am of those who think the smallness of the population an advantage. Firstly, the members are freed from the expense consequent upon living in large cities; and next, the chambers are removed from having their deliberations overawed or impeded by any of those sudden outbreaks of popular madness to which all people are prone, and to which the nature of this government more immediately exposes it, without possessing any power quickly to arrest or even control such licence.

Harrisburg is highly spoken of for the salubrity as well as the beauty of its site, and gives promise of becoming important in point of population; at present its inhabitants are about four thousand.

From this we steered away to the southward, until at Chambersburg we struck the direct road leading from Baltimore to Pittsburg. We had a rough night of it; but a halt of an hour at Chambersburg in the morning, enabled me to make a comfortable toilet and get an excellent breakfast. Here we took the first spur of the mountains, and from this were on a continual ascent.

Up the longer and steeper hills I constantly walked, and was often an hour in advance of the stage. This mountain region is certainly a very fine one, and I do not think its grandeur has ever been done justice to in description. Its attributes are all gigantic: it has the picturesque ruggedness of the Appenines, without their barrenness; since the valleys lying between the ridges, wherever they have been cleared, give evidences of the richest soil. A view from any hill top, however, shows these clearings to be mere specks in the surrounding forest, which yet clothes richly the sides of each interminable ridge you cross, fringes their most rugged summits, and waves over the loftiest peaks.

At Bedford Springs there is a most excellent inn; but the one at a miserable village called Macconnelville, presented an aspect anything but inviting: the precaution of Mr. Head, however, had made me independent of supplies. On quitting the Mansion-house he had fitted up a small basket with sundry comforts, which were of infinite use to myself and comrades, they served as a speedy introduction and a durable cement to our friendship.

I like these Western men; their off-hand manner makes you at once at your ease with them: they abound in anecdote growing out of the state in which they live, full of wild frolic and hardy adventure, and they recount these adventures with an exaggeration of figure quite Oriental, in a phraseology peculiar to themselves, and with a manner most humorous.

Much amongst strangers, they have a quick appreciation of character; and, where they take a dislike, are, I have no doubt, mighty troublesome customers; they are, however, naturally courteous, and capable of genuine and inbred kindness, as a little anecdote of my present trip will serve to illustrate.

On the morning of our second night out, I observed the Major and his friends holding a council just as we were stepping into the coach. We were eight persons, which gave three sitters to two of the seats and two to the third; by way of relief, my servant or myself frequently mounted the box, enabling the parties to separate,—a luxury of no mean importance. On this occasion I noticed, on being about to take my seat, which was the front one, that it was unoccupied, Sam being on the box, and three persons on each of the other seats. On requesting that one of the sitters by my fat friend would share the vacant front with me, the Major informed me that the arrangement was preconcerted, as they knew I was not quite so well used to rough roads as they were, and had work before me on getting to my journey's end; begging me to fix myself comfortably on the seat, and try and sleep for an hour or two.

This being a piece of unpurchasable, unthought-for consideration and civility, I conceived it as well worth notice as the many instances of brutality which ill-used travellers put on record; but it is by no means the only example I have seen of these rough subjects' innate kindness, and, I may add, good-breeding. There is, with them, a give-and-take system whilst thus roughing it in company, they seek no exclusive advantage, and evince no selfishness; but they are quick-sighted and shrewd observers, and I would recommend any who desire to travel comfortably with them, to carefully suppress any exhibition of over-regard for self.

With this precaution, let a stranger, and a British subject, be only known as such, and if a preference should occur, I will answer for his standing a good chance of getting it.

Here I enjoyed my first lesson in what is familiarly termed riding a rail; and from all such railways I hope to be spared henceforward. The term is derived from a fence-rail being occasionally used to supply the place of a broken thoro'-brace, by which all these stages are hung; and these are, in fact, the only sort of spring that would endure the load and the "rough breaks" their virtue must go through.

We broke down by a sudden plump, into a hole, that would have shaken a broad-wheeled waggon into shavings. Our driver did not approve of any of the fence-rails in the vicinity, so plunged into the wood, accompanied by one of my Western companions; and in ten minutes they returned, bearing a young hickory pole, that the driver assured us was "as tough as Andrew Jackson himself,[10] and as hard to break, though it might give a leetle under a heavy load." This was shoved under the body of the carriage, and rested upon the fore and hind axles: it was lashed fast, and the spare part of the spar was left sticking out behind, like the end of the main boom of a smack. The coach body, when rested upon this, was found to have a considerable list to port; but to have brought it to an even keel would have been a work of time, — not that such a thing was contemplated for a moment. The driver was enabled by this ingenious substitute for a carriage-spring to "go ahead:" the rest was luxury, which the "Good-intent line" did not bargain for; so we were left to trim ship to our liking. Contrary to all my experience, I insisted that the heaviest part of our cargo should be stowed at the bottom, for to have had my countryman's eighteen stone of solid stuff to prop up, for twenty miles, would have required the shoulders of Atlas.

Whilst walking up the mountains, I frequently overtook settlers moving with all their worldly goods over to the great Western valley. I generally exchanged a few words with them, and with the more communicative now and then had a considerable long talk. Most of them were small farmers and mechanics from the Northern States, who followed here in the wake of kindred or neighbours, their plan arranged and their location determined upon. One or two heads of families, however, told me they were just going to look about, and did not know rightly where they might set up.

I overtook one old couple attending a single-horse waggon up Laurel-hill; and surely, if any laurels awaited them at the summit, they were hardly enough won. The appearance of this pair attracted me as I approached the rocky platform where for a moment they had halted to breathe: the woman was a little creature, dressed in an old-fashioned flowered gown, with sleeves tight to the elbows, met by black mittens of faded silk, and a very small close bonnet of the same colour. She had small brass buckles in her shoes; a cane, like those borne by running footmen, in one hand, and upon the other arm a small basket, rolled up within which lay a tabby cat, with which she held a conversation in what sounded to me like broken French and English.

The man was a son of Anak in altitude, somewhat bent by years, but having a soldierlike air. His white hair was combed back, and gathered behind into a thick club: he wore a long greatcoat, which, if made for him, gave testimony to a considerable falling-off in his proportions, for it hung but loosely about him; had a very broad-leaved hat set jauntily on one side of his head; and supported his steps upon a sturdy stick.

I saluted this singular-looking pair, and was by the lady honoured with an especially gracious curtsey, whilst the gaunt old man bade me good day in an accent decidedly foreign. I patted the cat of the basket, addressing it in French, and was in a moment overwhelmed by the delights of its mistress, who *ciel'*d, and *mon-Dieu'*d, and *quel-plaisir'*d, until, if her tall *mari* had not stepped in to the rescue, I do not know to what lengths her delight might not have carried her.

The horse was sufficiently rested; the man who drove it was ready to proceed; and the ancient Parisienne, for such she was, had once more to ensconce herself beneath the canvass covering of the waggon, into which I had the honour of assisting herself and her cat, amidst thanks and excuses blended with all the graceful volubility of a well-bred Frenchwoman, — for well-bred she was, beyond a doubt.

"My poor little woman!" said the old giant, as, after the twentieth adieu, I joined him where he waited a little in advance of the waggon, and quickened my pace to keep up with his strides, — "she is made too happy for to-day to hear a gentleman address her in her own language, and by whom she can be understood;" adding, "You are not a Frenchman, sir?"

"I am not," said I, smiling; "but should imagine you are, by the compliment you so adroitly infer."

"No, sir," rejoined mine ancient, "I am a Biscayan; bred a ship-builder, but at present a house-carpenter."

"But you speak English like a native: how is that?" inquired I, desirous of continuing the dialogue thus begun.

"I have been forty years in this good country, and have made better progress than my poor little woman, though she is well educated and I have no learning to help me."

"Madame, then, is not Spanish?"

"No, sir, she is of Paris; and, what is very odd, that is nearly all she ever told me of herself. It was in the winter of 1792 that I first met my poor little woman: I had slept within a few miles of Havre, and was just turned away from the cabaret, when a little boy joined me, requesting that I would let him walk with me to the town. We fell into chat, when I discovered that my new friend had no passport, but that he had money, and was desirous to escape from France, no matter to what place. He was in great trouble; cried much; said he had lost all his friends, and begged me not to desert him.

"It would be too long a story to tell you all the trouble I had to get him on board ship with me; but, sir, that little boy is now in the waggon where you handed him."

"Your wife!" exclaimed I, affecting surprise, and really greatly interested. "But when did she disclose her sex to you?"

"Why, sir, there was no great need of disclosure after we once got to sea; her cowardice told her story, but I kept her secret till we arrived at Philadelphia, where we married; and in the lower part of this State we have lived ever since quietly enough, until lately."

"And what, at your age, could induce you to cross the mountains, my friend?"

"Why, sir, work was scarce in our country place, and I'm told there's a heap of building raising about Pittsburg, that's one reason; but the truth is that our politics have changed a good deal in Pennsylvania of late. In a scuffle at the bar of our hotel, this last election, I got knocked down and trodden on; my arm was broken, and I a good deal hurt; and my poor woman took such a horror of the little bit of mobbing we had that she would make me pull up stakes, and here we are on our last move."

We walked on side by side, until the waggon was left far behind and the coach came up. We had a long talk on the subject of politics; and, although a stanch American and a republican, I found my friend was opposed to "the removal of the deposits," — the universal test of the day, — and by no means a whole-hog man. But he said, "It is a fine country and a fine people; I am a citizen, have lived here forty years, and hope to die here."

Wishing that his desire might have a late fulfilment, I shook the honest veteran's hand; and we parted for ever, after an intercourse of three hours had created a sort of fellowship between us. Here was an humble chapter from the romance of real life, gleaned, where such an adventure was least expected, in one of the passes of the Alleghanies.

The walk up this hill was, independent of the good companionship I enjoyed, in itself fine: the road circling about dark ravines, from whose thickly-wooded deeps rose the hollow murmur of closely-pent currents, whose waters had rarely reflected the rays of the sun; and in other places clinging to the steep precipice, from whose side it had been cut, and which was yet burthened with the half-burnt trunks of hundreds of noble trees that had fallen to make place for it. The view, too, from the summit was glorious; and I thought as I looked below, northward and eastward, where two wide openings gave a boundless stretch of valley to the eye, that my journey was well repaid: but it was not over yet; and, before we reached Pittsburg, I do not know but that there were moments when I would have retracted this burst of enthusiasm.

The third afternoon and night it rained incessantly; the road from Youngstown, or Greensburg, being nearly as bad as that memorable Washington turnpike. The delays, too, were unnecessary and frequent; at some of the changing-places the servants had to be roused, and this was no easy task. Now and then, an extra independent hand refused to get up, or denied us help when he was up; in which case the poor devil of a driver was left to his own resources, with, now and then, the aid of a half-naked, wretched negro.

The travelling of the "Good Intent," taking the roads into consideration, was a capital pace, the horses excellent; but I have set down, that, on a pretty fair estimate, making allowance for the exaggerations of discomfort and ill-humour, about nine hours on the whole line were lost for want of the commonest attention, and the passengers greatly inconvenienced without any advantage accruing to the proprietors.

At length we emerged from the slough, and about daylight on the third morning were rumbled over the *pavé* of Pittsburg.

The inn was closed; but the rough assault of my Western friends soon roused the bar-keeper, who got his door open just in time to save his lock from a huge paving-stone, with which the angry Major purposed to test its power of resistance.

"Why, you're in an uncommon hurry," exclaimed the half-awakened bar-keeper.

"That's more than we can say of you, stranger," retorted the Major. "What was you about that you didn't hear the coach? Maybe it was the rain made such a noise you couldn't?"

"No; does it rain that hard, though?" gaped the matter-of-fact mixer of liquids.

"I guess it does; and if it wasn't that you've got the key of the liquor, it would be only right to put you out into it for an hour; for you are the hardest-hearted white-man I ever come across, this side the mountains, or you'd a' moved quicker to let in a dog on such a night."

A rousing fire and some hot whisky and water soon restored our good-humour: a bed was quickly arranged for me by a good-natured negro, who had, I verily believe, just crawled out of it; a fire was lighted in the little hole it occupied; and in half an hour I was fast asleep on the banks of *la belle rivière*.

FOOTNOTE:

[10] "Old Hickory" is one of the familiar names by which his lovers delight to designate the venerable President.

PITTSBURG

My first visit, at an early hour on Monday morning, was to the banks of the Monongahela, which ran by the bottom of the main street, wherein I was lodged. The water was at this time low, being fifteen feet under its highest level: the point of junction with the Alleghany lay, as I discovered, some way below. The opposite heights, which rise boldly from the water's edge, looked dark and drear enough, covered as they are with a stubble of blackened stumps, and a few blasted trees, the ghosts of the ruined forest. The political economist, however, would find ready consolation in the mounds of coal-dust, the dingy low-roofed buildings, together with the swinging of a hundred cranks, worked by the engines whose smoke is seen curling along the face of the steep hill. It is to give place to these iron giants that the forest has been felled; and to supply these with fire, the mountain is in this direction pierced to its centre.

Nature has supplied this place with wharves; and the people appear quite contented with her handiwork, for they are left as she made them. I counted fourteen steamboats all busied in taking in or discharging freight; and the river was here and there dotted by keels of a rude, picturesque construction: everything, indeed, gave evidence of active and prosperous trade.

I from hence made a circuit of the principal part of the town, which is soon accomplished, for it offers nothing externally to arrest the passer-by for a moment: the streets are narrow, irregular, and ill-paved; the houses as dirty as the smoke of bituminous coal can make them, and, though substantially built, are in general wholly destitute of neatness or ornament.

Upon Grant's Hill, a spur of one of the surrounding heights, that thrusts itself boldly into the heart of the delta on which the town is built, I found a Gothic edifice almost completed, the magnitude and tasteful design of which attracted me: I entered it, and perceived at once that it was a place of Catholic worship. From a communicative little man, whom I observed for some time eyeing me with a sociable look, I learnt that this was the cathedral; and it stands a pleasing memorial of the liberality of the sects of this town, having been raised by voluntary subscriptions made among the numerous congregations of the place.

It is a grateful task to record such evidences of the existence of true Christian charity; they reconcile one to one's fellows, and serve to balance the barbarous acts of bigotry and blindness which yet occasionally disgrace the age and degrade humanity. This edifice, when completed, will be an attractive object, both from its commanding site and the character of its architecture, which is of the florid Gothic, tastefully sustained throughout.

Descending the steep bluff of Grant's Hill, I entered the theatre, which lies within its shadow. This building was not yet a year old, and offered one of the neatest-formed interiors possible, calculated to contain about one thousand persons. It had all the offices and appointments of such an establishment, well and conveniently arranged; and in this respect might serve as a model to more important-looking houses. The ornamental parts of the interior were already disfigured by the smoke which fills this atmosphere day and night, and fully exonerates the people from the charge of being wilfully regardless of neatness and *propreté* in the arrangement of their dwellings.

I found the manager, Mr. Wemyss, at his post, and all things in tolerable order. At night the house was filled; though how the people made their way home again I do not know: even the short distance I had to explore on the line of the principal street, I found beset with perils; loose pavement, scaffold-poles, rubbish, and building materials of all kinds blocked up the *trottoir* in several places, which were to be avoided by instinct, for light here was none, natural or artificial. At length, after a few stumbles, I was securely housed in a small room, which I was promised the exclusive use of, and wherein the cheerful light of the bituminous coal, that blazed like pitch-pine, in my mind made ample amends for the dust it created, and of this, the amount was by no means trifling.

The next day I was joined by Lieutenant I——d, of the cavalry corps about to advance on an expedition through the prairies, and across the hunting-grounds of the Nomade tribes, ranging over the still slightly-explored regions lying between the Mississippi and the Rocky Mountains. We were ancient comrades of the spur and snaffle, having harried the low country in company far and wide; and, the morning being fine, we were quickly mounted for a raid through this new land.

Crossing the long bridge over the Monongahela, a muddy, turbid-looking river, we commenced the ascent of Coal Hill, so called from the great quantities of this material it supplies; along its base lies a range of busy manufactories, and the roar of the steam-engine resounds on all sides. Here, too, is a growing town, called Birmingham; but it must overleap the mountain, or, following the galleries by which the miners have already penetrated to its centre, become a subterranean city, before it can hope to rival even a suburb of its gigantic sponsor.

We had much difficulty in scaling the hill; the track was knee-deep in heavy mud, and in trying to follow a narrow ledge, by which we calculated to avoid this impediment for a hundred yards, I— —'s horse made a false step, and fairly rolled down a precipitous descent of some fifty feet into the road beneath, to the infinite amusement of a group of miners, who had probably been "guessing" that such a termination to our scramble was likely: they now swore that a better Racker[11] down hill they had never seen. I— —d had thrown himself adroitly out of his seat on the upper side of the ledge the very instant of the brute's slip, and, being unhurt, soon caught the astonished nag, which remained quietly looking about by the bottom of the precipice, half buried in an avalanche of shingle and small coal he had loosened in his course.

Once on the summit of this coal-hill, the plan of the growing city of manufacture lay displayed as on a chart beneath our feet, together with a great extent of country, and the course and character of the two fine rivers which, combined at this spot, take henceforward the name and style of the Ohio, or River of Beauty.

The course of the muddy Monongahela is north-west; and, from about north-east, the clear, lively Alleghany comes bounding into it, breasting its turbid waters, and bearing their heavy mass back by its brisk charge close against the western bank, whence, side by side, they take their downward course, but each preserving its distinctive character and colour for a considerable distance; divided by a pretty verdant island, about a couple of miles below their junction, they each embrace a moiety of it, renewing their churlish fellowship once more when this obstacle is passed.

The town stands upon a small alluvial delta, of a triangular form, at the exact point of union between the rivers,—a spot so lovely, that, as I looked upon it, much as I respect manufactures, I found myself involuntarily wishing that fate had reserved it for some less dirty purpose. As the city grows, it must of necessity climb the steep bluffs by which it is encompassed;

and on these it is not too much to imagine, at no far period, the squares, terraces, and crescents of a wealthy and public-spirited community; whilst, within the crowded triangle beneath, the clang of the noisy steam-engine and the black smoke will lie drowned, and along the narrow strips of level soil skirting its rivers will rise the warehouses and wharves of its commerce.

To the north of the Alleghany you see the little town of that name, with one or two buildings conspicuous, at this distance, for their size: this, too, is united to Pittsburg by a bridge of great apparent lightness and strength.

From the abutting hill whence we took our first long survey of this congeries of future cities, we took a western course, following the line of the Ohio; but holding to the high lands, till coming back, when we made a *détour* to the north, and thus got frequent and fine views of the neighbourhood.

The country appears generally hilly, with rich glens and valleys lying between, having numerous streams of clear living water, and presenting every proof of exhaustless mineral wealth; hence its adoption by the industrious swarm whose fires darken the sky by night and day.

The day after this, I— —d embarked on board a steamer for Louisville, on his way to join the head-quarters of his corps, somewhere upon the Missouri. The Republic allows no sinecure pay to its soldiers: most of these gallant men pass the best half of their lives upon the frontier, wasted by sickness, removed far from society or sympathy, poorly paid and worse thanked, enjoying very little present consideration, and without hope of future fame. It must require an ardent imagination, and all the romance with which poetry has invested sword and feather, to keep an American soldier to his colours in this time of peace; as, on a sober worldly view, his appears the least enviable condition to be found in the community.

I on this day took a solitary ride up the Monongahela, and visited the scene of Bradock's defeat and death. I found it all snugly fenced in, and under good cultivation. An intelligent farmer, who was on the spot, good-naturedly undertook, in answer to an inquiry I made, to act as *cicerone*. The localities appeared like a book to him: he told where the French lay *perdu*; pointed out the cover from whence the British advanced, to be repulsed headlong; where they, according to his legend, were re-formed, and once more thrust forward, to be again, and finally, overthrown.

I understood the minutest details of the whole affair, as well as the positions occupied by French, English, Indians, and Virginians, before my good-natured guide appeared quite satisfied; at least, I was forced, out of consideration for my own time and his patience, to say so much, and with many thanks to leave him: not, however, until he had urged me strongly to come home and take tea with his wife, or at least take a drink with him; one or both of which I pledged myself to do on a future occasion.

It was not a little amusing, at this distant day, to observe the ardour with which my guide canvassed the lost fight, of which he had read, as he informed me, twenty different accounts.

"It was a shame," he said, "a right-down sin, and a throwin' away of men's lives, ever to have put them under Bradock's command," whom he accused of having "no more military gumption than a goose." — "Why," he said, "two companies of British grenadiers would have eat every *crapaud* on the ground, if they'd bin let to go round and in at one end o' the ditch, instead of walking right straight up hill agin' the loaded muzzles of guns they couldn't see, only by the smoke out o' the long grass."

Then he would take off his hat, wipe his brow, and fairly knock it against his knee with vexation at the British defeat.

"Why, sir," he said, at the same time grasping my thigh, where I sat in my saddle, with an energy that brought tears into my eyes, — "why, mister, just do you look up at that little knoll to the right; the place warn't cleared then, and there was a heap o' dead timber lying there-bout. Well, sir, Washington sent, out of his own head, — for he warn't a deal thought on then, you see, — a company of Virginians to try the trees for it. Well, now just look where they were fixed by that move, right over the *crapauds*, — every mother's son o' them Virginians good for a squirrel at fifty yards. I'm d — — d if they wouldn't have used up every human of a Frenchman behind the drain, if it had been left to a settlement between them, and if the English would only quietly ha' looked on, and kept Johnny from breaking cover and treeing it."

"And why the devil didn't they use them up?" I here demanded, to give my vexed informant time to breathe.

"I'll tell you why, if you don't know. Why, because that d — — d Bradock was blind as well as deaf, and took the Virginians for inimies; so, not bein' able to get at Johnny, he slamm'd it right smash into them, and killed the biggest half on 'em as they were tryin' to run back to their own side. Sir, it was nothin' better than an eternal murder, and Bradock ought to have swung for it; but he was shot down, somehow or other, and died amongst better men, only shootin' was a sight too good for him."

Taking the statement of my friend for the ground of my opinion, I left him, at once amused by his enthusiasm and informed by his intelligence.

I did purpose keeping tryst with my new acquaintance, and having the battle fought over again, when I might have been able to do some justice to the force and spirit of his narration; but other routes were to be visited, and my time was limited to a few days: so we met no more.

On another day I rode by the United States' Arsenal, a fine building, inclosing some acres. It is well situated, near the banks of the Alleghany, about two miles out of the town. This is one of the most considerable *depôts* for arms and ordnance stores to be found in the Western country.

From this I pursued my way up the river for a mile or two, to where, at a pretty quiet spot, I observed a boat just leaving the bank for the north side. I hailed the ferryman, and he returned immediately, when, adding myself and nag to his freight, he again commenced pulling up the stream, assisted by a couple of curly-headed urchins, his sons, two out of twelve, as he laughingly told me; adding, that they were capital helps.

We had a couple of market-waggons aboard the flat, each drawn by a pair of horses. The river, I fancied, was here about as wide as the Thames at Southwark, running clear and strong; the banks tolerably bold, very regular, and fringed by a luxuriant growth of various trees and water-loving shrubs. On the other side I fell on the Pennsylvania canal, and I for a mile followed the line by which it approaches the town of Alleghany, till, coming to a rough high hill, I was tempted to try the ascent, which, after a good deal of ducking and scrambling, I accomplished.

The prospect from the summit amply repaid me: at my feet lay the growing town of Alleghany, which stands on a fine alluvial plain affording ample space for a city as large as Pekin; with two ports, one on the Alleghany, the other on the Ohio. I here traced the course of the canal to the aqueduct on which it crosses the river. Two fine steamers, with their galleried decks tier over tier, were stemming the current, each looking like the old wood-cut of Noah's Ark, — houses built upon rafts, of three stories high, with balconies running round them, the whole being covered by inclined roofs. Many of the picturesque-looking keels found here were also working up for the quays; and the waters just before the busy town presented a strange contrast to the view either up or down the rivers, where all was tranquil and solitary as when the light *pirogue* of the adventurous *voyageur* first timidly skimmed along by their rich shores, sending the startled deer to the mountain and drawing the watchful savage down.

How to get back was now a consideration without retracing my steps, to do which I had neither the instinct nor the inclination. I pushed for a near wood, from which I perceived smoke stealthily curling over the tree tops; and, after a long threading of the thicket, stumbled upon a little colony of charcoal-burners, the blackest and the merriest devils I ever met: they might have been Iroquois, or negroes, from their colour; but the first reply I got to my hail rendered any inquiry as to country unnecessary.

"Hola! my friend," shouted I at the top of my voice, as a tall, half-naked being stalked out of one of the huts, from which I was separated by a deep ravine; "pray step this way for one moment."

The man did as I desired, without a word; a couple of attendant imps hanging on to the strings of his knees.

"I'm sorry to trouble you," I added, as he drew within easy speaking-distance; "but the fact is, I have lost my road, and fear to lose my dinner."

"I'faith, thin, sir, if you'll tell me where-abouts you lost the road I'll find you the dinner, and go and look for the road while you're atein' it: with the blessing o' God, it will be the first road I seen since I've bin this side o' Pittsburg, to say the laste."

"Maybe you've seen a fine aisy-goin' road betune Cork and Cove?" I replied, in the same accent.

"Maybe I hav'nt," grinned the pleased charcoal-burner, laughing from ear to ear. "Och murder! you're the devil, sure! wasn't it the last ten miles I ever toed of Irish ground? Long life to you, sir! wait till I call the wife. Molly ashtore, come out av id, for here's a witch of a gintleman here. Jem, you robber, go and bid your mammy stir herself and come here."

Away ran Jem and his brother, or rather flew, for their feathers were fluttering in the air. I laughed immoderately whilst my countryman, with the most puzzled air, exclaimed,

"Och murder! but it's the quarest thing alive. Sure you must have know'd us?"

He was now joined by his wife and two or three others of the little family, who all appeared nearly of an age. Poor Molly, the Mistress, looked weak and haggard, and told me she "had the shakes on her for the last six months." She was affected to tears when her husband told her of my witchcraft, in knowing where they were from, and joined in begging that "I'd come round and take a bite o' cake and a sup o' spirits and water, to keep me from feelin' faint till I got to my dinner."

I requested, however, as my time was short, that one of the little ones might at once put me on the nearest track by which I would reach the bridge; and finding I would not accept their hospitality, the father of the family, attended by Jem, walked along with me to where a bridle-path led on to a waggon-track, which he desired me to pursue. Here I left my friendly countryman, and with a "God send you safe home, sir!" he turned to his own humble dwelling, to think with a full heart of that distant home my chance visit had recalled in all its freshness, and which, although he may never look to revisit, no son of poor Ireland ever forgets.

A circuitous route led me on to the main road, pursuing which I soon reached the bridge; but on my way through the street was struck with the growing air of this place, which I cannot help thinking is one day destined to be the great city of the river of beauty.

I entered the smoky Pittsburg, more than ever charmed with the scenery amidst which it is seated, still beautiful despite the ravages of the miner and the pollution of steam, smoke, charcoal, and all the other useful abominations attendant upon the manufacture of iron, glass, pottery, &c. The wealth and various attractions of this rich heiress of Nature have proved her undoing.

The greatest ravage which I had to mourn, because it appeared carried to a wanton and heedless extent, was the havoc everywhere making with barbarous and indiscriminate zeal amongst the neighbouring timber. I looked about upon the nearest hills, many of which are already bare, denuded of every shrub; and sorrowed to think that even such others as yet rejoiced in their rich forest garb were but enjoying a brief respite from the axe and flame, being assuredly condemned and marked for destruction.

Every man here, in fact, is at work "for his own hand;" and as each proprietor is desirous to make the most he can of his acres, these burn and destroy on all sides, never feeling satisfied that their land is cleared whilst a single tree lives to tell where once the forest waved.

In noticing the well-fenced fields, the comfortable dwellings, substantial offices, and generally excellent condition of these farms, one can hardly credit the history of the settlement of this Western country, when it is considered that, amongst these well-cleared and well-cultivated fields, within the memory of living men, the Indian ranged and the uncouth buffalo herded, and that the first "white-man" born west of the Alleghany is still living: by the way, a whimsical anecdote relating to this gentleman is current in Pittsburg, and which I here relate as I myself received it.

At a public dinner, Mr. R— —, the person alluded to, being present, had his health proposed and cordially drunk, as "the first white man born west of the Alleghany." Now Mr. R— — happening to be very dark-complexioned, a waggish countryman of mine, who was seated next to him, could not help adding, with a sly air, having repeated the toast, "and not particularly white either."

"Why that's very true," returned the subject of this jest, with much good-humour; "and the reason assigned for the exceeding redness of my skin is in itself not a little illustrative of the late condition of our country, which is, in fact, the true subject of this toast.

"Shortly after my father had located his family on the Ohio, my mother was, whilst in the act of fetching water from the stream a little way outside the stockade within which our dwelling stood, startled by the near whoop of an Indian warrior, and, on raising her head, perceived close beside her a chief of the neighbouring tribe; she instantly fled like a deer; and, being young and active, gained the shelter of the stockade, within which, however, she fell exhausted, but was so preserved. Some time after I was ushered into life; and the darkness of my complexion was always referred to the chance of my mother having been thus frightened and followed by the young Indian."

"And a mighty natural mode of accounting for the same," replied Pat; adding with a most provoking air of simplicity, "but may I ask did you ever hear your poor mother say whether the Indian overtook her or not?"

The last night I acted here was made memorable by the jovial condition of a couple of the leading members of the corps dramatic, and as it chanced, diplomatic. The play was "The Irish Ambassador," and the first news I had of my principal colleague, his Excellency the representative of his most Catholic Majesty, was, that he had arrived, but in a state unfit for our purposed conference, having been rendered utterly incapable by an imprudent application of gin cock-tail, prescribed, as his Excellency himself assured me with tears in his eyes, as a sovereign remedy for a disorganized state of nerves, to which he was unhappily subject.

An excuse was made for the unavoidable absence of the Spanish minister, on the score of ill-health; and the indulgence of the meeting requested for one of the *attachés*, who had boldly undertaken to read the absent diplomatist's instructions at first sight. This point got over, we proceeded smoothly, as might be expected, until the period when his Highness the Grand-duke was required in person, when it became evident that, through sympathy or some cause less sentimental, the Prince too was royally rocky: availing himself of his rank however, he made shift to reach a chair, and, aided by the support it afforded, maintained his place at the conference.

Nothing could exceed the charitable forbearance with which this republican assemblage looked upon the fallen condition of royalty: whether they judged that it was no way out of character for a German sovereign and the possessor of a hock-cellar to be fuddled, or whether they considered that this was no bad specimen of royalty to exhibit to their children's contempt, I know not; but, happily, the signs of their displeasure fell lightly on his Highness, and our negotiation was at length, though lamely, brought to a conclusion.

On Tuesday the 8th of April, at eight o'clock P.M. I once more took my place in the Good Intent, to re-cross the Alleghanies; when, turning our backs upon the River of Beauty, we slowly traversed the dark streets of its sooty neighbour; for, strange to tell, although the material for gas lies at their doors in exhaustless abundance, and although they use a great quantity of coal-coke for manufacturing purposes, the streets remain as dark as the extremity of their deepest mine on a holiday.

This too, I found upon inquiry, was by the good citizens laid to the account of the "removal of the deposits." "It is enough," they say, "for one side to originate a question, however obviously excellent and desirable, to have the antagonist party oppose it, and make the measure a new watchword to try battle on."

I was informed of one spirited individual having offered to light the place with gas on his own risk, but, as a matter of course, he was immediately opposed by both parties; and so matters will rest, until the good people, wearied of being kept in the dark, open the eyes of their divided corporation; and in those days will the Pittsburgians cease to walk in darkness, and become what, considering the quantity of coal they possess, they are well entitled to be, — a gas-enlightened community.

It was raining when we departed, and continued to rain all night, as we weltered through the mud. Next morning, although a shower yet fell, I became so weary of the close confinement of the stage, that I alighted at the foot of Laurel Hill, and, putting stoutly forth, pushed on ahead of the heavy vehicle. The road winds about the steep side of the mountain, and from several points affords grand views of the forest, valleys, and humbler hills below. The early shrubs were already putting forth abundant leaf and blossom, for the winter had been singularly mild, and the quiet air was impregnated with sweetness.

When very near the top of the mountain, — for the ascent is full four miles, — I encountered one of those groups which appear in constant progress along the great Western line. The extent, however, of the present caravan made it peculiarly interesting. It consisted of five long, well-covered waggons, each drawn by eight or six horses, was attended by three or four led nags, and a number of dogs of various denominations. The occupants of the waggons were women and children: the faces of the chubby rogues were all crowded in front to look upon the passing stranger, with here and there a shining ebony phiz thrust between; the chief freight appeared to consist of household furniture and agricultural implements.

By the side of these waggons first rode four or five horsemen, well mounted, who might be the principals of the party, for they were men past the meridian of life; straggling in the rear, or scattered along the edges of the forest, walked eight or nine younger men, rough-and-ready-looking fellows, each with his rifle in his hand. Wild pigeons abounded along the cover-edge, and the sharp crack which every now and then rang through the thin air of morning told that the hunters were dealing upon them.

From the construction of the waggons, as well as because their owners evinced no inclination either to hold communion or exchange civilities with a passing wayfarer, which no Southern ever fails to do, I concluded this to be a party of New England men, who, abandoning their worn-out native fields, were pushing on for the "far West" with the lightness of heart consequent on the surety of reaping a brave harvest from a soil which withholds abundance from none who possess hearts and arms to task it.

With what apparent indifference, if not positive pleasure, do the people of this country quit their ancient homes, and wander forth in search of new ones, to be again, in turn, deserted, if not by themselves, by their restless and enterprising children! The Tartar habit of movement and frequent change, which is, I fancy, natural to man, finds in no country at the present age such inviting facilities as are offered in this, nor could a people be found who more fully enjoy them.

I looked upon this well-ordered, sober party with much pleasure; and as I stood upon the mountain top, and thence watched their downward track, I found my mind actively employed picturing their after progress and accompanying the line of their long travel. First, came their repose and rest, as in their plentifully-furnished flat they slowly drifted down the smooth course of the near Ohio; then, their after-journeying through the wilderness in search of a pleasant spot on which to rear their huts and make to themselves a home; now followed their early and long-enduring toil, accompanied perhaps by the sickness of their children and the pining of their women, whose sensibilities, more acute than those of men, ever revert in seasons of sadness to the far-off places their young days made pleasant; and, lastly, when, after years had passed away, and that their well-fenced fields were teeming with a plenteous harvest, I beheld their sons gathering together their inheritance and setting forth in search of another new country, within which they might resume the toil of their fathers. Man may change the scene of his labour, but the evil of his condition is not to be evaded; and alike, from the most fertile as from the most barren soil, by the sweat of his brow must his bread be won.

I here waited, sheltered by a rocky projection, until the stage came up. The continuance of the rain effectually prevented me from indulging in any more walks this day; the tedium of the journey however, whilst light lasted, was greatly relieved by the constant changes of mountain scenery, as viewed through an atmosphere now wildly clear and again thick and gloomy.

I found considerable amusement also in calculating the fair odds against our being pitched into some one of the many deep ravines along whose edge we were, when going down hill, whirled with startling speed. It was at these descents that the driver sought to pull up his lost time; and this he did with a recklessness of consequences that led me, after mature consideration, aided by the experience of much rough travel, to come to the following conclusion, — that, in crossing the Alleghany mountains, when the roads are rotten and slippery, the chances for and against a broken neck are so nearly equal that no sporting man, of any liberality, need desire to seek odds, should he feel inclined to make a bet before commencing the journey.

We at times encountered a string of waggons at some narrow sharp turn of the corkscrew path, and were whirled by them, with our off-wheels curiously circling the unguarded ledge of a precipice some four or five hundred feet deep, where a wheel-horse suddenly jibbing, or a leader shying or falling, would, in all human probability, have provided the wolves and bears with a banquet, and the journalists with a neat paragraph, headed, "Melancholy result of fast driving, attended with serious loss of valuable lives."

The practice is for the team to be put on a run the moment they gain the summit of a hill; and, if all things hold out, this is kept up until the bottom be reached: the horses are excellent, and rarely fail. On my asking the coachman, — by whom I rode as much as possible, — what he did in the event of a wheel-horse coming down in a steep pass, he replied, "Why, I keep driving ahead, and drag him along;" — an accident which he assured me had occurred more than once to himself when the roads were encrusted with ice and snow: the passengers at such times are placed in sleighs, which are perhaps less dangerous.

On the morning of Thursday we once more arrived at the frontier town of the low-lands of Pennsylvania, — Chambersburg; and here I quitted the

"Good Intent" line, transferring myself, servant, and kit to the Baltimore stage; and at three o'clock A.M. on Friday, I was set down, cold and weary and wet, at the door of Barnum's hotel. A few thundering knocks brought down the porter, and I was admitted within shelter of the well-warmed hall, with

"Och murther alive! Mr. Power, is it yerself, sir? Why, thin, you're welcome!"

And in five minutes after, I was in a comfortable chamber, and a blazing fire of wood rising under the inspection of my Irish porter. Anxious to conclude my journey, I desired him to rouse me in time for the eight o'clock stage to Washington, though, Heaven knows, I could have slept for twelve hours at the least; and so tumbled into bed whilst the man was yet regretting the "mighty haste" I was in.

By nine A.M. I was once more rolling off the pavement of the monumental city. But what a change was I experiencing! The sun shone cheerily, as though rejoicing in his conquest over the cold mass which had so long imprisoned him, and all around appeared to hail his presence with gladness: the wind was light and mild, the road, which I had seen two months before all but impassable, was now, by comparison, excellent, and the surrounding country, then so bleak and bare, was now rejoicing in the beauty of early spring. My fatigue was all forgotten, and I enjoyed my present ride as though I had not before known what a bone-breaking jolt was.

At two o'clock P.M. Washington once more lay beneath me, with the broad Potomac beyond, looking like a currentless transparent lake, clipped about by finely wooded irregular heights, and navigated by faëry barks. Such was the aspect this noble river presented, and just such the little fleet of fishing-boats scattered over its bosom, busied in pursuit of the shad and the herring, now coming into season.

To my great joy, I found my excellent friend, Captain B— —n, was still resident at Fuller's: my old rooms had that day been vacated for me, a few hours beheld me comfortably installed, and the rough-work of the past trip across the backbone of the continent only served to enhance my present enjoyments.

The Impressions left by my present residence I have already given in an embodied form to the reader. I shall therefore beg him to accompany me back to Philadelphia, and thence *viâ* Princeton to New York.

May 26th. — A lovely morning: landed from the Delaware steamer at Bordenton, and rode thence to Princeton on horseback, sixteen miles; passing two royal residences by the way, first, that of Joseph Buonaparte, and next a queer-looking, low, quadrangular building, inhabited by one of the sons of Joachim Murat, ex-king of Naples. On reaching the hospitable house to which I was bound at Princeton, I encountered the prince, paying a visit to my friend Mr. T— — n. He is a tall, robust-looking personage, very fat, and fond of race-horses; but has not, as I learn, been over-lucky on the turf.

One can never meet and contemplate any of these far-flung fragments of Napoleon's mighty empire without reverting with renewed interest to the founder of so much unlooked-for though brief greatness. Sheltered beneath his Titan ægis these new-made monarchs flourished, and ruffled it with the best of Europe's princes; until, grown vain of their fancied power, they deserted their shield and shelter, leaving it to abide unsustained the assault of an outraged world, and, whilst, forgetful of their origin, seeking to stand alone, were shattered into atoms by its fall!

What a capricious climate is this! On Tuesday the 27th of May, I rode from Princeton to Brunswick, on a day as sultry as a July afternoon ever is in England; the heavy showers of the 25th had so saturated the sandy soil that no particle of dust could float, and the verdure of wood and valley was bright and refreshing to look upon. Yet here we are in New York, on the 28th, with large fires burning within, a north-east wind blowing without, attended by alternate sleet and showers, with fog and every other atmospheric misery most grievous to humanity. This sample of "the spring-time of the year" continued tolerably regular until

June 6th. — This day the sun is fairly on duty again. Rode to the course on Long Island, the third day of the present meeting, to witness a race which had called up North and South to arms. Trifle — a little mare of Colonel Johnson's, the Nestor of the American turf — had come on from Virginia to be entered against Shark, the property of Captain Robert Stockton, about to run his first four-mile race, a horse much was expected from. Alice Grey, the mare which I had seen beaten easily by Trifle at the fall meeting, was the only other entry expected to be made good; so that the thing was considered as a match between the two horses first named. For the only time I saw ladies present in considerable numbers, and was sorry that the gallantry of my sporting friends had not provided them with a more becoming stand.

All was tiptoe expectation; but the anticipated sport fell through, owing to the ill condition of Shark. He was, from some cause or other, as completely out of order as an animal could well be, and ought properly to have been drawn. His spirited owner was, however, absent in Europe, and the friends who acted for him decided that he should do his best. Two heats, run in very indifferent time, decided the affair; and the little pet of the Southerners was once more hailed *victrix*.

FOOTNOTE:

[11] Racking is a sort of shuffling gait, easy, I believe, to both horse and rider, when both are broken to it, and much followed throughout the West.

THE HUDSON

With expectations highly raised, and for a long time cultivated and encouraged by an eager inspection of all the prints I could collect, and a perusal of glowing descriptions in both prose and poetry, did I at length wake on the morning which was to introduce me to the beauties of this vaunted river.

My first act was to rush to my window, and throw open shutter and sash. It was six o'clock, the sun was up, and the sky cloudless; thanking my lucky star, which had prevailed to my wish, I hurried through my toilet, and away to the foot of Courtland-street, from whose wharf the steamboat Champion was advertised to start at seven A.M. Punctual to the hour, we slipped our moorings, and in a minute were gallantly heading up the Hudson, breasting its current at the rate of fifteen miles per hour.

Hoboken and its Elysian fields were passed like lightning. Casting one backward glance, I perceived Jersey city floating indistinctly in the golden haze of morning; whilst the yet more distant heights of Long and Staten Islands, with the dividing Narrows, showed like two dusky clouds with a pathway of silver drawn between.

I was first struck by a near view of that singular range of cliff, the Palisadoes, so named from the face of the rock bearing a resemblance to a gigantic stockade rising from the bank of the river, along whose southern side it is continued for a considerable distance. Lee's Fort is pointed out; the Tappan Zee is next entered, upon whose border lies the scene of poor André's capture; and farther on is the point from which the traitor Arnold made his timely flight.

All these, with other memorable sites, are in turn pointed out, glanced at, and rapidly left behind. But I am free to confess historical associations were lost upon me; they awakened no sympathy in my mind; it was absorbed, filled, bewildered, in the admiration which each rapidly-opening point awakened, for never before this fair morning had such a succession of matchless river views passed before my delighted eyes.

"Write down your first impressions of scenery when fairly viewed, and your descriptions will at least have correctness to recommend them."

Somebody, I know, says something very like this; and I have hitherto quoted it as an axiom: but alas! what rule, however sage, but meets exceptions; for what man endowed with any ordinary share of devotion to Nature, and admiration of her handiwork, dare venture to set down his first impressions of this enchanting Hudson whilst the overwhelming influence it creates is yet dazzling his imagination! I say overwhelming, because such, in sober truth, was its first effect on me.

I was at times unable to venture the expression of all I felt even to myself: I sought to avoid the intelligent friends who accompanied me, and am not ashamed to add, that, albeit "unused to the melting mood," I here was affected almost to weakness. There might, perhaps, have been chords awakened that helped this fancy; but in no mood could an enthusiast of Nature, I think, feel otherwise than "rapt" when free for the first time to view, on such a day, such glorious magic pass before his sight; for, in our rapid flight, I could compare the effect of all I saw to glamour only.

The grape-covered steeps of the old Rhine, the mountain-enshrined lochs of our Hielans, with their clear blue waters, and the sweet valleys in which the little lakes of Killarney are set like gems, — all are lovely, and all of these appear to me to have contributed models for this masterpiece, each to be equalled, if not surpassed.

But I must check my pen, since disjointed eulogium will do little towards satisfying the curious or silencing the sceptical; and for description in reasonable detail, worthy the subject, only one hand in our age has existed endowed by nature to grapple with such a task, and that wizard hand lies mouldering now beneath the ruins of Dryburg Abbey!

Above West Point and the pass of the highlands the river expands grandly, forming the Bay of Newburg. The town of this name lies prettily spread along the face of a gently rising hill; and in a meadow at the foot of the town stands a venerable-looking stone-built house, rendered memorable from having been the residence of Washington when at this place; which, bordering upon his stronghold, the highlands, was often his head-quarters.

On the opposite side of the river, deep within the bight of the bay, lies the stirring town of Fish-kill, occupied by a colony originally from the island of Nantucket, who carry on from this place their adventurous trade of whale-fishing; and appear, indeed, to have roused their neighbours of Newburg and Hudson to imitate their enterprise; many ships, the joint property of the most spirited of the community, being now yearly fitted out in these places, and sent to hunt the sperm-whale about the world.

Above this bay the river again narrows, and the scenery upon its banks assumes a softer character: spacious meadows with well-cultivated lands stretch widely to the distant wooded heights; the bold outline of the highlands is drawn about the rear; and in front the loftier Catskills push their rugged peaks amongst the clouds.

From Poughkeepsie, numerous country seats occupy the now park-like banks of the river to the north, which, although lying from eighty to one hundred miles distant from New York, may be yet considered reasonably near; for six or seven hours brings the boat up, and in the course of the day there do not pass fewer than five or six. On this morning I met on board the Champion Messrs. W— —'s and L— —e, on their way to the summer abode of their families: they were landed at Hyde Park, ninety miles distant from New York, before one o'clock.

By half past five we were laid alongside the wharf of Albany, having steamed one hundred and sixty miles in ten hours and a half, including many stoppages of perhaps a couple of minutes each; and nothing can be more readily executed than one of these pulls-up, with the discharge or reception of luggage or passengers.

ALBANY

This is the capital of the powerful state of New York, and promises at no very distant period to wear an aspect worthy its rank. No situation was ever chosen better adapted to display; for the town is built over the face of a lofty and steep hill, which only affords space for one or two streets about its foot, and this is chiefly occupied by docks and the several canal basins connected with the Hudson.

The principal avenue, a regularly built, grandly proportioned street, with a railway running through its centre, climbs directly up the hill, and is terminated by a well-kept public square, or *Grande Place*, as the French would call it, about which the State House, City Hall, and other public buildings are ranged. These striking objects, from the nature of the ground, stand boldly out, and have all an appearance sufficiently imposing; whilst here are some buildings that possess strong claims to architectural beauty.

Nearly all the more important public offices have lofty and well-proportioned domes; and these being uniformly covered with tin or other bright metal, impart a gay and picturesque effect to the general mass; and, indeed, the city, viewed from a little distance, with all these cupolas and towering domes reflected in the setting sun, assumes quite an Oriental appearance: one is immediately reminded of the mosque and minaret of some Turkish capital: the fine marble too used in the construction of all public buildings, and indeed of many private ones, increases the effect which they derive from their style and from the bold eminence they occupy.

Albany was long almost exclusively Dutch, and may be said up to this time to have hardly kept pace with the rapid advance of the country generally: it must have marvelled at the spread of the numerous flourishing towns which have grown up around within a few years, and which threatened to eclipse, if not extinguish it wholly. A movement, however, has of late taken place: the inhabitants have awoke, new colonists have superseded the family from Sleepy-hollow, or imparted to them a share of their energy; and Albany begins to assert her claims on the productive country by which she is backed, and to turn into her own channel a portion of its commerce. Building is everywhere going forward; land has doubled and trebled in value; improvements are in steady progress; and, should the present prosperous course of things meet with no untoward check to paralyse the industry of the people, Albany will in a few years assume an importance more profitable to its citizens than the empty honour it derives from being styled the capital of the State.

There are several excellent inns here: one kept by an Englishman, a Mr. Thomas, in which I dined once or twice with friends, and which bears a high reputation; another, wherein I always resided on my several visits here, kept by Mr. Crutenden; and if henceforward any stranger who relishes good fare, loves Shakspeare, and would choose to make the acquaintance of a Transatlantic Falstaff, passes through Albany without calling at the Eagle, and cracking a bottle with "mine host," he will have missed one of those days he would not have failed to mark with a white stone.

Soberly, I do not remember ever to have met with a face and figure which, were I a painter, I would so readily adopt for a *beau-idéal* of the profligate son of mirth and mischief as those of mine host o' th' Eagle. He has a fellow feeling too with "lean Jack," is as well read in Shakspeare as most good men, quotes him fluently and happily, honours and loves him as he should be loved and honoured, and in himself possesses much of the humour, much of the native wit, but not a single trait of the less admirable portions of the fat knight's character.

Indebted to Mr. Crutenden for many pleasant hours, I will offer no excuse for making this indifferent sketch of him here, since it in no way trenches upon the rule I hold sacred of eschewing comment on private persons, or details of social intercourse, where indeed, men speak oftener from the heart than from the head. Mr. C. I look upon as a public character, and thus I am enabled to say how much I esteem him. Should he be wroth, I vow, if I ever should visit Albany again, never to make one at the "Feast of Shells." On the contrary, I'll fly the Eagle; forswear "the villanous company" of mine host; I'll disclaim him, renounce him, "and d — n me if ever I call him Jack again."

The theatre here is a handsome building, and well adapted to the purpose for which it was designed; but is, I believe, worse supported than any other on this continent. I had been advised not to visit the city professionally; but being strongly solicited by the worthy manager, "mischief lay in my way, and I found it."

I feel compelled in honesty to state the facts of this trip, though no way flattering to my powers of attraction: however, if there be anything unpleasant to relate, I ever find it better to tell of oneself, than leave it to the charity of good-natured friends. The only disagreement I ever had with an audience, in fact, occurred here, and roundly, thus it happened.

On the evening when I was advertised to make my *début* to an Albany audience, I at my usual hour walked to the house, dressed, and was ready; but when, half an hour after the time of beginning, I went on to the stage, there were not ten persons in the house. The stage-director and myself now held a consultation on the unpromising aspect of our affairs. He ascribed the unusually deserted condition of the *salle* to the sultry and threatening state of the atmosphere, which had deterred the neighbouring towns of Troy and Waterford from furnishing their quota,—those indeed being his chief dependencies. I was opposed, on policy, to throwing away our ammunition so unprofitably; and so after due deliberation, the manager agreed to state to the few persons in front, that "with their permission" the performances intended for this night would be postponed until the evening after the next following; as, in consequence of the exceeding smallness of the audience, it was to be feared the play would prove dull to them, as it must be irksome to the actors.

Nothing could be received with better feeling on the part of the persons assembled; not a breath of disapprobation was heard. They instantly went away; but soon after I reached home, I found, by the report of one or two gentlemen who had since been at the theatre seeking admittance, that a considerable excitement prevailed, and that at the public bars of the neighbourhood the affair was detailed in a way likely to produce unpleasant effects on my first appearance.

The appointed night came, the house was filled with men, and everything foreboded a violent outbreak; the manager appeared terrified out of his wits; but, as far as I can judge, behaved with infinite honesty; disavowed the truth of the imputations connected with the dismissal, and which it was sought to fasten upon me; and affirmed that he was fully prepared to place the facts simply before the audience, in the event of my suffering any interruption.

It was now found that an actor or two needed in the piece were absent. These worthies, the chief agitators in this affair, were, in fact, in front of the house to assist in the expected assault upon a stranger and one of their own profession. On this being explained to the manager, he said he was aware of it, and had threatened to discharge the individuals; but relying upon the affair terminating in my discomfiture, they did not fear being sustained by the same intelligence which they now directed against me.

On my appearance the din was mighty deafening; the volunteer champions of the public had come well prepared, and every invention for making the voice of humanity bestial was present and in full use. The boxes I observed to be occupied by well-dressed men, who generally either remained neutral, or by signs sought that I should be heard. This, however, was out of the question; and after long and patient abiding, "for patience is the badge of all our tribe," I made my bow and retired, when the manager, who had on the night in question dismissed the house, made his bow, and, after silence was obtained, begged that the audience would give me a hearing, assuring them on his own knowledge that I had not contemplated insulting them.

I again came forward, and after some time was permitted to say that I could in no way account for a simple matter of business being so misrepresented as to occasion this violent exhibition of their anger; that, before the audience in question was dismissed, its permission had been obtained; that, had I really contemplated insult, it is hardly probable I should wait two days to encounter the anger of those I had sought to offend. I farther said, that on the common principle which they professed, I was entitled to a hearing, since the sense of the majority was evidently with me; and that, if the disorder continued, I should, for the sake of that respectable majority, sincerely regret this, since the character of their city for justice and hospitality would be more impeached than my prospects be injured.

After this the row was resumed with added fierceness: not a word of either play or farce was heard; but I persisted in going through with the performance, being determined not to dismiss a second time.

At the fall of the curtain I begged the manager would not again announce me; as although, for the sake of the many who I could see were opposed to this misjudged outrage, I had gone through the business once, I could not again subject them to the annoyance of such a collision, or myself to continued insult.

I was, however, happily induced to change this determination at the request of many gentlemen of the place, who assured me that the whole thing arose from stories most industriously circulated by one or two ill-conditioned actors, backed by inflammatory handbills and a scurrilous print.

Out of this affair, which threatened me serious annoyance, I really gathered a new proof of the kindness of the people of this country, for I found persons on all sides interesting themselves for me, although I entered the place without an acquaintance; and, had I not stood in need of help, so in all probability should I have quitted it: but in this hour of annoyance, men not of theatrical habits put themselves actively forward to shield a calumniated stranger from insult or injury; in consequence of this interposition, on my next appearance, nothing could be more orderly than the conduct of the audience.

I concluded my engagement, which was only for four nights, and left the theatre with a promise to return, which pledge, at some inconvenience, I redeemed; and I have never been able to regret a momentary vexation which obtained for me many friends, and made known to me the sterling good feeling existing in Albany, of which I might otherwise have remained ignorant.

The rides about Albany are numerous, the roads the best in the country; and the little city of Troy, with its Mount Ida, worthy even the celestial visitants who honoured its less beautiful predecessor with their presence. Higher up lies Waterford, a thriving place, also charmingly situated; and, near this, the Fall of the Cohoos, one of the finest natural objects in the country. Indeed, a morning's ride in this direction offers a succession of views that can nowhere be surpassed, and which I do not remember to have often seen equalled.

Approaching Albany from the west, and looking across the Hudson over the finely-wooded slopes and verdant meadows on which it fronts, it appears a city bordered by an ornamental park; to the south tower the cloud-capped Catskills; on the north are the blue mountains of Vermont; and about the verge of the landscape on all sides runs a line of boldly undulating hills, whose rugged outline forms no inappropriate framing to this very beautiful picture.

It had been my intention from Albany to proceed directly for Niagara, and thence returning to Buffalo, join a steam-boat, which was advertised to make the tour of the great lakes, Superior and Erie, touching at Detroit and one or two other points of interest, then after visiting the new entrepôt for the territory of Michigan, Chicago, was to return with her passengers to Buffalo; the trip being one of pastime, and calculated to occupy about twenty days.

This plan was, however, frustrated, through an application being made from the Polish committee of Philadelphia that I should act a night for the benefit of the fund raised for these exiles for liberty: back, therefore, I hurried to Philadelphia; arrived in the morning, acted at night, with the thermometer at ninety-seven, and was off again for New York by the mail-boat next day.

I was anxious to get away west, to make the most of my holidays, and, being Sunday, this mail was the only public conveyance permitted through the State of Jersey. I however caution all thin-skinned travellers against using it any time between the first day of June and the last of October; for to run the gauntlet at night through the legions of musquitoes quartered between the Delaware and the Raritan is no laughing matter, as I found to my cost.

The worst of this journey was, that, on arriving by the railroad car at Amboy, which we did at midnight, we were compelled to wait unhoused here until three or four in the morning, the steamer not departing until that hour for New York. The example those insatiable vermin made of me with four hours' leisure in which to work their wicked will, I even now sweat to think on; one of my eyes was hermetically sealed up, and my upper lip would have matched that of any Guinea negro, whilst my hands were so swollen that I could not close them without pain and difficulty: in short, as Roque says, there was not "a sounder-bitten bully in all Andalusia."

Halting for one day at New York, I proceeded by the morning boat to West-point with the intention of resting here a few days: but not having taken the precaution of writing on to secure a chamber, I was indifferently provided for; this charming spot only possessing one hotel, which is a concession made by government to the public, as it is properly only a military post, and the seat of the national Military College.

Much has been said and sung, well and ill, of the beauty of the place, but certainly not one word too much, for language can hardly convey any just notion of the variety of attributes Nature has laid under contribution, and here combined, for the embellishment of this most perfect spot.

In the cool hour of twilight I strolled a little way up the western hill, and thence looked back upon the hotel and the lines of tents beyond, for at this season the cadets were in camp; excepting the hum of myriads of busy insects, not a sound was to be heard; the fire-fly was filling the lower grounds with his dazzling light, and seemed the only thing that lived or moved there; when suddenly the sharp roll of a drum, followed by a bugle-call, broke in on this tranquillity, and disenchanted the scene which I had just decided must have been designed by Nature as a temple to Solitude.

The next morning I quitted West-point, and in the afternoon landed once again in Albany, where I took a couple of days' repose, and employed myself in making inquiries and settling my route to Niagara, the idea of visiting which wonder became all-absorbing; the long cherished desire was about to be gratified, the dream of years to be realized. All obstacles of business being removed, I grew restless and impatient of further delay; I had, however, pledged myself to make a visit by the way, and was only waiting for a couple of friends who were to be my travelling companions.

JOURNEY TO COOPER'S TOWN

OTSEGO LAKE

At three o'clock A.M. on a cloudy and somewhat chilly morning, left the door of the Eagle in a very comfortable extra coach, which was chartered to convey a freight of four persons to the mansion of Mr. C— —e, lying upon Otsego Lake, distant from Albany some sixty miles.

My companions were Mr. H— —e, whom I had with me at starting, and Mr. I. V. B— —n, for whom we had agreed to halt at his hotel on the top of the State House hill, and a long halt we had of it; for, having no great confidence in our punctuality, he had very wisely, as far as his own comfort was concerned, left orders to be called whenever we should appear: and not a moment earlier was he in the least danger of being roused, for we had to awaken one of the Irish waiters before he could be come at; a task of no small difficulty. After some half-hour's delay at the top of the hill, we set forward.

Mem. — In future, always arrange on all early expeditions to have my quarters beat up last.

Although the morning broke gloomily, the sun rose brave and bright, and managed throughout the day to keep the field against both wind and cloud, that sought to overcast him. For the most part, this line of country is very tame, and offers little to compensate for the bad road leading through it. The amusement, therefore, which a series of fine landscapes affords the traveller not being found here, we had to draw upon our own personal resources to banish weariness; happily these were not wanting: the youngest of my friends was the son of a leading Whig, or Oppositionist, and newly inoculated with the right degree of political fervour becoming the time and his age; the senior was a Tory, or of the Government party, possessed of much natural humour, and having a thorough knowledge of the people.

Previous to starting, the young politician was bold in his assertion that in Schoharie county, — that through which our route lay, — the Whig interest was in the ascendant; this assertion his better instructed opponent as stoutly contradicted, insisting on the contrary, that Jacksonism was the political creed cherished as orthodox amongst the country people.

The mode of coming at the true state of the parties was simple enough; we had only, whilst halting to change horses or bait, to touch upon the absorbing topic of the day, and the village loungers, landlord, bar-keeper, and guests, might have been placed upon a canvassing roll without a chance of error, so decidedly did they make "their love known."

I soon discovered that the "ould Gineral" had a hollow thing of it on this line of march, as, indeed, I have uniformly observed to be the case in all the agricultural districts; and although it may be argued that the confidence of these sons of the soil may neither be wisely nor well placed, it must, I conceive, be on all hands admitted that it is at least the result of honest conviction; for, if a stranger may be permitted to judge, I should say, a more virtuous and right-meaning class does not exist than the agriculturists generally of these States; indeed it appears clear to me that it is to this great body of truly independent electors the political seer must turn when he would desire fairly to calculate the probable changes likely to be worked out in this vast region. They are the owners of the land which their votes govern; they are invulnerable to the anarchist and the mad agrarian; they are observant and intelligent; and although liable, as are all men, to be for a time hoodwinked, or led astray, by interested brawlers, only let the veil be once lifted, and a glimpse afforded which shall inform them that their property or the country's freedom are endangered, and they will be found a rampart behind which all true patriots, the lovers of order and country, may rally, and which they may hold impregnable against the furious assault of the leveller, or the insidious sap of the disguised despot.

But enough of this: *chacun à son métier*; yet here I am betrayed into a homily where I only contemplated a jest. The truth is, my allusion to this topic at all arose from the vivid recollection I still have of the great fun I derived from this canvassing of my companions in support of their opinions previously expressed.

At each new stopping-place, my Whig friend would jump out with eager anticipations that here his majority would be made too palpable for denial; after him would quickly stride his long-legged, long-headed rival; and in a moment both were hard at it with the inmates of the house.

At places where a weak minority gave signs of hardihood, I usually adopted their side in argument; and, as I was fully *au fait* to all the slang of party at least, it became my business in promotion of fun, to fan the flame, which in one instance had nearly ended in getting myself and my allies turned out of an honest Jacksonian's house, who swore no such libellous Whigs should drink at his bar. In fact, my ears being kept on strict duty during our noisy debates, in order to determine the exact moment for prudently backing out, I, in this case, concluded it wise to anticipate the expulsion which was decreed by a large majority, having caught certain ominous disjointed words, which, by the aid of a copulative conjunction or two, would have read, "Take 'em down and duck them in the river."

About two o'clock we reached the neat little village called Cherry Valley, and, in a couple of hours after, entered upon the well-kept domain of Mr. C— —e. The view of the lake and mansion, as it is approached from the main road, is exceedingly good; and, when the spirited proprietor's tasteful designs shall be completed, will have no equal in this country.

Our reception at Hyde-hall was as hospitable as heart could wish. It was the birthday of our host's son; and we found a large party assembled, amongst whom were three or four remarkably handsome women.

Otsego, or, as it is commonly called, Cooper's-Town Lake, has been best described by the novelist of that name, in, I think, his admirable American book, "The Last of the Mohicans." He looked upon it with the eye of a poet and the love of a son; for he was born and passed his boyhood upon its banks, and in the pretty town reflected in its clear water the name of his father is perpetuated. The son has founded his name upon a yet surer basis: towns may fall as they have risen, and their founders be forgotten; but the pleasure we derive from genius enshrines its possessor within our hearts, and transmits his name to be a household word amongst our children. Ages may pass away, and empires may flourish and may fade, but the hand of a Cicero will ever be found to pluck the weeds from the tomb of an Archimedes!

This mansion, at which I continued for three or four days, is built upon a natural terrace, part of a fine hill that juts out into the lake, and creates a little bay that laves its south side, and forms a safe harbour for the boats of the family, in one of which I remember to have had the pleasure of making an exploring cruise under the infliction of as pitiless a shower as ever a party of fair voyagers was pelted by.

On either hand range the bold finely-timbered hills by which the lake is bordered, until, gradually rounding at the southern extremity, it affords space for one of the neatest little towns I ever visited, and whose white buildings and glittering vanes give a charming termination to the view from Hyde, from which it is distant some eight or nine miles; but the character of the vista, and there being only water between, makes it look nearer by half this space.

On Monday, June 30th, after abiding three cold, wet days, quitted Mr. C— —e's family, drove along the bank of the lake to Cooper's Town, and thence took stage for Utica, accompanied by my young Whig companion, who now had the field of politics to himself; for our Tory friend had turned upon his steps for Albany.

We did not reach Utica till late in the afternoon, the distance being forty miles, and our rate of going not exceeding six miles per hour: we made no halt here, but, hiring a carriage, immediately pushed for the Retreat at Trenton Falls, which we did not arrive at until after ten o'clock P.M. The people, however, were yet up, and with much civility set to work to provide us with a broiled chicken and a fresh trout, over which we quickly forgot a very rough day's ride.

TRENTON FALLS

On awaking here in the morning, I rejoiced to hail the beams of a fine warm sun breaking into my little chamber; it had been a stranger for the last few days; and the weather, after having been prematurely hot, had at once jumped back into March, and become wet, boisterous, and cold to a most provoking degree.

After an early breakfast we set out, with the din of the waters sounding an alarum in our ears, and directing our steps.

Immediately on quitting the hall of the Retreat, we entered upon a grove of fine trees overhanging the bed of the torrent, and thence descended by several flights of ladders planted *en échelon*, for some hundred and sixty feet, until we at last stood on a level with the swift dark stream, and, looking upwards, beheld the forest high overhead bending from either side, with a narrow strip of clear blue sky drawn between. The first fall was visible about five hundred yards to our left; its waters tumbling, as it seemed, over the tops of the intervening trees, to whose foliage the late heavy rains had restored the freshness of early spring.

Looking about from this first point, I could have readily imagined myself standing upon the floor timbers of a first-rate ship buried in a wooded ravine, so evenly were the sides of the rock scooped out; and this impression was assisted by narrow layers of different strata, which ran in slightly curved lines placed at equal distances, giving the effect of the ship's sheer and planking, whilst through her entrance or cloven bow the white foam rushed.

Walking upward, along a narrow strand of bare rock, with the forest pressing on you, as, bent almost double in some places, you stoop beneath the overhanging cliff on which it grows; then for a time closely shouldering the precipice, walk upon a ledge or projecting shelf of from one to three feet wide, the current below boiling and whirling along the while, of dazzling brilliance; I at one moment counted five rainbow arches, perfect and imperfect. What a succession of "Maidens of the Mist" might a lover of romance conjure up from these vexed waters on a fine moonlight night!

Proceeding onwards, you, on quitting this point, descend once more into the river's bed; and here the resistless power of the torrent when at its full is made manifest by the ruin which on all sides marks its headlong course. Trees of the largest growth lie twenty feet above its ordinary level; some with their roots uppermost, others sustained athwart the arms of their sturdier fellows, here decay and rot amidst their living leaves.

Passing the second fall, we mounted a few steps to a resting-place, named the "Rural Retreat;" and here, from a little box perched on the point of a huge rock which abuts right upon the great abyss, we had a scene before us and about us of great wildness and grandeur; whilst high over all waved the original forest, contemporary with the continent itself, — trees beneath whose shade the sachems of the warlike Mohawks had feasted and legislated.

The last fall lies about a quarter of a mile above this point; and immediately below is a dangerous pass, where the vast mass of falling water is hurled in its course against a deeply-serrated rock, over which rock the curious visitor is obliged to tread, making a step across an angle formed by the boiling whirlpool, clinging to a stout chain, and closely shouldering the rock; the river passing below, with a motion anything but composing for a nervous man to cast a sidelong glance upon. At all points of peril, however, lines of chain are securely riveted, affording a dependable holdfast; which after rains is indeed absolutely necessary, where a single *faux pas* would be fatal.

A little to our left the water of the river was collected into a basin of about one hundred yards' diameter; overflowing which, it found a narrow outlet between two rocks, and thence precipitating itself in a flood of the colour of amber, was bridged by rainbows dazzling to look upon, although a person of ordinary nerve has nothing to encounter really dangerous; yet, at this point, a very few years back, an accident of a fatal nature did occur, and under circumstances which give to it a melancholy interest and will ever keep it as a legend of the place.

A family party, consisting of father, mother, son, two daughters, and the betrothed of one of the latter, a fine girl of seventeen, arrived in company at the "Retreat," where the parents decided upon remaining whilst the rest of the company explored the more adventurous route succeeding.

On went the young people in high glee, — the last fall was at length achieved; here, after standing for a moment upon the table rock against which the strength of the fall bursts, one by one the attentive lover handed the merry girls up the dizzy step: he turned to offer to his young betrothed the last and dearest act of gallantry, but the rock was naked; the object of his care, who but the instant before smiled in his face, was here no longer.

Not a soul of the party had witnessed any movement of their vanished companion. Absorbed by the scene, they were struggling onward beneath the overhanging cliff, when the arrival of the distracted lover, his mad gesticulations and horror-stricken looks, recalled them to hear his loss and aid his search.

For a few minutes the hope that she had turned back, or concealed herself to cause a false alarm, held the worst conclusion at bay: but, on reaching a little cove a few yards lower down, this hope was crushed, and conviction of her fate placed before them; for here, quietly floating on the smooth eddy, lay a gaily-trimmed bonnet. It was at once recognised: the lover sprang into the river, snatched it up, and found within its hollow the comb of her they sought.

She had, in truth, slipped from off that giddy ledge, and, sinking at once below the influence of the whirlpool, lay calmly upon its rocky bed.

Next day, after much perseverance, the body was found, and rescued from beneath the very point off which she must have fallen; not a feature was discomposed, as it is said, or a garment ruffled: to use the words of my informant, who for thirty years has listened to the roar of this torrent, "She looked just as though she had lain down to sleep in the rain, where I saw her, stretched out upon the ledge here." The details of this story were given to me with added interest by the narrator, from the circumstance that, the very day previous, two of the party alluded to had revisited the spot for the first time since the chance which made it to them so memorable.

Our guide, I believe, related the particulars of one or two other accidents; but after this I had ears for no more. That the young and happy maid should in one moment be snatched from a world to her so bright and beautiful, and engulphed down deep in that cold pool, her brothers in her sight, her lover by her side, yet no hand held forth to save her, was a picture too sorrowful to be shifted for any other. I could not indeed forget it during the remainder of the day, and the rush of the water no longer roused me to exertion. From this spot we turned, and retraced our steps to the hotel.

Our next morning was devoted to an excursion down the stream, to a spot where a saw-mill was at work and a strong rude bridge in progress; we crossed upon it, unfinished as it was, and in a meadow upon the west side, Herkimer county, I believe, saw two youngsters herding a couple of fine cows. I called them to me, but the girl, at the sight of my companion and myself, ran off like a lapwing; the boy, a redheaded chubby rogue, about twelve years of age, was however soon persuaded to approach. When we questioned as to where his mammy lived, he pointed over the meadow to a thicket from out of which a little column of light smoke was rising; but in reply to one or two other queries, after a scratch or two at his head, our little squire boldly bolted out "No English!"

And sure enough not another word could we coax out of him: he was, however, quite willing and able to make it up in good Irish, and much did I regret not being able to have a "goster" with him. From one of the carpenters at work on the bridge I learned that the mother spoke only Irish, but that she managed her dairy and farm admirably; and that the father, who was just able, as they expressed it, "to tell what he wanted," worked at the mill, and got "a heap o' money jobbin' about at one thing or t'other."

These poor people had been in this neighbourhood about three years: they had arrived here destitute, friendless, ignorant even of the language of the country; but they were industrious and persevering, and at this time may have been said to possess independence; for they were owners of sixty acres of excellent land, a cow or two, a few sheep, with poultry, pigs, and other evidences of pastoral wealth. The situation of their little cottage might be envied by many a wealthy builder in search of a beautiful site, and the country about them is perfectly healthy.

We this day met at the hotel a new arrival or two, and sat down in company to a very neat dinner: the trout here is excellent, and the butter the best out of Philadelphia.

On the 2nd of July we left this comfortable house; and it was not without reluctance I so soon bade farewell to the Falls of Trenton, which, beautiful in themselves, are surrounded by a country possessing so much attraction that I felt a strong desire to become more intimate with it.

My companion, Mr. H— —, having met with a couple of friends here who were journeying our way, it was proposed that we should join company as far as Niagara, taking to our own use an extra. This we readily procured at Utica; the postmaster agreeing to forward the party to Buffalo by a route we laid down, for the sum of seventy-five dollars, the distance being nearly two hundred miles. We were by our agreement entitled to halt as long as we chose at any place on our route, and, moreover, were to be driven at the rate of seven miles per hour at the least.

All these points being duly arranged, we left the thriving city of Utica in as heavy a storm of rain as could well fall, the weather having once more become cold and cheerless: a more dismal night I never would desire to encounter. The rate of travelling soon fell below the minimum of our stipulated pace: to do the drivers justice, this was owing to no fault of theirs, but the roads were cut into gullies broad and deep, and the tumbling we got would have been of vast service to a dyspeptic subject. The state of the weather was the more to be regretted as we were passing through some of the best cultivated farms in this State; and, notwithstanding the disadvantageous nature of the medium through which I saw the land, this character appeared to me well deserved.

The farmhouses were very numerous, generally built of good brick, and putting forth strong claims on admiration in the shape of various ornamental flourishes; an ambition which distinguishes the rural architecture indeed of all this State, giving evidence of the ease and growing wealth, if not of the purest taste, existing amongst the proprietary.

Syracuse we passed through in the middle of the storm and the darkness of night; and about six A.M. were safely landed under the ample portico of the hotel at Auburn, celebrated for its prison, regulated upon what is called the "silent system."

Whilst my companions were making toilet I set forth to visit this penal abode, the character of which is made sufficiently evident as you approach the lofty walls that encompass so much of misery and guilt. At regular distances upon these battlements I perceived sentry-boxes, with men keeping watch, musket in hand.

A small sum is here paid for admittance. On my arrival at the lodge, I was informed that the prisoners were at breakfast, during which time visitors were prohibited: I therefore had to wait some minutes in this place; and, except the occasional fall of a heavy bolt, did not hear a sound; the very turnkeys seemed infected by the system which it was their duty to enforce, and they moved in and out in silence, or spoke in monosyllables hardly above a whisper.

Following the gaoler, I was passed within the square at the very moment when the prisoners were moving out from their breakfast-hall on the way to renew their several labours; and the sight was to me one of sickening melancholy.

They were marched from the building in squads, using what is called the "lock-step," and were jammed together as close as they could possibly tread: they moved in quick-time, and fell out singly, or in pairs, as they arrived at the point nearest to the scene of their employment.

I observed that, notwithstanding the regularity of labour, and the unquestionably wholesome diet provided here, the faces of the individuals composing these ruffian squads were uniformly pale and haggard; yet, on saying so much to my guide, I was assured that disease is comparatively rare amongst them, and that many who enter here with broken constitutions recover their bodily vigour and are made whole men again.

The cleanliness of this prison-house, the convenient distribution of its various offices, and, indeed, the evident excellence of its general arrangement, must strike every stranger with admiration, and doubtless presented to the commissioners of inquiry recently appointed from England many hints worthy of adoption for home use. Of the merits of the system itself it does not become me to speak; it has been well considered by wise and worthy men, who continue to watch over its working with a philanthropic spirit; but I confess that the impressions I received from my visits to these prisons were anything but in its favour.

At eight A.M. we quitted Auburn, the weather clear and mild: we crossed the head-water of the Seneca Lake upon a well-built bridge, a mile and a quarter in length, and, with this exception, observed no point of interest until we approached the Lake of Geneva.

This is one of the lions of this route, and in no way disappointed our raised expectations. Gradually winding about the eastern bend of the lake, the road affords to the traveller a continuous view of the location of the little city; and certainly nothing was ever more happily chosen than the fine hill over whose side it is built, its streets rising gradually from the edge of the clear water in which they are reflected.

Entering the main street, I observed that the stores were large and substantially built; there was a great bustle, and an air of business too, about most of them, which it was pleasant to look upon. The hotel at which we drew up was a large, well-appointed house: the landlord, finding that we were strangers, civilly invited us to ascend to the gallery upon the roof; and certainly the view it afforded was one I should have been sorry to miss.

The environs appear to possess an unusual number of tasteful villas; on all sides these might be distinguished, giving and receiving adornment from the situation. The lake itself looked like a huge mirror; and from its polished surface was clearly reflected every turn of its shores, and each cloud that floated over it. Its characteristics are softness and repose; of a certainty it must have been a feminine spirit that presided at the creation of this spot, for its features are all of gentleness and beauty.

At Canandaigua we stopped to dine at a very large, and, I should imagine, good hotel: the landlord was exceedingly obliging. The regular dinner of the house was long past, but he managed to get us a very tolerable meal; and what was wanting in this he made up by giving us an excellent bottle of wine.

In the environs of this place, as at Geneva, I observed a number of well-built and neatly-appointed villas; indeed, this sort of country residence is better kept, and built in better taste, in this western country than I have elsewhere observed in the States.

About nine P.M. we arrived at Avon Springs; and here we called a halt for the night, not a little pleased with the prospect of a comfortable bed, which the appearance of the inn gave promise of.

This place is a good deal frequented of late years by invalids, its mineral waters being found of great service in dyspepsia, — the most crying complaint of the country next to the removal of the deposits, and certainly more universal.

I here found my excellent friend R— — d, who, together with his young bride, had accompanied his father-in-law, who was desirous of testing the salubrity of these springs. He described the surrounding country as beautiful, and the little place itself as agreeable enough for a short sojourn.

The fourth of July, the anniversary of American Independence, was to be duly celebrated by a ball, for which my friend had received an invite printed upon the back of the nine of hearts; a medium now obsolete in England, but conserved here in its integrity.

A less amusing remembrancer of the glorious event began to parade the avenue at an early hour in the shape of a patriotic drummer, having an instrument, to judge by its sound, coeval with the first fight for that freedom it was beaten to celebrate. If anything could have kept me awake, this cracked drum would; and, in truth, I had my fears, when, on entering my room, I heard my hero ruffing it away immediately in front of the window; but they were groundless apprehensions, though his efforts were varied and unceasing, for I undressed to the tune of the "Grenadiers' March," stepped into bed to the "Reveille," and dropped fast asleep to the first part of "Yankee Doodle!"

At six A.M. of the 4th we were once more in motion; the vapours of night were yet hanging thick and low; but through the dense atmosphere, as we rolled down the avenue, I heard the indefatigable functionary, who composed the military band of Avon, determinately beating "Hail Columbia!"

At the village of Caledonia we found that a ball was afoot, and we pushed on eagerly for Buffalo, anticipating, from the importance of the place and the wealth of its citizens, something in the way of display worthy of their loyalty and of the occasion.

Between Le Roy, a town of remarkable neatness, and Batavia, I encountered my first sample of a corduroy-road, or, as it is sometimes facetiously termed, a Canadian railway.

Our driver, a merry fellow, called out that we must look out "not to get mixed up of a heap," and rattled at it. I did not require much experience to decide that travelling over a road of corduroy was by no means going on velvet; but the effect was not so bad as I had expected to prove it: by holding fast, one could keep one's seat tolerably well, without much fear of dislocation; but I would strongly recommend any man having loose teeth, to walk over this stage, unless he desires to have them shaken out of his head.

From Batavia the road is execrable, and the country without a feature to interest or amuse, uncultivated, wild, and dismal. It was about half an hour before sunset when we entered Buffalo, the City of the Lakes, the entrepôt for these inland oceans.

BUFFALO

America is, perhaps, in our day, the only country wherein these infant capitals, these embryo cities, may be seen, and their growth noted, as they are gradually developed before living eyes.

A very few years back, this frontier, now so populous and thriving, was only known as "the Wilderness;" and upon the edge of this, washed by the waters of Lake Erie, has Buffalo sprung up. The great source of that gratification which is felt on a near view of this, and other places of similar origin, is to be found in the feeling that they derive their being from the prosperous industry of our fellow-men, and that in their increase we behold its happy continuance. They are the vouchers which America may fairly produce to show that the fruition of liberty has been with her productive of increased energy and spreading enterprise.

These places have not, like St. Petersburg, been raised up in obedience to the policy or the caprice of a despot; the work of bondsmen, founded amidst pestilence, and cemented with blood and tears. The unfinished palace of the half-savage prince already the tomb of hundreds of its miserable builders; a city of marble founded upon a marsh.

Here, it is true, was a wonder having no parallel, of which the living of the last century might have observed the progress,—one may add, the completion, as, should its lord so will, the present generation may look upon its abandonment and depopulation;—but the cause of the existence of St. Petersburg calls up no generous sympathy with its progress, because we know that the labour was constrained; and from its story, when fairly told, we rise, not with pride in the power of our kind, which had overcome so many obstacles, but with pity for the suffering and debasement of humanity constrained to such exertion. On the contrary, these yet humble cities of America, so humble as sometimes to draw from the far-travelled a sneer upon the application of the word, are surrounded by a healthful, moral atmosphere: their infancy is vigorous, giving promise of a long endurance and ultimate greatness, only to be limited by the will of the King of kings.

From the roof of the Eagle, a very large hotel, I took a general view of the wide-spread frame of Buffalo, whose many as yet barely definable streets are in the keeping of houses so thinly scattered, that they reminded me of lines of sentries placed to denote occupation. I traced the course of the great Erie canal from the Niagara river to the lake, whose busy harbour was filled with steamers, schooners, and other trading craft.

After sunset we descended from our lofty observatory, and followed the line of the main street, witnessing the rejoicings called forth by this anniversary of American Independence. The feeling of the community at large could only be guessed at, since it made no sign; but if the body politic of Buffalo might be considered fairly represented by some hundred or so of active urchins who were congregated in a square near the centre of the main street, nothing could be more ardent than this city's gratitude, for these delegates beat drums, blew fifes, fired crackers, and huzzaed until the welkin rang with their shrill small yells. We found, upon inquiry, that there was no ball, dinner, or other public demonstration; the reason was ascribed to the extreme violence of party politics, which at this period completely divided the community, and were carried out to an extent without precedent in their brief annals.

The street was chiefly occupied by a number of Indians of the Seneca tribe, dressed in a costume part native and part European: these holiday-keepers lounged lazily about in all the delight of utter intoxication, the men invariably in groups by themselves, and the ladies of the tribe trapesing after them at a long interval with stoical indifference.

Nothing can be more subversive of the poetry one's early recollections connect with this race, than a first rencontre with the outcasts by whom it is represented on these frontiers, who daily degenerate where all else seems to thrive, and who perish in the midst of an abundance, which, for all but them, increases with each year.

I am not sure whether it would not be more humane to deal upon the natives as summarily as with their forests; for the fall of the former before the advance of civilization is not, though slower, less certain.

They may at present be likened to girdled trees, about whose vigorous trunk the axe of the woodman is but lightly drawn, yet whose fall is assured past remedy; the springs of health and life are stopped, upon their fading leaves the sun rises and heaven's dews descend in vain; for a little while they continue to wave their naked crests in the gale, and hold forth their gaunt limbs as if life were in them, objects exciting at once commiseration and disgust; until, crumbled into decay, the unseemly skeletons lie prostrate athwart the roots of their once fellows, who were stricken down in their bloom, and so perished by a quicker and more merciful sentence.

NIAGARA

I felt interested with Buffalo, and had promised myself much pleasure from a visit to the country occupied by a branch of the Seneca tribe in its neighbourhood; but Niagara was now within a few hours, — the great object of the journey was almost in sight. I was for ever fancying that I heard the sound of the "Thunder-water"[12] booming on the breeze; so, with a restlessness and anxiety not to be suppressed, I got into the coach on the day after my arrival at the capital of the lakes, and was in a short time set down on the bank of the swift river Niagara, at the ferry, which is some four miles from Buffalo.

We found the little rapids about the shore occupied by fishers of all ages, who required but a small share of the patience which is deemed so essential a qualification to the followers of this melancholy sport, for they were pulling the simple wretches out as fast as the lines could be baited and offered.

The shipment was quickly effected, and in a few minutes our faces were turned from the dominion of the States. The vessel was a large horse-boat; that is, a flat propelled by paddle-wheels similar to those of a steam-boat, only wrought by horse-power, — an animal tread-mill in fact. Whether the horses working this were here on good behaviour, or not, I could not rightly ascertain, but certainly they were scampish-looking steeds, their physiognomical expression was low and dogged, such as one might expect from the degrading nature of their unvarying task.

On the larboard gangway of our flat the American jack floated, and over the starboard side waved the Union flag of Old England; they fluttered proudly side by side, a worthy brotherhood, and so united may they long be found!

The ride along the Canada shore was very fine, the noble stream being constantly in sight: the country appeared thickly populated; but the land poor, the cultivation of it, I believe, is not found very profitable.

We halted to water the team at a public-house that stands upon the ground where was fought the battle of Chippewa, which, as the Yankees say, "eventuated just no how." This was the twentieth anniversary; and, on alighting from the box, I was exceedingly amused to find the host and a smart wayfaring young man, with mutual vehemence well worthy the cause, fighting the battle over again.

From this house the eternal mist caused by the great fall may be plainly seen curling like a vast body of light smoke, and shooting occasionally in spiral columns high above the tree-tops; but not a sound told of its neighbourhood, although we were not five miles distant from it, and the day was calm and clear. At about three miles from this, as the vehicle slowly ascended a rise, I heard for the first time the voice of the waters, and called the attention of my friends within the carriage to the sound.

Never let any impatient man set out for Niagara in one of these coaches; a railroad would hardly keep pace with one's eagerness, and here were we crawling at the rate of four miles per hour. I fancied that the last three miles never would be accomplished; and often wished internally, as I beat the devil's tattoo upon the footboard of the coach-box, that I had bought or borrowed or stolen a horse at Chippewa, and galloped to the wonder alone and silently.

At length the hotel came in view, and I knew that the rapid was close at hand.

"Now, sir, look out!" quietly said the driver.

I almost determined upon shutting my eyes or turning away my head; but I do not think it would have been within the compass of my will so to have governed them; for even at this distant moment, as I write, I find my pen move too slow to keep pace with the recollections of the impatience which I seek to record.

It was at the moment we struck the foot of the hill leading up to the hotel that the rapid and the great horse-shoe fall became visible over the sunken trees to our right, almost on a level with us. I have heard people talk of having felt disappointed on a first view of this stupendous scene: by what process they arrived at this conclusion I profess myself utterly incapable of divining, since, even now that two years have almost gone by, I find on this point my feelings are not yet to be analyzed; I dare not trust myself to their guidance, and only know that my wildest imaginings were forgotten in contemplating this awful reality.

A very few minutes after we were released from the confinement of the coach saw myself and companions upon the Table-rock; and soon after we were submitting to the equipment provided by a man resident upon the spot for persons who chose to penetrate beneath the great fall, and whose advertisement assured us that the gratification of curiosity was unattended with either inconvenience or danger, as water-proof dresses were kept in readiness, together with an experienced guide. The water-proof dress given to me I found still wet through; and, on the arrival of the experienced guide, I was not a little surprised to see the fellow, after a long stare in my face, exclaim,

"Och, blur an' 'oons! Mr. Power, sure it's not yer honour that's come all this way from home!"

An explanation took place; when I found that our guide, whom I had seen some two years before as a helper in the stable of my hospitable friend Smith Barry, at Foaty, was this summer promoted to the office of "Conductor," as he styled himself, under the waterfall.

And a most whimsical "conductor" he proved. His cautions, and "divil a fears!" and "not a hap'orth o' danger!" must have been mighty assuring to the timid or nervous, if any such ever make this experiment, which, although perfectly safe, is not a little startling.

His directions, — when we arrived at the point where the mist, pent in beneath the overhanging rock, makes it impossible to distinguish anything, and where the rush of air is so violent as to render respiration for a few seconds almost impracticable, — were inimitable.

"Now, yer honour!" he shouted in my ear—for we moved in Indian file, — "whisper the next gintleman to follow you smart; and, for the love o' God! shoulder the rock close, stoop yer heads, and shut fast yer eyes, or you won't be able to see an inch!"

I repeated my orders verbatim, though the cutting wind made it difficult to open one's mouth.

"Now thin, yer honour," he cried, cowering down as he spoke, "do as ye see me do; hould yer breath, and scurry after like divils!"

With the last word away he bolted, and was lost to view in an instant. I repeated his instructions however to the next in file, and, as directed, scurried after.

This rather difficult point passed, I came upon my countryman waiting for us within the edge of the curve described by this falling ocean; he grasped my wrist firmly as I emerged from the dense drift, and shouted in my ear,

"Luk up, sir, at the green sea that's rowlin' over uz! Murder! bud iv it only was to take a shlope in on uz!"

Here we could see and breathe with perfect ease; and even the ludicrous gestures and odd remarks of my poetical countryman could not wholly rob the scene of its striking grandeur.

I next passed beyond my guide as he stood on tiptoe against the rock upon a ledge of which we trod, and under his direction attained that limit beyond which the foot of man never pressed. I sat for one moment on the Termination Rock, and then followed my guide back to my companions, when together we once more "scurried" into day.

"Isn't it illegant, sir?" began the "Conductor," as soon as we were well clear of the mist.

"Isn't it a noble sight intirely? Caps the world for grandness any way, that's sartain!"

I need hardly say that in this opinion we all joined loudly; but Mr. Conductor was not yet done with us,—he had now to give us a taste of his "larnin."

"I wish ye'd take notice, sir," said he, pointing across the river with an air of authority and a look of infinite wisdom. "Only take a luk at the falls, an' you'll see that Shakspeare is out altogether about the discription."

"How's that, Pat?" inquired I, although not a little taken aback by the authority so gravely quoted by my critical friend.

"Why, sir, Shakspeare first of all says that there's two falls; now, ye may see wid yer own eyes that it's one river sure, and one fall, only for the shtrip o' rock that makes two af id."

This I admitted was evident; whilst Pat gravely went on:

"Thin agin, only luk here, sir; Shakspeare says, 'The cloud-cap tower;' why, if he'd ever taken the trouble to luk at it, he'd seen better than that; an' if he wasn't a fool,—which I'm sure he wasn't, bein' a grand poet,—he'd know that the clouds never can rise to cap the tower, by reason that it stands up above the fall, and that the current for ever sets down."

Again I agreed with him, excusing Shakspeare's discrepancies on the score of his never having had a proper guide to explain these matters.

"I don't know who at all showed him the place," gravely responded Pat; "but it's my belief he never was in id at all at all, though the gintleman that tould me a heap more about it swears for sartin that he was."

This last remark, and the important air with which the doubt was conveyed, proved too much for my risible faculties, already suffering some constraint, and I fairly roared out in concert with my companion, who had been for some time convulsed with laughter.

Whoever first instructed the "Conductor" on this point of critical history deserves well of the visitors so long as the present subject remains here to communicate the knowledge; indeed, I trust, before he is drowned in the Niagara, or burnt up with the whisky required, as he says, "to keep the could out of the shtomach," the present possessor of this curiosity in literature will bequeath it to his successor, so that it may be handed down in its integrity to all future visitors.

Next morning at an early hour I revisited the "Termination Rock," but excused myself from being accompanied by "the Conductor." I next wandered down the stream, and had a delightful bathe in it. Accompanied by a friend, I was pulled in a skiff as close to the fall as possible, and in short performed duly all the observances that have been suggested and practised by curiosity or idleness; but in all these I found no sensation equal to a long quiet contemplation of the mass entire, not as viewed from the balconies of the hotel, but from some rocky point or wooded shade, where house and fence and man and all his petty doings were shut out, and the eye left calmly to gaze upon the awful scene, and the rapt mind to raise its thoughts to Him who loosed this eternal flood and guides it harmless as the petty brook.

There never should have been a house permitted within sight of the fall at least. How I have envied those who first sought Niagara, through the scarce trod wilderness, with the Indian for a guide; and who slept upon its banks with the summer trees for their only shelter, with the sound of its waters for their only *réveille*.

Now, one is awakened here by a bell, which I never can liken to any other than a dustman's, and can hardly find a spot whereto parasols and smart forage-caps intrude not.

I would even include in my denunciation the tower which is now erected upon the piece of rock that abuts upon the great fall, and standing in whose gallery you actually hang suspended over the abyss; not but that the tower is in itself rudely simple, and in good taste perhaps, but that one feels this place needs no such accessories, and, instead of deriving advantage from them, is degraded into a mere show by their presence; and, in saying this much, I feel as though the application of the term was a profanation.

I only saw three natives near the fall during my stay; but these formed a little group I would like much to have had Landseer look upon.

I was walking one morning before breakfast about a quarter of a mile below the fall, when I suddenly came upon a squaw leaning against a tree: as many of the Tuscaroras understand a few words of English, I addressed her with "Good morning, good morning!"

With a calm bend of the head she placed her fingers over her lips by way of return to my salutation, turning herself at the same time a little away as if to avoid further notice or intercourse: curiosity, however, overcame good-breeding in me, and mounting the little bank to a level with the shady tree against which she passively leaned, I immediately became aware of her object.

Coiled up, on the earth, by her feet lay an Indian, his head and shoulders wrapped close in his blanket; upon this motionless mass her eyes were calmly fixed: against the opposite side of the tree sat a very handsome lad, about eight or nine years old, who never lifted his head to look on the intruder: near the boy crouched a half-starved hound of the lurcher kind, a red-coloured, wire-haired brute, with a keen cold Indian look, and as apparently incurious as the best-taught warrior of the tribe: there was no wagging of the tail in friendly recognition, as might be expected from a kindly European dog; neither was there the warning growl and spiteful show of bristled crest and angry teeth, nor any suspicious circling round the stranger, with tail tucked close and thievish scrutiny, so common amongst low-bred white curs; this hound of the Red-man, on the contrary, deported himself in a manner creditable to his race, and to the tribe of his adoption: I do not believe his eye was ever once raised to survey me; or, if it was, the movement was so well managed that I did not detect it.

Supported against the tree stood a long rifle, over whose muzzle was hung a scarlet shoulder-belt and pouch, richly worked with an embroidery of blue and white beads; by a thong of hide was also suspended from the rifle a sheath of leather, through which protruded a couple of inches of the bright broad blade of a knife: these I readily conceived to be the appointments of the sleeping man; and the trio thus patiently watching his slumbers, — his wife, child, and dog.

I looked upon this savage group for some minutes, and no happier scene could have been found for such a rencontre: — the grassy knoll which the family occupied; the rich foliage of the butter-nut tree that shaded them; the wooded heights above, and the deep-channeled river flowing by; together with a stillness made more thrilling by the sound of the cataract, for a moment rumbling like near-coming thunder, and then dying away into a continuous moan, soft and absolutely musical, whilst afar off its light vapoury masses gently rose and fell, converted by the morning sun into clouds of silver tissue. I have often, amongst other vain wishes, sighed for the possession of the painter's power, but never more than at this moment; and as I silently looked upon the unchanging group, and called to mind the artists whom such a chance would have repaid for longer travel, I grieved to think it should have been given to one whose attempts by description to image it must prove so tame a record.

After a long pause, pointing to the coiled-up sleeper, I ventured on a second inquiry, saying, "Man,—he sick?"

The squaw fixed her fine eyes upon me, and comprehending my inquiry, nodded once or twice, articulating in a low musical voice, "Man sick,—whisky too much—make bad!"

Again her head drooped, and her eyes rested upon the motionless mass before her; the little imp and the hound meanwhile never by a sign indicating their knowledge of the presence of an intruder. I now turned back towards the hotel, which I had left to watch the sun rise on the fall from the bed of the river. My early stirring was every way fortunate, for the morning was fresh and unseasonably cool, consequently the misty abyss into which the river tumbled was bridged by beautiful rainbows in every direction; whilst, to crown all, with the exception of the group I have mentioned, no unhallowed foot broke on the holy place.

The family had not appeared on my return to the house; so seeking my little chamber, whose window commanded the rapids and the great fall, I flung myself upon my bed, and gratefully reviewed all the beauty of earth and sky which I had been so happily permitted to behold and to enjoy.

The days I passed here must always be recalled by me as days of unalloyed enjoyment; I felt an indescribable calm steal, as it were, over my spirit. Generally active, impatient, and inquiring, I have seldom found any neighbourhood which I did not compass in a few days; but from the vicinity of this spot I had no desire to stir. Finding that the dinner-hour was two o'clock, which would have destroyed the day, I requested the proprietor of the hotel, one of the most obliging persons I ever met,—an Englishman,—to give our little party dinner at five; and from breakfast to this time I believe our time was usually passed lounging dreamily about Goat Island, to reach which you cross the river below the falls to the American side, and then pass over the rapids on a bridge, which is in itself a wonder.

The turf of this island, its trees and flowers, retaining in summer the freshness of spring, the delicious purity of its atmosphere, and the brightness of its waters, render it most charming. The solitude here has no drawback; the strong currents of air by which it is encircled defy the powers of the musquito, — that bane to all thin-skinned people with pastoral inclinations, and not an insect in the least venomous or annoying is to be found here.

This Island of the Rainbow, as it has been poetically and not inappropriately named, is situated exactly between the falls; surrounded, and intersected in part, by rapids frightful to look on. Before American enterprise and ingenuity spanned these with the bridge that now connects the Iris isle with the main land, the approach to it must have been attended with great difficulty and much danger; indeed, I believe it was very rarely attempted; at present it is occupied by one or two poor families, who tend a garden now in progress, under the care of the proprietor of the place.

Within these few years, a young man of good appearance was known to have taken up his abode here; he shunned all observance, only holding communion with a poor family who procured him what necessaries he needed. After a residence of two years he died, without leaving the slightest clue to his name or country. That his condition was gentle may be inferred from his accomplishments: a flute and a guitar, on both of which he is said to have played much and well, with a drawing or two, are all that remain of the recluse, although the man who attended upon him says he sketched and wrote much.

Certainly no anchorite ever selected a pleasanter summer solitude: how he got through the severity of a five or six months' winter in a place so exposed can only be imagined, since the hermit died and "made no sign."

I visited the other lions of the place, but took little heed of them. The sulphur springs were exhibited, and the gas ignited, by a remarkably fine old man, who was full of anecdote of the late war: one or two of his stories I took good note of, and purpose availing myself of them at some future time.

On one afternoon I forced myself away to visit the Devil's Hole and the Whirlpool, situated about five miles below the falls; and a wilder scene it is impossible for imagination to conceive than the deep rocky basin into which the river is precipitated, and from which it issues at right angles from its previous course, bearing with it portions of the wrack accumulated within the black vortex of this fearful pool, into whose gulf it is impossible to look without a shudder. The drive through the forest was delightful; and, if any sight could have repaid me for leaving the neighbourhood of the falls, this fitting *pendant* would be that sight.

The bad weather which occurred so late in the month of June, and, indeed, continued through the first days of July, had retarded the advance of visitors. At the period of our stay there were but two or three strangers here besides ourselves; and, not dining at the public table, these I never saw except at a distance. The weather during the day was warm without being oppressive, the evenings and nights deliciously cool.

I had brought my companion, Mr. H——e, thus far on a promise of returning with him in a few days, and never did I feel more urged to break faith: but knowing that he was compelled to return in a certain time, and had accompanied me out of sheer good-nature, I could not reconcile it to myself to let him journey back alone; for our companions were bound on a wide tour through the Canadas.

After a halt here of only three short days then, I finally crossed the Niagara for the American shore, and immediately took a coach for Tonnewanta, to intercept the boat on its way from Buffalo by the Erie canal, intending to journey by this route as far as Rochester.

At Tonnewanta, a pretty little village, we were detained two or three hours; and here I once more encountered my family of Tuscarora Indians. The man was at this time wide awake, but still half drunk; and, although a fine-made fellow, had that horrid brutal look which accompanies continued debauch. He was attended as I at first saw him, only that now, as he stood by the public-house door talking with a couple of negroes, the boy and the hound only were beside him. I looked about for my lady of the tribe, and perceived her squatted on her heels against the wall, about fifty paces lower down, "burd alane."

From a slight furtive glance of the urchin, I perceived that he recognised me; he spoke a couple of words to his father, who, turning his head in the direction where I stood, muttered an interjectional "Ugh!" and resumed his previous calm attitude, contrasting oddly with the *insouciant* look and merry grimaces of his negro companions.

I next walked on to the solitary squaw, in hopes of claiming acquaintance; but she kept her eyes fixed upon a necklace she was playing with as gravely as a devotee might tell her beads, and by no sign of recognition deigned to flatter me.

Miserable and degraded race! on whose condition much care has been vainly bestowed, much generous sympathy idly wasted! I say wasted, since the aborigines of this continent are either above or below sympathy. I confess my feeling for them has been much changed by a near view of their condition and a better knowledge of their history and habits; and whatever complaints they may advance against the rapacity of the white man, he must at least be admitted a generous historian.

I shall have occasion hereafter to revert to the unpopular view of this question, which I have adopted against my inclination in obedience to my judgment, and meantime must quit my family of the Tuscaroras—what a name to adorn a tale!—for the canal boat arrived, and in a moment we were hurried to embark.

FOOTNOTE:

[12] The Indian name "Niagara" signifies Thunder-water.

ERIE CANAL

PACKET-BOAT.—HEAT.—CEDAR SWAMP, LONG SWAMP, AND MUSQUITO SWAMP.—UTICA

This day, up to the meridian, had been temperately warm, but not in the least sultry or unbearable. The boat was exceedingly clean, not over-crowded; and I sat down within its neat cabin, anticipating a couple of days' quiet travel, which, if a little monotonous, would be at least unattended by the fatigue and dust of a stage journey between this and Utica.

The boat for a few hours went on merrily; the eternal forest closed about us, and the sound of our horses' feet alone broke upon its silence. Towards evening the heat became great, and after sunset the southern sky began to give forth continuous sheets of flame, along whose pale surface would occasionally dart lines of red forked lightning, whilst the breeze gradually died away. My first idea was, that we were about to be favoured with a refreshing storm of rain and thunder; but vain were my hopes: I watched and listened, but no drop fell, no sound was heard.

Meantime, the heat increased as the night closed in: the little cots, however, were duly hung one below another along the sides of the cabin. I had procured an upper berth, with a window by my side; and having exhausted my patience, and wearied my sight watching the fiery sky, I at last ventured to creep below. Although a hotter atmosphere can hardly be imagined, I slept tolerably sound; but, on waking, found myself anything but refreshed. The sun was not yet above the horizon when I crept forth on to the deck: it was that hour of morning which, of all others, one expects to be invigorating and cool, as indeed it usually is in all climates; but here, enclosed within the banks of the canal, and surrounded by swamp and forest, there was no morning air for us. My mind was made up to leave the boat at the first place where a stage might be procured.

All this day the air absolutely stood still. At our places of halt we were joined by men who had left the stages in consequence of those vehicles not being able to travel. Our pace was reduced considerably; and the cattle, although in excellent condition, were terribly distressed. At Lockport we found business nearly at a stand-still; the thermometer was at 110 degrees of Fahrenheit. We passed several horses dead upon the banks of the canal, and were compelled to leave one or two of our own in a dying state. Here more persons joined than we could well accommodate, and I found positively that all movement by the stage route was at an end, forty horses having fallen on the line the day previous. To attempt abiding in any of the places along the canal, I was assured would be an exchange for the worse; so the only course was to endure the "ills we had," and certainly these did not become the lighter through practice. Towards the second night our progress became tediously slow, for it appeared to grow hot in proportion as the evening advanced.

The south-western sky was again banked up by black clouds, from which the sheet lightning never ceased to burst. Under other circumstances the scene would have been viewed as one of infinite grandeur; but, at present, every consideration became absorbed by our sufferings, for to this the affair really amounted.

This night I found it impossible to look in upon the cabin; I therefore made a request to the captain that I might be permitted to have a mattress on deck: but this, he told me, could not be; there was an existing regulation which positively forbade sleeping upon the deck of a canal packet; indeed, he assured me that this could only be done at the peril of life, with the certainty of catching fever and ague. I appeared to submit to his well-meant arguments; but inwardly resolved, *coûte qui coûte*, not to sleep within the den below, which exhibited a scene of suffocation and its consequences that defies description.

I got my cloak up, filled my hat with cigars, and, planting myself about the centre of the deck, here resolved, *malgré* dews and musquitoes, to weather it through the night.

"What is this name of the country we are now passing?" I inquired of one of the boatmen who joined me about the first hour of morning.

"Why sir, this is called the Cedar Swamp," answered the man, to whom I handed a cigar, in order to retain his society and create more smoke, weak as was the defence against the hungry swarms surrounding us on all sides.

"We have not much more of this Cedar Swamp to get through, I hope?" inquired I, seeking for some consolatory information.

"About fifty miles more, I guess," was the reply of my companion, accompanying each word with a sharp slap on the back of his hand, or on his cheek or forehead.

"Thank Heaven!" I involuntarily exclaimed, drawing my cloak closer about me, although the heat was killing; "we shall after that escape in some sort, I hope, from these legions of musquitoes?"

"I guess not quite," replied the man; "they are as thick, if not thicker, in the Long Swamp."

"The Long Swamp!" I repeated: "what a horrible name for a country! Does the canal run far through it?"

"No, not so very far, only about eighty miles."

"We've then done with swamps, I hope, my friend?" I inquired, as he kept puffing and slapping on with unwearied constancy.

"Why, yes, there's not a heap more swamp, that is to say, not close to the line, till we come to within about forty miles of Utica."

"And is that one as much infested with these infernal insects as are the Cedar and Long Swamps."

"I guess *that* is *the* place above all for musquitoes," replied the man grinning. "Thim's the real gallinippers, emigrating north for the summer all the way from the Balize and Red River. Let a man go to sleep with his head in a cast-iron kettle among thim chaps, and if their bills don't make a watering-pot of it before morning, I'm d— —d. They're strong enough to lift the boat out of the canal, if they could only get underneath her."

I found these swamps endless as Banquo's line: would they had been shadows only; but alas! they were yet to be encountered, horrible realities not to be evaded. I closed my eyes in absolute fear, and forbore further inquiry.

Here I remained throughout the whole night, dozing a little between whiles, but never foregoing my cigar for a minute. Towards daylight the dew descended like rain, but brought with it no coolness to earth or man: it felt exactly as though it had been boiled the day before, and had not been left long enough to get cool.

During this day many of our men frequently threw themselves overboard, clothes and all on, that is, in shirt and trousers, these being all of habiliment that could be worn; I really feared that some of them who had been a little too free in their cold applications, that is, of iced water and brandy, would have gone mad.

This blessing of ice we were seldom many hours without, the poorest hovel on the canal being commonly provided with it in sufficient abundance to give us a supply. The inhabitants, I found, were suffering from the unusual continuance of heat as much as strangers: at night they built huge fires of pine before their doors, so that the thick smoke might penetrate the dwelling, and scour the infernal musquitoes out of it. At these fires we would find the poor women sitting in the smoke at the risk of suffocation; pale, haggard, with their hair neglected and dishevelled, looking like worn-out ghosts rather than living beings. The oldest inhabitants on the line of the canal assured us they never remembered any heat of three days' continuance which could compare to this; and I believe them, since no man could long endure such a visitation.

This evening our condition was in no way improved, except that we heard the sound and felt the presence of a strong current of northerly wind; but it blew as though issuing from a furnace, and afforded no present relief. The sky continued to show "fiery off," and the musquitoes of that ilk did credit to the genealogy my informant ascribed to them: but there is a period beyond which even suffering ceases; this happy insensibility I had attained; and when after midnight we were landed at Utica, I felt as though I could have slept soundly and well even beneath the heated deck of our canal packet.

I got an excellent bed at the hotel, however; and at daylight awoke to feel once more the delightful sensation of coolness. In the night heavy rain had fallen; a light but pleasant breeze was blowing; and the past was already a subject for merriment, although it was such matter for jest as I never willingly will undertake to collect again.

LITTLE FALLS

SARATOGA.—BALLSTON.—
ALBANY.—MOUNTAIN-HOUSE.—
CATSKILL.—HYDE PARK.—LYNN

The early hour of six A.M. saw us once more in motion for Schnectady, by way of Little Falls. We pursued what is termed the ridge road, running along the valley of the Mohawk.

The day was bright, and not over-warm. The sun's rays being tempered by a delicious north-east breeze, the condition of the atmosphere completely re-invigorated the almost prostrate body, whilst the loveliness of the prospect delighted and cheered the mind. No valley in the world can present charms more varied or more beautiful; even making every allowance for the happy change from musquitoes, swamps, close confinement, and suffocation, to freedom, exercise, and healthful breezes, with the satisfaction consequent upon the re-enjoyment of all these.

We frequently ran along the line of cuttings for the railroad now in progress between Utica and Schnectady. The rocky nature of the ridge whose line they pursue, offers formidable impediments; but the work was proceeding with great rapidity notwithstanding. This railway, when complete, together with the canal by whose side it runs, will afford a facility of communication between New York and Utica, which, for speed and convenience, can have no rival.

We breakfasted at Little Falls, a small town built on what was, at some period or other, the very bed of a torrent, amidst the huge piles of rock riven from the mountains in its course. Although overshadowed by the steep heights that wall the ravine in which it lies, it is kept cool and healthful by the constant current of air following the rapid fall of the river, which is here precipitated over a series of rocky ledges in a wild and hurried course, giving to the ravine and town the name of Little Falls. A more picturesque, romantic site no painter could desire. I felt vexed to be compelled to leave it after about an hour's halt; and should yet more regret this, did I not hope to revisit it.

Arriving at Schnectady, we found the railroad train about to start for Saratoga springs; and, taking our places, we arrived at this Malvern of America about ten at night, after a delightful day's ride.

Next morning I got up early, and took a lounge about Saratoga. The nominal attraction to this place is its water, which is much in vogue, and may be procured all over the States, being bottled and sold under the name of Congress water; as in all such places however, pleasure, not health, is the end pursued by the majority of visitors.

The day was again close and hot: the street was a foot deep in light dust, so that every carriage moved in a cloud, and not a breath of air could rise without bearing this nuisance on its wing. I could not but think, considering the abundance of water, that there was a lack of charity in thus withholding a sprinkling from the road, especially as the resident invalids would, I am sure, have as much benefited by this mode of application as by any other; since to breathe for any length of time an atmosphere constantly impregnated with impalpable powder, must be anything but salutary.

The chief attraction presented to my eyes was the piazza of the hotel where myself and friend had our quarters. This was of immense extent, full twenty feet wide, boarded throughout, and covered by the roof of the house, which was supported by lofty pillars of pine. About these columns grew, in the greatest luxuriance, the wild vine of the country, or some other Clematis, covering them from ground to roof, and forming a continuous rich drapery throughout the whole extent of the long piazza.

This forms a promenade for the residents of the house and their visitors; and, were it out of reach of the dust, it would be difficult to create one more elegant and agreeable. There are several hotels here, whose exteriors present all the attractions of cleanliness and great size, both exceeding good points in so hot a climate as this now was. Of their internal arrangements I know nothing; for after partaking of a breakfast, in common with some hundred and fifty elaborately well-dressed ladies and gentlemen, in a room every way proportioned to the number of the *convives*, with the thermometer at about 88 degrees, I declared off, and made up my mind to decamp by the next train to seek quiet and coolness on the summit of the Catskill mountains.

On our way we halted for a few hours at Ballston, the quality of whose water is, I believe, similar to that of the Saratoga springs: the place itself I liked better, simply, I suppose, because it had less of bustle and pretension. At the hotel, whose pillared piazza, was, like that I had just quitted, clothed with the freshest and most luxuriant clematis, I met a gay young belle of New York, who was resident here with her family, recruiting a sufficient stock of health to carry her through the fatigues of a winter campaign. By this lady I had my prepossessions in favour of Ballston confirmed; she assured me that the society here, though exceedingly small by comparison, was infinitely more pleasant; that there was less of dress or ceremony, and consequently more real comfort and sociability. I left this place with a strong inclination to remain for a few days at least: but my time of *relâche* was short; and my misery was that I had much to see, and many points to visit lying far asunder, therefore was bound to hasten on, leaving agreeable realities as soon as found, to seek for something better, which too often proved a shadow when overtaken.

Arrived at Albany, however, I found a right substantial welcome awaiting me from "mine host o' th' Eagle," in the shape of a six o'clock dinner of trout and woodcock, which would have recommended itself even without the aid of a hot day's journey and a ten hours' fast.

Passed the evening with the K— —s, one of those families of women which, if I did not value their delicacy more than my own inclination, I should like to describe, in contradiction to those who, viewing only the surface of American society, have so flippantly passed judgment upon its members.

And how many of these little circles have I encountered, and been admitted into, in various parts of these States, composed of women who have seen little of what is called the world; but whose information, intelligence, and spirit would have made them the ornaments of any country; and whose manners, refined, feminine, and naturally graceful, might with infinite advantage be studied by some of the ungentle censors whose tone of criticism is so *prononcé*.

It has often, when visiting in the country, been a matter of surprise to me to meet with so many women every way presentable, yet who have had such slight opportunity, as it is called, of acquiring that perfect ease and repose of manner by which truly well-bred women are readily distinguishable.

The fact is, in the cities, where numbers congregate, society is apt rather to catch its tone from that which is most showy and prominent than from what, though more refined, is less obvious. In cities, also, strangers are often presented, and, from a deference to European fashion, observed and imitated, whose manner might with more profit be viewed as an example of what ought to be eschewed than held out as a model for adoption.

But this is a digression I must close here, and which, indeed, the recollection of my fair friends at Albany alone could have betrayed me into. Acquainted with so much that is attractive and admirable in private life in this country, I should be less than honest did I not feel a desire to do it such poor justice as the expression of my feeling may render: I have only to regret that a rigid sense of propriety condemns me to deal in generalities only upon a point where I could individualise with such absolute truth.

At seven o'clock A.M. went on board the Erie steamer, and a little after ten my companion and myself were landed at Catskill.

A stage was in waiting at the landing-place, which quickly took us up to the town; and here we hired a carriage to proceed directly to the Mountain-house, which we had marked from the river as the morning sun lighted it up, looking like a white dovecot raised against the dark hill-side.

In consequence of some bridge having been recently washed away by a flood, we were compelled to make a considerable circuit in order to ford the river; this, however, we accomplished, and continued our ascent under the happiest auspices.

I will say nothing of our winding rocky road, or of the glimpses we now and then had of the nether world, which "momentarily grew less," as, whilst, halting for breath, we curiously peeped through the leafy skreen, flying from the faded leaf and drooping flower of scorching summer, and finding ourselves once more surrounded by all the lovely evidences of early spring.

We took nearly five hours to win the house aptly called of the Mountain. I walked more than half way, and never felt less weary than when I rested on the natural platform, which, thrust from the hill-side, forms a stand whence may be worshipped one of the most glorious prospects ever given by the Creator to man's admiration.

In the cool shade we stood here, and from this eyrie looked upon the silver line drawn through the vast rich valley far below, doubtful of its being the broad Hudson, upon whose bosom we had so lately floated in a huge vessel crowded with passengers: for this vessel we searched in vain; but, by the aid of a telescope, made out one of the same kind, which appeared to flit along like some fairy skiff over a pantomimic lake made all radiant with gold and pearl.

How delightful were the sensations attendant upon a first repose in this changed climate, enhanced as these were by the remembrance of the broiling we had so recently endured! I never remember to have risen with feelings more elastic, or in higher spirits, than I did after my first night's rest upon this mountain: the rooms were small but very clean, and the house with but few inmates; a circumstance I rejoiced in exceedingly, although it was perfectly incomprehensible to me, considering the state of the atmosphere below.

I found next day that here even there was a lion, in the shape of a waterfall, to be visited before one could be permitted to take absolute rest; so away I went to visit it, — a sort of waggon-omnibus being in preparation to take the inmates through the wood to the fall.

A ride of some three miles brought us as close as might be to the spot, and a walk of as many hundred yards presented to view a scene as well suited for a witches' festival as any spot in the old Hartz.

In the season of melting snow this must doubtless be a grand affair, for the fall is full three hundred feet deep; at present a mere rill crept over the centre of the rocky amphitheatre, and, long before it reached the basin beneath, it was changed into a silvery shower of light spray. We found a mill-dam had appropriated all the surplus of the weakened torrent, close by the head of the fall: as here was a day and night to recruit in, a trifling bribe induced the sawyers to raise their floodgates for our especial benefit.

The bargain being completed, we descended into the bed of the river near the basin, and, giving the appointed signal, were indulged with a momentary glimpse of the scene under better form; but still, I am certain, received no idea of the effect produced here when the machinery is complete.

After wandering a little way down the rugged bed of this misused river, — for surely Nature never designed that its waters should be arrested in their course to turn a saw-mill, — the party collected to return: with two others, I decided upon walking back, and pleasant it is to walk through these quiet wild wood-paths, where the chirp of the birds and the rustle of the leaves alone break in upon the repose.

These mountains are everywhere thickly clothed with wood, saving only the platform whereon the house is built; deer abound on the lower ridges, and the bear yet finds ample cover here. A number of these animals are killed every season by an indefatigable old Nimrod who lives in the valley beneath, and who breeds some very fine dogs to this sport.

I did promise unto myself that during the coming November I would return up here, and sojourn with the stout bear-hunter for a few days, for the purpose of seeing Bruin baited in his proper lair; but regret to say my plan was frustrated. It must be an exciting chase to rouse the lord of this wild mountain forest on a sunny morning, with the first hoar frost yet crisping the feathery pines; and to hear the deep-mouthed hounds giving tongue where a hundred echoes wait to bay the fierce challenge back, and to hear the sharp crack of the rifle rattle through the thin air.

Or, whilst resting upon some crag under the blue sunny sky, to watch the sea of cold clouds tumbling about far below, and think that they o'er-canopy a region lower still, about which one's fellows are at the moment creeping with red noses and watery eyes, or rubbing their frozen fingers over anthracite stoves, utterly unconscious, poor devils! that

"The sun, when obscured by the clouds, yet above

"Shines not the less bright, though unseen."

On Tuesday at five A.M. was roused to breakfast, and descended into the lower world to meet the Albany steamer.

I opened my casement and looked forth upon the ocean of mist, whose huge waves rose and fell as they kept rolling by. It seemed as though river, valley, and mountain had been overwhelmed by this restless deluge, whose course was yet unstayed. The sun as yet wanted the power to shine through the mist; all was dark, chilling, and almost fearful.

Before breakfast I had a last palaver with our guide; he said that the extreme denseness of the fog gave assured token of "an awful hot day."

At six A.M. our muster was completed, and the party for the lower regions duly told off. As the carriage slowly crept down some of the steepest portions of the tortuous way, time and opportunities were afforded to steal a look under the cloudy canopy which the sun was quickly drawing upwards, and thus good assurance was afforded that the guide had prognosticated rightly.

It did look "awful hot," to be sure; a golden-coloured haze seemed to float over the whole land like the subdued reflection of a bright flame. It made one feel uncomfortable to look upon the glowing landscape: the long snaky river gave no idea of coolness; it had a dead shiny look, only to be likened to a stream of molten lead.

Meantime we mournfully beheld the green moist leaves, the yet half-open buds, together with all the other pleasant signs of spring, vanish with our too hasty fall, and to these succeeded parched grass, dry yellow leaves, and sickly flowers drooping and over-blown.

At half-past ten we quitted Catskill in the steamer, and by half-after twelve were landed at Hyde Park. Mr. W— —ks was awaiting our arrival, and a pair of his trotters soon set us down at his very pretty country-house, which is one of a cluster of charming residences scattered along this portion of the north bank of the river.

A pleasant house and an agreeable party, with the sweetest possible scenery to ride or walk through, with a river and boats, and every accessory the frankest hospitality could furnish, might reasonably be presumed attractive enough to arrest a wayfarer in search of comfort: one drawback alone was to me insurmountable, mine ancient and implacable foes the musquito tribe were in full possession. These verdant shades form a portion of their hunting-ground on the Hudson; with them the war-hatchet is never buried; I had no sooner taken up my position therefore, than hostilities were re-commenced; my defence was creditable enough as I flatter myself; but Hercules himself might have shunned such fearful odds; I saw no reason therefore why I should abide to have every vein in my carcase breathed by these Cossacks, in obedience to a mere point of honour; so, shortly after dinner, I fairly cried peccavi, and decided to decamp.

I was almost ashamed to declare my motives of flight to my hostess, whose hospitality I had accepted for a few days; especially as I saw others, and women too, heroically abiding the assault: but the truth is, my residence on the mountain had made me effeminate; Catskill proved my Cannæ. Freed from every accustomed annoyance in that "shady, blest retreat," I had absolutely begun to doubt whether there could be any longer found in the world below either heat or musquitoes; with the confident presumption of restored vigour, I stooped from my security, and reaped the harvest of my folly.

My first idea was to return to the hills, but I had made an appointment to sail from Nahant down the east coast for a day or two with a friend, who I knew would expect me; and thither I resolved to push, the more especially as I was informed musquitoes were not strong enough on the wing to abide the rough breezes blowing in the bay of Massachusetts.

It was nigh midnight when the night-boat touched, in its way down, at the pier of Hyde Park: bidding adieu to my friends, I stepped on board, and was again cutting through the dark river.

The boat was crowded; and what a scene did the cabins present! But to describe it is impossible: indeed, the glance of curiosity I was tempted to take was an exceedingly brief one. Let the reader only imagine some two hundred men stowed away in double tiers of berths, or lying in rows upon stretchers placed close together, between the decks of a steamer, on one of the hottest, closest nights of a North American summer, and he may imagine a picture it would be very difficult to describe correctly.

The night was very beautiful however, and almost reconciled me to passing it sleepless. Many persons kept the decks, which were yet ample enough to afford solitude to those who desired it. Myself and H— —e quietly lighted our cigars, and philosophically roughed it out till six o'clock A.M., at which time we were landed in New York.

We knocked up the lazy varlets of the hot baths, and with this luxury balanced the loss of sleep.

I found myself back in New York sooner than I had anticipated on starting for the west; but, in the course of the day, discovered that the good city was yet too hot to hold me. W— —n, who by good fortune was yet holding out here, invited me to dine with B— —r and himself at the club; and, could we only have contrived to ice the atmosphere, nothing would have been wanting to our comfort. I found these last of the Romans were off in a day or two for the Springs, after the rest of the world; so, nothing being left to hold me, I took my passage next evening for Boston.

Roomy as is the "Benjamin Franklin," I found on this occasion every berth already taken: the captain, however, resigned his room to me with much good-will; so my mischance proved fortunate, as I found myself installed in a neat cabin having a window opening on the water, which indeed the heat of the night made most necessary.

There were two or three southern families on board, bound for Rhode Island: they appeared worn out by heat and long travel. The women especially pay dearly, I fear, for their sunny possessions; and what return can compensate for loss of health? Many of these are natives of the north; but, marrying southern gentlemen, they follow the fortunes of their husbands; the distances are great to which they are removed perhaps; and the necessity for a continuous residence on the plantation through two or three succeeding summers, saps, for ever, the constitution of a delicate female.

The appearance of two or three of these young matrons now on board the packet excited my more than commiseration; attenuated in form, sallow-visaged, and fragile as the aspen, they appeared to shrink from the very breeze, to seek whose freshness they had journeyed so far. Two of them possessed the remains of positive beauty; their dark hair was of gossamer fineness, and their handsome eyes sparkled with that unnatural light which shines as it were from the tomb. No man could have looked upon them without pity; so attractive, so young, yet so evidently past all earthly cure.

Landing at Providence, five hours' ride over a most dusty road brought us within sight of the State-house of Boston, when a thunder-storm, which had been for some time threatening, fell upon us with merciless fury. The overburdened cloud appeared as though it fairly rested upon the house-tops, and out of it ran a torrent of rain such as I should only have looked for under the line, or on some tropical island.

I was outside, and had I even desired to seek shelter, the assault was of so sudden a nature, and so vigorous, that the worst one could expect from a complete ducking was effected in a moment: I sat it out therefore, and arrived at the Tremont uncommonly uncomfortable.

July 22nd. — Still on the move, seeking some cool spot where I may fold my tired wings and take "mine ease." One night's halt convinced me Boston was no quarter such as I desired just now; the house was crowded, the thermometer high, and my room as high as the glass, for it was one hundred and something up four flights of stairs. My good friend, Mr. T — — r, took compassion on my condition, and volunteered to drive me down to Nahant; so off I was again. We passed across the harbour by one of the little steamers; and from hence to the pretty town of Lynn, there is nothing in the landscape particularly attractive. Over the destinies of this said town of Lynn St. Crispin holds absolute dominion; for the entire population, man, woman, and child, father, son, and brother, appear devoted to the calling in whose practice the princely saint was brought up.

Vast quantities of shoes are here manufactured for the Indian markets; the amount exported annually is something enormous. The place wears an air of great prosperity; the dwellings being of remarkable neatness, and the public edifices of a size and character highly creditable to the ambition of these worthy citizens.

This caste-like monopoly of certain callings is a singular feature in the economy of the New England republic, there being many of its towns where trades are exclusively exercised, and the practice of them handed down as an inheritance from one industrious generation to the next in succession; and notwithstanding the many arguments lately raised at home against hereditary honours, I do not find that in Massachusetts a souter is considered likely to make a shoe, a cooper a cask, or a farmer grow onions, with less ability, simply because their fathers did the same before them.

The drive along the sandy beach from this place to Nahant was a most agreeable change from the dusty road on a warm July morning, especially with the prospect of a fresh breeze and a fish breakfast crowning the rocky peninsula rising boldly in the distance.

The first happily encountered us before we reached the hotel, much to our relief; and the second was very quickly provided on our arrival. The precise day of the month when this place becomes fashionable had not yet arrived; although the heat, which alone could render such a residence desirable, had; consequently, there were few visitors, and my fears about want of room proved groundless. A choice of chambers was proffered me, and I selected one having an eastern aspect, with a window that commanded the north-east coast of the vast bay of Massachusetts; whilst just within reach lay the snugly-sheltered cove and rocky islet about which, according to the most authentic reports, the "great sea sarpint" delights to disport him when in a merry mood. "Who knows," said I to myself, when all the advantages of my location became known to me, — "who knows but that on some morning, bright and early, I may behold the monster combing his venerable beard amongst the rocks below, or see him lift his head to the level of my window — the height not being over a hundred feet — in civil search of a bit of old brown Windsor to shave withal?"

Here, then, will I fix my head-quarters until the prompter's whistle shall once more summon me to commence a new campaign at New York; — six weeks nearly, with nothing to do, — it will require some management to complete this task without weariness!